The Search for American Political Development

The Search for American Political Development is the first full-scale assessment of American political development ("APD") as a field of inquiry in political science. The book surveys its foundations in the origins of the discipline, evaluates the current state of its institutional and cultural investigations, and addresses the challenges APD scholars confront today. The authors seek to move the enterprise forward with chapters devoted to the concept of political development and to its methodological and substantive implications for the study of politics.

Karen Orren and Stephen Skowronek are founders and managing editors of *Studies in American Political Development*. Karen Orren is Professor of Political Science at the University of California, Los Angeles. Stephen Skowronek is the Pelatiah Perit Professor of Political and Social Science at Yale University.

THE SEARCH FOR AMERICAN POLITICAL DEVELOPMENT

Karen Orren
University of California, Los Angeles

Stephen Skowronek
Yale University

CAMBRIDGE
UNIVERSITY PRESS

PUBLISHED BY THE PRESS SYNDICATE OF THE UNIVERSITY OF CAMBRIDGE
The Pitt Building, Trumpington Street, Cambridge, United Kingdom

CAMBRIDGE UNIVERSITY PRESS
The Edinburgh Building, Cambridge CB2 2RU, UK
40 West 20th Street, New York, NY 10011-4211, USA
477 Williamstown Road, Port Melbourne, VIC 3207, Australia
Ruiz de Alarcón 13, 28014 Madrid, Spain
Dock House, The Waterfront, Cape Town 8001, South Africa

http://www.cambridge.org

First published 2004

Printed in the United States of America

Typeface Sabon 10.25/14 pt.   *System* LATEX 2ε [TB]

A catalog record for this book is available from the British Library.

Library of Congress Cataloging in Publication Data
Orren, Karen.
The search for American political development / Karen Orren,
Stephen Skowronek
p. cm.
Includes bibliographical references and index.
ISBN 0-521-83894-0 – ISBN 0-521-54764-4 (pb.)
1. United States – Politics and government. 2. Political development.
I. Skowronek, Stephen. II. Title.
JK31.O77 2004
320.973 – dc22   2003065414

ISBN 0 521 83894 0 hardback
ISBN 0 521 54764 4 paperback

*For J. David Greenstone, in memory, and Theodore J. Lowi,
teachers of us both*

Contents

Preface

This book is the product of a long, sometimes exasperating, sometimes exhilarating collaboration. Certain values helped us through, chief among these the value of friendship. We began more than twenty years ago when casual conversations about politics and history led us to create a journal outlet for scholars with similar interests, *Studies in American Political Development*. Among the benefits of editorship has been regular contact with a wide range of perspectives and participation, however vicariously, in each. In this way, our collaboration has included the unwitting persons whose names are found on *Studies'* tables of contents.

That said, we are inclined to add something more than a routine statement absolving others of responsibility for what we have written here. While in editing the journal we seek to present historical research by political scientists in all its variety, in writing this book we set out to craft a statement of our own. The title of the book is meant to capture the dual nature of "the search" for American political development as we see it today: in part, it is an effort to bring a story – the story of America's political development – into sharper relief; in part, it is an effort to bring into sharper relief an academic subfield, "APD," within the discipline of political science. How this subfield defines itself will have a lot to do with how it tells the story, and the time seems ripe for a considered treatment.

Our aim throughout has been to describe the distinctive set of interests that drives research on American political development, to do so in a way that is true to what scholars associated with this field actually write, and to convey to others – students with a general interest in politics, scholars working in other subfields, prospective

APD recruits – why we think these interests are worthy of sustained attention. It was apparent to us at the start, however, that merely surveying the different avenues of research currently explored by historically oriented political scientists in order to reach for some elusive consensus among them would not do much to distinguish, much less advance, the common enterprise. In our review of the literature, we will explain what we see as the current uncertainty about APD's nature and scope, but to do this and no more, did not seem sufficiently helpful either. Doing more, in turn, made our task more complicated and inevitably more controversial.

To clarify our own thinking, we decided that the best course was to let the subject be our guide. Rather than try to fit issues posed by the study of American political development to the recent trends and received canons of research in other precincts of political science and of history, we decided to work the other way around. We asked ourselves two basic questions: What does a historical analysis of American politics entail, and what, exactly, is political development? Proceeding along these lines promised a way to uncover the contributions that a field with this name might make to the understanding of both politics and history, and also a way to assess those elements of research design that distinguish this literature from that of related undertakings.

We argue that APD is best understood neither as the political history of the United States nor as the use of history as a source of data for testing theories of politics based on non-historical assumptions. Our contention is that APD is worthy of consideration as a field of inquiry because it harbors an approach to political analysis all its own: it grapples with what we describe as the historical construction of politics, and with political arrangements of different origins in time operating together. It will be seen that the analytic stance is different from that generated by other research programs in the study of American politics, even when the subject matter of that research is historical, and also from that afforded by earlier studies of political development. The template we provide takes account of the unraveling of teleological assumptions about development found in those earlier studies, while, at the same time, allowing us to retrieve "development" as a signal attribute of politics, one that holds out a wide-ranging agenda for substantive research and theory building.

Just as essential as a template for historical analysis is a clear definition of the concept of political development itself. By reclaiming this concept for the study of American politics we are, in a sense, defining the dependent variable, describing in general terms what APD as a field of inquiry ultimately needs to explain. Readers will find that our definition is heavily weighted toward political institutions, for we locate political development in the reconstruction of authority relations in governance. A definition that references authority, in both its formal aspects and practical operations, provides a reliable empirical indicator of political development without closing off further debate about what factors might explain development as it occurs. We do not expect our definition of development to settle anything once and for all, but we do think that by spotlighting the substance and accumulation over time of changes in governing arrangements, our definition puts politics at the center of developmental analysis and situates political action at its most consequential.

What follows, then, are the results of our search as it has proceeded to date. Readers familiar with our previous writings may recognize some of the themes in this book. Reworking them in the context of questions currently confronting the subfield as a whole has altered our thinking and deepened our appreciation for the issues that surround the historical study of politics. In the final analysis, this is our bid to revive a venerable conversation about the development of the American polity, to reexamine traditional themes and rework them into a timely research program. We intend it as a guide, one of many ways into our subject, and as such, the conclusions we draw speak for us alone.

To those who have read and criticized various versions of these arguments in working papers, discarded chapters, and full manuscript drafts we are especially grateful. They include: Bruce Ackerman, Richard Bensel, Terri Bimes, Walter Dean Burnham, Daniel Carpenter, John Coleman, Steven Dunn, David Ericson, Morris Fiorina, Daniel Galvin, Matthew Green, Jacob Hacker, Marc Janssen, Victoria Hattam, Ira Katznelson, Rogan Kersh, David Mayhew,

Bruce Miroff, Cassandra Moseley, Ruth O'Brien, Andrew Polsky, Elizabeth Sanders, Eric Schickler, Adam Sheingate, Colleen Shogan, Rogers Smith, Kathleen Thelen, Daniel Tichenor, and Keith Whittington. We are grateful to Ed Parsons and Lewis Bateman at Cambridge University Press who acquired the manuscript at a "critical juncture," expedited the production process, and accommodated our separation anxieties with grace and good sense. We also thank, by no means least, a few personal and intellectual confidants, friends who withstood our moods and were willing to act as sounding boards for good and bad ideas as we worked the manuscript through: Joyce Appleby, John McCormick, Eileen McDonagh, Susan Jacobs, Carroll Seron, Steven Smith, Stephen Werner, and Ellen Meiksins Wood.

ONE

The Historical Construction of Politics

The circumstances which accompany the birth of nations and contribute to their development affect the whole term of their being.
Alexis de Tocqueville

THE STUDY OF AMERICAN POLITICAL DEVELOPMENT is a substantive inquiry guided by a theoretical precept. The substantive inquiry
covers the full range of politics in the United States: past politics
and present politics, political action and political behavior, political thought and political culture, movement politics and institutional
politics. The theoretical precept is this: because a polity in all its
different parts is constructed historically, over time, the nature and
prospects of any single part will be best understood within the long
course of political formation. Studying politics through history is
nothing new; adherents to a developmental approach spurred the formation of political science as an academic discipline at the end of the
nineteenth century. However, after several decades during which history was relegated to a decidedly minor role in the study of American
politics, interest in historical approaches is resurgent. Recent years
have seen the rise of a veritable cottage industry of political scientists
engaged in historical investigations of one kind or another, and for
the first time, we hear American political development referred to as
"APD," a subfield with its own name and acronym.

Why this new attraction to Clio? One explanation is that political
scientists stepped into a void left when younger academic historians
who specialized in the United States turned away from the study of
government and leadership to concentrate on other things.[1] There
may be some truth to this. Though historians do not depend on

government for material to analyze, political scientists do rely on history; arguably, then, when historians discovered other, less-well-attended interests, political scientists were obliged to undertake the necessary spade work for themselves. But the circumstances go deeper. Political scientists were drawn to American history first of all by events in the polity itself. The revival of interest in America's political development coincided with the "movement culture" of the last third of the twentieth century, with popular mobilizations, one upon another, that challenged long-established social relations and called for a new inventory of America's political resources. Associated with these were insurgencies within the major political parties, first from the left and then from the right, that undercut the received wisdom of liberal consensus and thrust the legitimacy of American state institutions to the center of political controversy. The quandaries presented by this fast-moving scene prompted scholars to step back for a longer view.

Not surprisingly, they began to see things in a new way. The theory of American politics dominant in the middle of the twentieth century had offered explanations for its stability and continuity; under the sway of "group-process" or "pluralist" ideas, political scientists had distinguished American government by the ease with which its institutions accommodated changes in society and by the seamless precedence of its liberal ideology. Pluralist scholarship postulated an American state open and responsive to interest pressures, an American society only loosely attached to legal foundations, an American Constitution ultimately dependent on informal "rules of the game," rules that, at the level of the individual citizen, sanctioned the operations of the existing system. In the unsettled decades that followed, historical research was enlisted in the service of a theoretical critique. The first matter of intellectual business was to bring to light what the reigning synthesis had missed, and for anyone who cared to look at the past in this way, there was much to be found. Scholars attuned to the discord between state and society discovered the persistence of ancient institutions, impervious to social pressures; scholars attuned to the vicissitudes of society discovered the impositions of formal authority; scholars suspicious of the rules of the game and of liberalism discovered an extensive record of ideological conflict, quashed alternatives, and broken promises.

The force of this critique shaped the study of APD as we find it today. Texts setting forth these broad revisionist themes became the canonic works of the new subfield.[2] They suggested new lines of inquiry into the past, inquiries into the politics of state formation, identity formation, welfare provision, sectional relations, race relations, and cultural antagonism generally. They also encouraged political scientists to move investigations close to the ground, to delve into the intricacies of political conflict and governmental operations in particular historical settings. The result has been the rapid accumulation of a broad-based historical literature on American politics and government, a literature that aspires to meet contemporary standards of research in the disciplines of history and political science. Propositions are now more subtle and exacting; findings are more fully documented; claims are more methodologically secure. Skepticism toward grand theoretical systems of all kinds continues to drive APD's advance, but what has been lacking in synthesis has been compensated for thus far by the new topics addressed, the new techniques applied, and the new findings of substance.

The future is another matter. A theoretical critique may substitute for a positive research program for a while, but it is unlikely to do so indefinitely. The outstanding question is just how long this subfield can sustain itself as an open-ended, freewheeling interrogation of historical dynamics and the causes of past political episodes. One aspect of this question is whether such an enterprise can hold its own amid the research agendas that currently anchor history and political science departments separately – whether historically minded political scientists can resist being pulled more directly into the orbit of scholarly communities boasting a more positive sense of purpose. The other side of the same issue is whether APD, as it is currently practiced, augurs any fresh and coherent statement about the nature of politics itself, a statement of its own that can be readily understood as such even by those who think about politics and history differently.

On all counts, there is reason for concern. Though political scientists are doing more, and arguably better, historical research on

3

American politics, the bonds forged of a common critique of prior thinking are getting weaker, and the insights being offered are becoming more localized and dispersed. Scholars formulate historical propositions that are more subtle and exacting, but they have less to say than scholars in earlier generations about the development of the American polity overall. Until recently, the study of American political development offered research strategies and concepts for reaching general insights afforded by longer time horizons; that was its comparative strength as an approach to political analysis. Currently, as APD research begins to look more like work in the rest of political science and the rest of history, its distinctive contribution is becoming less clear. Indeed, at a time when social, economic, and strategic conditions – a "new" multiculturalism, a "new" globalism, a "new" U.S. hegemony – all but trumpet the irrelevance of America's past, the absence of more comprehensive thinking about the relationship between past and present is conspicuous and might well be counted the most serious shortcoming in APD's recent revival.

Our hope is that this little book will recapture the enduring value of research into America's political development, that it will add some forward thrust to the enterprise and recommend its further elaboration as a field. The aim is to tap the fuller significance of ongoing research in the context of an overall reassessment of the APD project. By "fuller significance," we have in mind what it is that APD might teach us about how past and present politics are connected, by what bridges or processes; about how time comes to exert an independent influence on political change, apart from the notion that time "passes"; about how these things illuminate the nature of American politics, including whether, and in what sense, it may be said to "develop."

The discussion framed by these questions is primarily conceptual in nature, an effort to characterize a mode of inquiry, cull its common themes, identify its current problems, and suggest responsive solutions. Research on the substantive side of APD is, as we have indicated, alive and well; what we add to that is largely incidental to our main interest in capitalizing on insights to be found in the existing empirical literature, in extending the implications of what scholarship in the field has recently brought into view. Moreover, though we strive for a general statement about the field of American political development, we do not present our own full-blown theory of American political development, offering instead a survey of the ground on which theory building might now profitably proceed and a preliminary road map as to where. As was once said of English lawyers, today's APD scholars work for the most part "with their heads down," immersed in the puzzles before them. We have taken the liberty of drawing out from their efforts a presentation we hope will be useful to anyone who wants to think about politics historically.

History and Change

The boundaries of the APD project are porous – receptive to influences from the rest of political science, from the other social science disciplines, and beyond. No membership card is required to participate; indeed, it is common for individual researchers to move closer to the central concerns of APD in one study and far afield in the next. This openness to other areas and the ease of movement and exchange across related inquiries have been important, continually informing and enriching the APD enterprise. But this book is not about the interests APD shares with other research programs or about the potential, however real, for mutual enrichment; it is about APD's own core features. To bring the enterprise into sharper relief and provide an overview of issues to be pursued in later chapters, the remainder of these introductory remarks survey what we take to be the distinguishing marks of research into America's political development.

For instance, the characteristic that most readily identifies APD scholars among other political scientists is their dedication to analyzing American politics through intensive research in American history. What do they expect to find there? Are they closet historians who somehow ended up in the wrong Ph.D. program, or are they after something in particular?

The answer likely to gain the widest assent from scholars who identify with the APD project is that they hope to learn more than

5

is already known about how, and with what effect, American politics changes over time. As is often the case with simple answers, this one will require further explanation to be meaningful, but even by itself, it should dispose of any idea that practitioners study history for background, because they think the political issues presented in the past are somehow more interesting or important than the issues of our own day, or because every theory of politics necessarily refers to history, if only for data to analyze and test theory against. The answer might serve also as a preliminary characterization of APD as a "theory-driven" enterprise. APD does not use history as a grab bag of examples; it does not approach the past as a benign proving ground for a theory of politics constructed on other foundations. Its aspiration is to build theories of politics that are more attentive than others available to specifically historical processes of change and the political issues that those processes pose. It should be equally apparent that APD researchers want to know more than just "what happened" in the past; their aims characteristically go beyond getting the narrative of characters and events – the story – down on paper as accurately and meaningfully as possible. Taking care to get the facts right is important in this as in all forms of social science. APD's primary interest, however, lies in grasping processes of change conceptually, in general terms, and in considering their broader implications for the polity as a whole.

One procedure to this end is comparison. Comparisons in APD research appear in many different forms, but alternative points of reference are seldom far from view: What happened at other times in American history? What happened at the same time in other parts of American government? What might have happened had things followed the path prescribed by some normative standard of politics? What happened at similar points in the history of other countries? The strong comparative bent of APD research, and its intellectual debt to comparative historical theory, stems in part from its interest in generalizing beyond a particular set of historical events and in part from an interest in counterfactuals broadly considered, that is, in analogous material that might help reveal how outcomes vary in relation to different historical circumstances.[3] Why, for example, did the labor movement in America turn out the way it did rather than some other way?

There are limits to this interest in thinking about American politics as a branch of comparative political studies; the comparisons featured reflect APD's own particular purposes. For instance, when politics in the United States is situated against politics in other countries, it is likely that the comparisons will be used to highlight what, if any, problems or characteristics of change are peculiar to the historical configuration of government and politics in the United States. This has important advantages, bringing the United States into sharper relief while guarding against unexamined claims of American exceptionalism. With or without the use of comparisons, APD's single-country focus avoids the side-stepping that sometimes accompanies cross-country data and seeks instead to grapple with political change as it occurs, or not, in a specific place, the United States. It examines the terms, conditions, and meanings of change as these might be understood for this polity. The experiences of other countries are, in this sense, part of the backdrop, helping to set the stage for the issues that APD puts front and center: How is this polity put together? What constitutes significant change within it? How does that occur? Does political change in America build to something new or merely reshuffle old forms? Is there a discernable direction to political change in America over time? Answers to these questions appear study by study, as scholars organize American political history into patterns, political regularities observed over time.

Pattern identification is the sine qua non of the enterprise.[4] Without patterns – representatives get reelected, wars build states, electoral realignments occur about every thirty years, African Americans vote Democratic – American political history would be just "one damn thing after another," a relentless succession of events impervious to any larger meaning; sorting through and making sense of the innumerable details that attend every political situation would be difficult, perhaps impossible. Discovering patterns helps to locate the key components of a situation and demarcating them helps to identify meaningful points of change – before as opposed to after Congress reorganized itself; at the start as opposed to the end of the war; before the civil rights movement as opposed to after the mobilization of African Americans into politics. Political history, as we come to analyze and understand it, is always an arrangement of time into patterns.

APD research is not alone in the search for patterns; pattern identification is one of the most common of all research techniques. The basic procedure, the same everywhere, may even be said to subsume comparisons of the sort described earlier in which politics in, for example, France, Great Britain, and the United States, is treated essentially as different sets of patterns. As applied generally, the technique is first to classify historical material according to certain general characteristics and the circumstances of their occurrence and then to employ this classification in the analysis of material drawn from other times or places to determine the presence or absence of these same general characteristics and circumstances. The pattern, the regular appearance of a particular set of political characteristics across time or space, opens to explanation or to being discarded as uninteresting coincidence.

Though the technique is widely used, there is considerable variation in the kinds of patterns featured in different fields of research, and here again, particular uses tell a lot about the purposes of these fields themselves. Without pressing the point too hard, it is perhaps fair to say that historians characteristically stick closer to chronology in their search for patterns than do APD researchers, especially contemporary APD researchers. Moreover, when they address large-scale patterns, historians are apt to bundle contiguous years into bounded "eras" and to identify consistencies across institutional and cultural settings in ways that serve to synthesize politics within a period of time – the "age" of Federalism, the "age" of Jackson, the "party period," the Cold War era. Even when historians identify patterns that recur over broad stretches of time – for instance, the republican ideology of the Founding era as it reappears in subsequent decades – it is the repetition within bounded periods rather than the mechanisms that move politics from one period to the next that holds sway.

APD research is, in contrast, characteristically more aggressive in its manipulation of patterns and more radical in its departure from

8

a chronological view of history. The patterns it brings to light are as likely to overlap one another in an irregular fashion as to neatly align within a period, and the patterns of interest often range across broad swaths of time. These might be patterns of the present that extend all the way back to the origins of the Republic and before – like religious "awakening" – or patterns of the past, which, though seeming to fall away, leave traces that affect the operation of the new ones set in motion – like royal prerogative. Illuminating patterns of this sort, APD research indicates political movement *through* time rather than a polity bounded in time and highlights connections *between* politics in the past and politics in the present rather than the separateness and foreignness of past politics.[5]

By looking at what APD scholars do, we begin to see a bit more clearly what they are after. By giving their own twist to standard tools of comparison and pattern identification, they are better able to discern the separate elements that comprise the American polity, to see how these are arrayed and configured in time, and to examine how and with what effect the array changes over time. Their purposes are not entirely coincident with those of others who use one or both of these same techniques, with those of, for instance, historians, comparative theorists, or Americanists working in other precincts of political science. Nonetheless, their use of comparison and pattern identification emphasizes essential aspects of politics and political change neglected elsewhere.

Continuity and Change

Thinking about patterns in APD research immediately presents a paradox. Though centrally concerned with political change and its significance, the patterns scrutinized with greatest frequency in the APD literature – arguably the most important in lending APD coherence as a "field" – are patterns of constancy, displaying little or no apparent change over time. These are features of American politics that appear to be the most resilient, that seem to have remained the same in certain essential characteristics over the better part of two centuries. The Constitution, with its foundational structure of federalism, separated powers, and fixed and staggered elections, is the subject of one such claim of no-change; the failure of radical ideologies, in particular of socialist movements, to take hold in the United States is another; the two-party system is a third; sectional divisions in the political economy a fourth. These constants present the master problematic of APD research: how to calibrate the significance of change amid so much apparent continuity in the fundamentals?

Though prominently featured, these continuities are not taken at face value in APD research; on the contrary, scholars characteristically put them up against other patterns that circumscribe, modify, or otherwise impinge on their fixed status. Cyclical patterns produce one sort of modification, for example, new party coalitions form every thirty years, with each new formation significantly altering the meaning and effect of constitutional relationships.[6] Other changes, related to patterns, are imprinting events, breakpoints in time, that alter aspects of politics decisively from before and with far-reaching consequences for operations elsewhere later down the road: the revolt against Speaker of the House Joseph Cannon in 1910 marked a sea change in the internal operations of the Congress and eventually made itself felt on institutional relationships throughout the government.[7] Another pattern appears in the breach, in some defining void, which operates as a "boundary condition" of politics in this polity: the absence of full-blown feudalism in America's past circumscribed its politics long into the future, wedding it seemingly forever to a liberal ideology.[8] And there are relationships formed by the sequencing of patterns: the franchise in the United States was extended widely prior to the development of central administrative controls; like a boundary condition, this sequence influences rather than signals change or no-change.[9]

Cycles and other recurrent patterns found in American political history are of special interest in assessing relations of continuity and change because they suggest that breakpoints themselves sometimes take the form of patterned events. Recent observations of recurrence in the APD literature include recurrent moments of constitutional reconstruction,[10] recurrent modes of presidential leadership,[11] recurrent cultural outbursts contributing to the secular growth of government,[12] recurrent backsliding from liberal advances,[13] and recurrent waves of antitrust agitation.[14] In each case, the mode of change itself suggests a certain kind of continuity, a more encompassing regularity operating at some deeper level that calls for identification and explanation in its own right. Explaining these modalities is likely to involve a characterization of the operations of the American polity overall as well as to encourage a more circumspect characterization of just how different American politics is from one period to the next. In this way, recurrent patterns of change provide a point of entry into some rather subtle questions: whether, and in what sense, do we observe the same constitution or the same political culture at work across major periods of political change? How, and in what sense, are these constants actually implicated in the changes themselves?

But there is a more general and important point to be made about APD's interest in relations of continuity and change. Constants, cycles, watersheds, boundaries, breakpoints – all are seen in APD research to exert themselves on political action in the moment at hand. They are not factors in the background but constitutive elements of the situation under analysis. At any given moment, the different rules, arrangements, and timetables put in place by changes negotiated at various points in the past will be found to impose themselves on the actors of the present and to affect their efforts to negotiate changes of their own. How, for example, is each successive wave of anti-trust agitation affected by interim changes in corporate organization? Likewise, when random, unpatterned events intrude on a scene – a natural disaster, a foreign attack, the death of a leader – their impact is revealed in the extent to which they disrupt patterns in play and counter the effects of past actions, sometimes without leaving a mark, sometimes causing a new pattern to begin.

Suffice it to say at this point that when continuity and change are given their maximum play in the analysis of political history, chronology gives way to a fuguelike motion of stops and starts, with backtracking and leapfrogging not readily captured on a calendar. Some lines persist; others recur; new lines form; others disappear. Addition, subtraction, repetition – all have their effect on what ensues. Take, for instance, a constant of American politics, the electoral college. Close study shows that in the late nineteenth century, the electoral college had an important impact on how congressmen voted on public policy, supporting their leaders' attempt to shape a coalition of states wide enough to win the White House. By the midtwentieth century, however, this impact had largely vanished. The electoral college had not disappeared; the change occurred, rather, because new congressional rules and new resources in the office of the president had intercepted and altered its effects.[15]

It is precisely in its combination and juxtaposition of patterns that politics may be understood as *shaped* by time. That is to say, politics is historically constructed not only by the human beings who from time to time negotiate changes in one aspect of the polity or another but also by the new configuration of patterns, old and new, that ensues. Put yet another way, the contours of the polity are determined in the first instance by those who seek to change it and by the changes they make and in the second instance by all the arrangements that get carried over from the past and are newly situated in an altered setting. If for political historians, time is primarily the stretch of years and politics finds itself along that expanse, for APD scholars, the calendar can often be dispensed with in favor of locating patterns and circumstances solely as they appear against one another. History in this sense is instrumental to APD's main object, which is to tell time politically or to tell time according to the juxtaposition of patterns old and new and their interactive effects.[16] Consider the sequence mentioned above, in which democratization precedes bureaucratization: its importance in APD is not merely that one came before the other but how early democratization in the absence of bureaucracy affected state building when it eventually occurred. It is through the structures and dynamics of political time that APD locates problems of political action and analyzes political change.

Analysts have found great variety in the historical constructions that shape politics. Some show a convergence of elements from different directions on a single alteration, as in the change in congressional voting mentioned above. Others are indicated in cross section, as an interaction effect among persistent, recurrent, and emergent elements.[17] Some indicate layering, with one set of patterns moving in parallel to another, seemingly related but without apparent mutual impact.[18] Others are configurative, like the sectional divisions of the American political economy, where change follows along preexisting parameters.[19] Even when historical constructions point to a resilient pattern in the current mix – to the persistence of sectionalism, liberalism, racism, sexism, capitalism, or some particularly robust institutional structure – they characteristically illuminate as well modifications introduced by the addition or subtraction of other elements or by a new arrangement among the component parts.[20] In this way, the relative impact of time on any political episode becomes an empirical question of its own.

Order and Change

Notwithstanding APD's strong commitment to historical research, the impulse to seek explanations in comparisons, patterns, and juxtapositions, to sort out relations of continuity and change, to formulate general concepts by which to identify these constructions and evaluate their significance holds APD within the discipline of political science. A closer look at priorities within the home discipline, however, suggests still other features that set the APD project apart. In particular, APD's emphasis on change over time, on movement in politics, which is in large part responsible for its strong historical bent, contrasts with the emphasis on order and stability in politics often displayed in other political science programs.

This divergence in emphases seems especially pronounced in the study of American politics, where the main lines of scholarship have sought ever more elaborate explanations for order – formal constitutional arrangements, informal rules of the game, open systems striving for balance, rational actors building institutions that will induce an equilibrium. It would not be going too far to say that the dominant mission of the study of American politics has been to expose and explain the pervasiveness of order within it, to discover sources of coherence amid the constant commotion and far-flung parts of this polity, to account for the stability of American democracy. Not so in

APD. This research exposes sources of disorder, introduces incongruity and fragmentation into depictions of the political norm, and pushes to the foreground an essentially dynamic view of the polity as a whole.[21]

To be sure, APD cannot, and does not, turn its back on questions of order entirely: how stability and predictability can obtain in a world beset by constant threats of discord and disruption is rightly one of the oldest in political thought. More mundanely, the importance of order in governmental affairs is obvious – and not only as order figures as an obstacle to change, as it certainly does. The presence of order is evident, for instance, in the very patterns by which APD tracks and assesses change and continuity. But if APD does not reject the premise that there is order to be discerned in political affairs, it does demote that premise to the status of a baseline, analytically and empirically, for a different research agenda.

The telling point of contrast will be found in how different kinds of political analysis account for change. In conventional political analysis, even when the subject matter is historical, change is usually regarded as an interlude between relatively permanent settlements, a transition from one steady state or stable path to another. Situated in time between the "normal" politics of order, change is seen as episodic and contained. Conversely, in APD, change is something inherent in politics as such; it is an integral feature of the juxtaposition of patterns that construct politics historically. Understanding change this way means that the alternative to a search for order need not be a capitulation to chaos; relaxing the premise of order in politics may in fact lead to a clearer understanding of it, its character, operation, limits, and significance.

APD brings this prospect into view by breaking down, so far as possible, the conceptual barricades that have been erected between order and change in politics and by devising new analytic strategies that indicate how each bears more immediately and continuously on the other. These innovations, it should be noted, invoke and build on a rather conventional definition of political order – that it is a constellation of rules, institutions, practices, and ideas that hang together over time, a bundle of patterns, in the language used above, exhibiting coherence and predictability while other things change around them. It is in this way that we understand terms like *the constitutional order* and the *Jacksonian regime* and the seniority system in Congress. But when the operating limits of these orders are scrutinized, and their surroundings more closely observed, it becomes less meaningful to talk about a political universe that is ordered than about the multiple orders that compose it and their relations with one another. Some might reinforce one another for a time, others might operate in constant tension with one another, and still others might simply parallel one another for a time with no apparent effect. The wider berth sought for studying the sources of change and for reconceptualizing change as an essential aspect of politics stems directly from the careful attention now being paid to the limits, contingencies, varieties, and incongruities of order.

A number of related strategies have been employed to this end, each of them involving the division or disaggregation of politics along separate dimensions into composite parts. One, a disaggregation along the dimension of time into patterns, has been described in the previous sections; still, it is instructive to consider how current thinking about patterns departs from prior practice in this particular respect. The contrast is most striking in the deployment of periodization schemes. In earlier years, APD scholars, not unlike historians, were inclined think in terms of synthetic schemes that would bundle together as much of American political history as possible between the fewest number of period breaks; in fact, one periodization scheme currently meeting criticism on this ground is one of APD's own founding paradigms – the "realignment synthesis" of American political history.[22]

In current scholarship, the preference runs the other way, toward periodization schemes that are more variable and multiform and less well aligned with one another. By identifying narrower, more discrete patterns that overlap and counteract and layer upon one another simultaneously, researchers produce a less consistent, more disjoint picture of the normal state of politics overall. Consider parties, for instance: recent research has shown that changes in the ideologies of America's two major parties do not move in tandem with changes in their coalitional alignment with one another but seem to follow a different logic with consequences of its own.[23] The same technique has been used to disaggregate elements within periods. Take the legislation of the Progressive era: here two impulses are engaged – one to promote corporate reform and social welfare, and the other to promote racial segregation and white supremacy. In other words, the "age of reform" did not push change in one way only but in two seemingly contrary directions at once.[24]

A second, closely related, strategy has been to scrutinize ordering mechanisms thought to induce a broad-based uniformity in political organization. In APD today there is deep skepticism about master ideas or processes alleged to arrange political affairs for extended periods of time or prime movers that claim to control political action in other important domains: the "liberal consensus"[25]; the "organizational synthesis"[26]; "elections, the mainsprings of American politics"[27]; "Congress, the keystone of the Washington establishment."[28] This skepticism extends to the most firmly ingrained conceit of all in this category – the idea that the Supreme Court is the final arbiter of changes in the constitutional rules of the game. Correcting the distortions introduced by a Court-centered view of who is in charge of these rules and pointing to the full variety of sources of constitutional innovation affords a new multisided picture of constitutional politics, one in which states, representatives, executives, and judges are all "in charge," vying with one another to determine the Constitution's meaning.[29]

With claims about prime movers and master organizing mechanisms held in abeyance, more circumspect specifications of order have been free to proliferate. This tendency is already far advanced in the study of the history of public policy, where scholars now speak of an "American health-care policy regime," for example, and an "American pension policy regime."[30] These are orders as we have always understood them (constellations of rules, practices, institutions, and ideas that hold together over time) but with the proviso that they are different from one another and that both operate at the same time. Thus, a health-care policy regime organized around public supplements to an extensive private provision of benefits operates alongside a pension regime organized around private supplements to a more extensive public provision of benefits. The language of "path dependency," recently picked up by students of public policy, calls attention to the tenacity of such orders and to their composition as bits of the polity that hang together internally even though there may not be much consistency among them. Surrounding orders and events are then analyzed for how they support or challenge the constellations specified, and comparisons are made between the course of different policy regimes in the same polity and with similar policies in different polities.[31]

Pushing these insights further, and bringing us closer to a reconceptualization of the relationship between political order and political change, are observations about tensions routinely introduced by the simultaneous operation, or intercurrence, of different political orders. For instance, in the 1830s the coexistence of southern slavery with an expanding democracy for white male citizens is not a refutation of order in itself, but rather evidence that any realistic depiction of politics in time will include multiple orders, as well as the conflict and irresolution built into their reciprocal interactions.[32] At every point in antebellum America, politics was framed by the competing entailments and mutually threatening movements of these two orders along their different paths, and these two orders at least – for certainly others were at work. Thus the order of church-state relations: changes within religious dominations at this time bore down on the institutions of democracy and slavery alike, both holding the antebellum polity together and breaking it apart, and with regional variation in the order of American states. The mix is, again, typical; in any given analysis it will be elaborated and refined.

Finally, APD has undertaken a reappraisal of the nature and role of political institutions. The traditional role played by institutions as ordering mechanisms in politics is prominently displayed in APD research, but in the effort to bring the study of order to bear more directly on understandings of change, this research has begun to stress other aspects of their significance. First, scholars have observed that these traditional bulwarks of order in politics are not only so many rules and practices that may, incidentally, restrain political change but also repositories of purposeful political action; indeed, institutions are composed of operatives who promote change, often in the course of resisting it from others.[33] Second, scholars have observed the impact of institutions, singly and collectively, on the formation of political identities among those subjected to their control and tied these order-inducing mechanisms more closely to strategies of action, be they strategies of compliance, resistance, or reform.[34] Third, scholars have observed that when institutions persist in the face of changes taking place around them, they themselves become implicated in the historical construction of the disjoint politics referred to earlier. This includes their tendency to delimit change and render it incomplete, to continue their operation in new historical formations that thereby come to be riddled with inconsistent mandates and purposes.[35]

All of this is explained and illustrated more fully as we proceed. Here we might pause to remark on the irony of a research agenda that has elevated the importance of government institutions, and of law, in the analysis of historical construction only to implicate them in a conception of political order that is inherently fragmented and productive of changes elsewhere in the polity. At bottom, this curiosity speaks to the distinctive understanding of politics that is implicit in recent APD research. Although institutions are by no means neglected by other research programs in political science, they tend to be subordinated by theories and methods that are essentially individualist, and their role is correspondingly attenuated. In both pluralist and rational choice theories, for instance, the institutions of government are at best first among equals, necessary scaffolding for interest group activity and for "game forms."[36] In APD, the importance of government institutions is conveyed directly as an ineluctable political characteristic: their built-in mandates for controlling behavior at large and through time. These mandates motivate institutions in ways that, to varying degrees, subsume individual operatives and their personal preferences. Moreover, the fact that these mandates are promulgated at different times rather than all at once means that institutions are frequently found at loggerheads with one another. Taken together, these considerations suggest that institutions designed to promulgate and enforce mandates – that is, the institutions of government – are in a category by themselves, theoretically and descriptively in the processes of political change. Indeed, the assertion of their pivotal position in the slogan "bringing the state back in" signaled APD's entry on the scene in the 1970s.[37]

In at least this respect, it might be argued that APD *has* had a unifying and enlarging effect on conceptions of "the political" even as it has disaggregated ordering mechanisms and problematized their impact on the whole. Just as attention to the outward reach of government institutions, setting and enforcing the rules by which all other institutions are established and perpetuated, serves to bring discussions of order more directly to bear on the analysis of change, it also serves to dissolve any stark analytic separation between state and society. As it has turned out, "bringing the state back in" has been less a matter of asserting the "autonomy" of government institutions than a matter of asserting the primacy of the categorical realm of authority within which social relations are organized, political identifies formed, and transformative ambitions directed. This is reflected in APD's own reach outward from government authority proper to race relations, church relations, industrial relations, family relations, and the like, pieces of the "polity" that qualify as such through their legal regulation but which were likely to be relegated in conventional political analysis to the status of "private" interests and "social" conflicts. No doubt it was this same intuition about the scope of government and politics that caused younger, politically minded historians to abandon conventional political history, with its all but exclusive preoccupation on the formal institutions of state and the elites who operate them.

Change and Method

We can now say with some confidence that APD's emphasis on change entails a distinctive approach to political analysis. Order continues to play an important part – usually it is an order of some kind that is displaced or modified by change – but the insistence on treating every state of affairs as in transition, a state, as it were, in the process of becoming, sets APD's understanding of politics apart. The meaning of any order becomes inseparable from what it has preempted; its significance is to be found in the tensions that accumulate within and around it over time and how these bear on its current stability and future direction. The primacy of order in other forms of political analysis is evident in the attention they give to how institutions operate internally, how they arrive at rules to begin with, how these are enforced, and how these rules spontaneously or otherwise break down – often because of external changes that are themselves left unexplained. APD's different emphasis moves the discussion from the normality of stasis to contingencies of status, from the coherence of internal relations to the external incongruities, from politics as a series of settlements to politics as the current configuration of conflicts. This move demands that change be accounted for comprehensively, that its agents and limits be specified, and that its precipitants and conditions be explained.

But how can this be done? In our remarks thus far we have invoked historical construction as the bridging operation that keeps politics past and politics present linked across changes, but we have said little about the way in which these connections are to be made analytically and how the insights inherent in that image are to be exploited. These are matters of method and research design, matters we address here provisionally by examining how APD scholars situate events, how they demarcate and survey the ground that exists prior to a transformation of interest. This is not a formula that is strictly followed – or to be followed – in every study, but it reflects a logic that directs much of this research. It can be indicated by a few orienting propositions.

Our first proposition is that all political change proceeds on a site, a prior political ground of practices, rules, leaders, and ideas, all of which are up and running. The site can be any definable political expanse – a geographical area, a policy network, a political institution. At first, this seems an innocuous claim; it is hard to imagine an analysis of change that did not begin with placement in time and space, without specifying the site. Consider a famous example that APD scholars would otherwise be quick to take issue with: John Locke's assertion in the Second Treatise on Government that "in the beginning, all the world was America." Locke meant "America" to conjure up in the minds of his readers a place sparsely populated by individuals who lived without money, property, or government. "America" described a platform for political development, laying out the circumstances that would have to be met and overcome if something new was to be created. Even in this metaphorical, wholly voluntaristic, and largely frictionless account, change confronts a prior state of affairs.

APD scholars proceed in a similar way with the important proviso that their sites are historical, set in real time. Locke sought to explain the construction of politics with reference to timeless principles of human action, and to that end, he was intent on stripping away as far as possible the trappings of actual historical circumstances. A historical site, in contrast, will display all the tensions and contradictions of prior construction. That is to say, no matter how far back we go in real time, change confronts political authority already on the scene. By virtue of its historical character, political change is always a *re*construction.

Because historical sites take in a web of existing relations among diverse individuals and institutions, they call for description at the macro or system level rather than the micro or individual level. Like other studies in political science, APD highlights agency – citizens' actions, legislators' votes, politicians' designs. It also makes some familiar assumptions about behavior – that agents are more or less rational in pursuing goals, that they understand rules, and that they have limited responses to coercion. But insofar as political change is at issue, the scene always includes those likely to be affected by what transpires – other persons or adjacent institutions – and the consequences that ensue, intended or not, immediate and long term. Thus the preference in APD literature is for "thick" over "stylized" descriptions of sites, descriptions that show an array of different pieces and how they are associated and also for process tracing – examination of the reverberations of a change and of carryovers that are largely unaffected by it. It follows also that the degree to which historical sites of change can be walled off from action occurring in other precincts remains an open question; boundaries drawn for heuristic purposes are themselves provisional propositions pending evidence of effects observed along a wider front. As we have observed already, and as we argue at length in later chapters, relations with outsiders are central to the "development" of politics.

It is also worth noting the special resonance of specifying historical sites of this sort with the study of political change in the United States, where political self-conceptions are famously attached to the possibility of creating things anew – a "new Adam," a "new order of the ages," a "New Deal," a "New Beginning." Specifying sites historically underscores the fact that no political transformation is complete, that even violent revolutions leave traces of earlier regimes, and that nothing follows on a clean slate. APD assumes that development occurs on sites that are more or less changeable but never empty, nonexistent, or inconsequential.

Our second proposition pushes a bit further: sites of political change are characterized by "full" or "plenary" authority; rules and agents designated to enforce them cover the territory, however it is defined. This idea might raise a few eyebrows: would it apply, for instance, to the lone adventurer in the 1840s making his way across an empty stretch of western prairie or to a nation verging on anarchy where the semblance of law and order has all but broken down? The answer is yes, for though enforcement problems may stimulate new developments, political development itself involves changing the prior set of rules by which a collectivity has been governed. A description of America's "beginnings," which took plenary governance as a guide, would include, for starters, the apparatus of religious conformity in seventeenth-century England, royal charters, compacts arrived at on-board ship to America, and the organization of the native villages already established there. In short, authority in different forms and in mutually impinging arrays permeates the field. Far from filling a void, political development on this site would very soon confront rules governing everything from the legitimate uses of land and work relations to the practice of religion and the relations of husband and wife.

With this view of the matter, Locke's "America" quickly gives way to other imagery: "in the beginning, all the world was downtown Tokyo." In historical construction, as in downtown Tokyo, empty lots are few and far between: building something new usually means disturbing something else (even minor improvements implicate adjacent installations and services), and several different projects are likely to be underway at any given time. Plenary authority means that changing any aspect of politics entails bumping against authority already in existence; if not immediately apparent (as with our friend crossing the western prairie) it may, at any time, descend. The question will always be how much of what is there gives way. What stays the same will be just as important for the specific effect it will have on the future staying power – the viability – of the change in question and important as well for the processes of historical construction that will move forward from that point.

The proposition of plenary authority counters deceptively simple and familiar understandings of political development like "the growth of government" as it is manifested in more public buildings, higher public expenditures, and more officials on the public payroll. Though the forms and instruments of government have changed substantially over the years, America in the nineteenth century was no less fully governed than America in the twentieth; more of some forms of authority indicates less of others, which, though they may have been less conspicuous, were not necessarily less suited to their purpose. At the same time, plenary authority need not imply efficient governance. It allows for competing and conflicting authorities on a site as well as any spaces that might be opened for new authority by ineffective enforcement mechanisms; it accommodates activities that might insinuate themselves between the lines of existing authority or in places where no rules have yet been laid down; and it acknowledges corrupt authority, with rules observed mainly in the breach. Furthermore, although plenary authority calls attention to change as a disruption of embedded governing arrangements, it should not imply that change always has to be wrenching. There are numbers of ways in which the disruption might be minimized: cooptation and preemption are well-known processes of this sort. Finally, the proposition that sites of political development are characterized by plenary authority should not be misunderstood to imply that political change can only shuffle things around, as the cards of a deck might be shuffled around a table. There is a big difference between the assumption that polities have always been fully governed in our sense and the assumption that all government is the same. Downtown Tokyo is continually being remade; the proposition of plenary authority emphasizes the status quo ante and in that sense also the channels of political invention.

It is by means of these two propositions that the historical construction of politics can be seen to play out in any given episode of change. A study by Martin Shefter of "regional receptivity to reform" during the Progressive era might serve as an illustrative example. The question Shefter poses is why the progressive reform impulse of the early twentieth century took hold more strongly in the western states than it did in the Northeast. The key step in his analysis is the specification of the two political landscapes as they appeared in the late nineteenth century. In the West, the critical role of railroad transportation divided communities politically along lines determined by their access to railroad service and rates. Railroad corporations financed elections and wove their influence deeply through the state governments, and over the course of the nineteenth century issues of corporate influence and political corruption dominated political conflict in the region. Farther east, where the establishment of parties preceded the rise of railroads, the political reach of the issues that dominated in the West was more attenuated. Parties organized eastern politics early on, and they were becoming even more adept at doing so during the late nineteenth century. They ran elections, organized state and local governments, and divided communities politically over the issues that they chose to contest, principally the tariff. The deeper inroads made by the Progressives in the West, it is argued, followed from the greater prominence of corporate control in that region and the greater difficulties of unsettling traditional party loyalties in the Northeast.[38]

Our third methodological proposition rounds out the above: political change ultimately registers its developmental significance in altered forms of governance. This assertion follows directly from the historical view of change provided by a description of authority relations as they are arranged on a site, demanding simply that significant political change manifest itself in a new array or new arrangement of authorities on the scene. Changes that do not leave a mark on authority relations – an idea stillborn, a movement crushed, a party abandoned – are topics of interest, but they tell us more about impediments to political development and the boundaries of political development than about the significance of political development. By the same token, due emphasis in this proposition should be given to the word *ultimately*, for APD is interested in the sources and processes as well as the fact of political change. The formation of associations, the building of parties, and the origin and dissemination of new ideas are all integral to America's political development and, in that sense, are important subjects for study in their own right. The point is that although any of these may figure prominently in an explanation, they do not and cannot complete an analysis of political development. Regardless of where the impetus comes from – an association, a party, an economic group, a sectional interest, a religious movement, a charismatic leader, or another institution – political change will move through or against extant forms of governance and, absent evidence of some new relations of governing authority, its significance must remain in doubt. Effects may be immediate or long term, direct or attenuated, and in tracing the relations between cause and effect intervening factors may be seen to hold great significance, but in the final analysis, we are looking for changes in how people are governed.

This third proposition serves the analysis empirically, for it has the virtue of concreteness. As a practical matter, the institutions of government, with their explicit mandates, methods of operation, and extensive paper trails, provide the more ready means for tracking and marking change, as evidence drawn from noninstitutional settings must often rely more heavily on interpretation and conjecture. Consider, for example, American populism. Populism was long considered a failure, despite its unmistakable presence in party politics, institutional struggles, and policy debates during the 1890s. It failed in that the Populist agenda for the reform of American government and public policy, which was presented most forcefully in the 1890s, was defeated. Recent scholars have challenged this conclusion, pointing to later organizational innovations for the mobilization of farmers and to populist policy commitments that dominated the national agenda and made their way into law long after the demise of the Populist party.[39] In both views the proof of Populism's significance ultimately turns on changes in governance; the question disputed is the extent to which the changes negotiated later can be traced back to the original movement and the extent to which later intervening factors altered their meaning and effect. This doesn't downplay the role of ideas or innovation or movement organization; it enhances and centers them within their purposes.

Change and Meaning

Assertions about populism's "failure" throw into the hopper one final set of issues, those of interpretation and meaning. Thus far, much of what we have said about APD could be applied to politics in any country, and the analytic template we have lighted upon may well recommend itself for use in other national settings. The *A* in APD would, in this sense, refer to one among many laboratories for research on the historical construction of politics and its significance. But there is more to it than that. A method that situates the analysis of change in the thick description of a site signals the intention of the analyst to enter into issues and problems as they are understood on that site, to address the historical formation under investigation as a configuration of political norms. The questions taken up by APD research are seldom disembodied from the life of the polity itself; more often than not, they are keyed to its changing circumstances and integral to its lived experience. If there is a single aspiration that has persisted throughout the long history of this enterprise, it is for a political science that will take its cues from the problems of American government and politics itself, a political science that will bring its own interpretations of the American "experiment" into a dialogue of practical significance with others interested in America's future.

Whatever else might be said of this aspiration, it clearly cuts against the grain, countering, first and foremost, the ever-stronger emphasis in political science at large on the scientific nature of its inquiries. The scientific emphasis narrows the potential audience even among professional political scientists, excluding all but small bands of specialists working in the same subfield. Wider meaning can be extracted from strictly social-scientific efforts: modeling committee behavior in the House of Representatives, for instance, can have important things to tell us about the requisites of order in a democracy, but those inferences will vary and must be made with caution. No less obvious is that the fragmentation of scholarship on American politics into the discrete subject areas that prove more amenable to rigorous scientific treatment – the Congress, the parties, the electorate – itself militates against conclusions about the condition or prospects of the broader polity, although whether this is a cause or an effect of normative reticence would be difficult to say. Fundamentally there exists today no impetus, intellectually or professionally, to raise or answer the "big" questions that have traditionally been the stock-in-trade of APD research; indeed, in some circles, these questions may be considered subversive of the purposes and rules of inquiry.

On another count, then, APD finds itself set apart. At issue is just what sort of theory APD aspires to build or, perhaps more accurately, whether in its aspirations to build a historical theory of politics, it can hold together and reconcile its own competing impulses. Although its conception of itself, in part at least, as an interpretive enterprise, engaged in a conversation about the past and future prospects of the American polity, may promote skepticism toward certain extreme forms of positivist social science, for the most part, APD scholars endorse the idea of a science of politics. They credit empirical research as the surest route to knowledge; they affirm the value of accumulating knowledge and not simply more timely interpretations; they hold their research to accessible standards of falsification and proof. No doubt, some are attracted to APD because they see it as a way to join empirical research to interpretative issues like liberalism, democracy, and modernity. But there is also a good deal of hedging on this score, a reluctance to renounce any part of this program, and at the same time an uncertainty of how to defend it. In fact, as things now stand, this uncertainty is well grounded.

As a preliminary matter, we might take stock of the many ways in which APD research serves to facilitate normative inquiry. One of them underscores a point made at times in writings on the philosophy of history: that the activity of studying the past is by its nature an interrogation of the past, a cross-examination of a set of allegations of interest to the investigator.[40] This seems amply borne out by existing APD research. In fact, the temporal patterns that may have seemed so abstract earlier in this chapter imply interrogation of just this sort. Boundary conditions, for instance, refer to alternatives foreclosed invoking, almost nostalgically, values and possibilities "lost." Cycles locate political actions in recurrent situations, and they alter how we understand individual motive and performance. The historical construction of politics, as we have presented it, and the idea of juxtaposition arguably have similar effects.

More direct support for a subtext of normative engagement is found in the topics prominently featured in APD research: sectionalism, populism, the welfare state, race, gender, and business regulation. These are not simply topics of historical controversy; they are topics of present-day controversy whereby history can be seen to bear directly on contemporary political dilemmas. They may or may not have been chosen for study for this reason; at a minimum they point to the fact that the history of the United States has been to this point a prolonged moral saga, self-proclaimed as such from its beginnings. When the U.S. post office is scrutinized, as it has been in several APD studies, it is viewed in the perspective of democratic office holding, political party building, and the spread of public communication.[41] Studies of state building divide according their stand for or against libertarian premises. To be sure, these studies are not only, and often not mainly, about these large themes, but there is no mistaking the inference that the results observed mattered for some set of purposes beyond the events analyzed.

Or consider the most prominent pattern of no-change taken up in APD research: the enduring precedence of liberal ideology. Liberal ideology has been offered up as an explanation of continuity and adaptability in political culture, in political institutions, and between the two; it has also served as a foil for highlighting evidence of disjunction, contradiction, and provincial foreclosure of other programs and worldviews. Some of these studies are forthrightly evaluative. Others, ostensibly more matter-of-fact, unpack liberal ideas to demonstrate their multiplicity, though they too reveal distinctively "meaningful" overtones of limitation and possibility at critical junctures of political choice. This preoccupation seems altogether appropriate given the continuing role of liberal ideology in American politics and its expanding aegis globally.

In all these ways, it is easy to see how the style and substance of APD research serve as a basis for normative inquiries. What is less clear is whether APD is, or will remain, more than a label that can be attached willy-nilly to historically based interpretations of this kind, or whether there is something added to these inquiries by the problem of political development itself. Of all the issues we have raised in this chapter, this is the one most likely to strike a raw nerve, for it finds APD disarmed on its home turf: on inspection there is today no operating definition of political development agreed on – or even debated – by any identifiable group of APD researchers. The current awkward silence surrounding the concept that names this field clouds all aspects of its ambition – theoretical, scientific, and interpretive.

This problem has been simmering on the back burner of the APD project for some time. In part, the collective reticence to speak cogently to its own core proposition is a reaction to the overweening certainties of earlier scholarship. As is shown in the next chapter, the founding generation of scholars who initially tied political science to questions about political development did not need to look hard for patterns of change, nor were they at pains to disentangle nuanced relations between change and order or to search out meaning in contemporary events. Both patterns and meaning were built into their narrative of liberalism's ascendancy worldwide; change over time consisted of institutional moves that promoted or deviated from that process, and the political issues of the day were open to assessment according to that standard. These scholars documented and commented on liberal progress, identified "stages of advance," and pointed out signs of "backwardness," and it was this understanding of "development" that held their enterprise together as, at once, interpretive, theoretical, and scientific. But this understanding did not stand up to scrutiny – it unraveled in the course of APD's own investigations. Its resuscitation as a premise for serious scholarship was not achieved by a like-minded modernization theory in the 1960s, nor is its respectability likely to be restored by the spread of liberal ideology and institutions in our time. With the demise of this substantive understanding of development as a guide to political study, it is perhaps not surprising that so many APD scholars today work "with their heads down."

Compounding the problem in recent years is the influence of the "postmodern" critique, a philosophical stance on historical interpretation and the status of narrative theory that casts aspersions of its own on the old talk of development while offering little that invites serious reconsideration of the concept.[42] This is of special concern, for whatever might be said of APD's ambiguous relationship to the scientific bent of mainstream political science, its interest in issues of interpretation and meaning have so far found a welcome reception among those who study and practice political philosophy, and the ease with which scholars have moved between political philosophy and the study of American political development has been a source of support for each.[43] Drawing on this support serves to keep interpretive issues alive in historical research on American politics; what is questionable is whether postmodern diffidence about development serves APD's other interests in theory building and political science. Arguably, this exchange too works to deflect attention from the arena in which APD is most likely to make its mark, which is new ways of thinking about the meaning of political change over time.

Development, as in "American political development," is much more than a word; that is why its overtones have rankled to the degree that they have and why scholars of such different stripes have been anxious to shut them off. But for better or worse, themes of advance and progress and reversals, although they can easily hinder objectivity in the hands of the analyst, are also intrinsic to the realm of political action. Persons and movements enter politics seeking to change government and politics, at least in some small aspect, or to hold change back; that is why we routinely speak of political actors as radicals, moderates, and conservatives. Not to ask about how the political world changes, not to ask about whether politics does move on over time, not to explain the processes of this movement or nonmovement, to renounce seeing the problem not only in bits and pieces but also "at large," is to distort the political action we set out to study – populist organizing, constitutional framing, policy entrepreneurship, voting – and to obscure as well the rationale behind its motivations, the rationale behind its strategies.

Regaining lost intellectual traction calls for a new definition of development that can withstand previous criticisms but is still robust in substance. The benefits of such a definition for the community of scholars proceeding under its name should be self-evident. Without it, in fact, it is hard to see how they can hold together, articulate a shared sense of purpose beyond a call for more history, or make an identifiable or lasting contribution. Prospects for their own productive accumulation of knowledge will remain, at best, uncertain, and far from overcoming the fragmentation of contemporary political scholarship, APD research is likely to reinforce it. More positively, by concentrating on a basic dimension of politics that other scholarship does not directly address, a definition can identify the common research program, offer commensurability across the many different substantive subjects that are pertinent to take up, provide a way of summing up results and bringing them to bear on the findings of others. Perhaps most importantly it would facilitate interpretation, allowing for more sure-footed, less ad hoc assertions about what American politics has "meant" to participants in the past, and where, if anywhere, American politics is heading (toward liberalism or against liberalism, somewhere else, or nowhere at all? – politics as just "one damn thing after another.")[44]

In the course of this book, we try our hand at providing a definition that taps this potential. Our strategy is to separate the definition of development proper from the issues, many of them normative, that surround the concept. This definition, we believe, must distinguish between what is political development and what is not. It should also be neutral with respect to any particular trajectory; that is to say, the definition of development should be independent of substantive findings or characterizations, one way or another, about the pattern of political change over time. A definition of this sort is not an all-purpose solution; it is simply a good place to start. If it does its work well, it should help immeasurably in strengthening the empirical, scientific side of APD and in refocusing attention on the larger issues that have always offered the most compelling rationale for its existence as a field.

This, then, is where we are headed in this book. In Chapter Two, we return to the origins of the study of American political development in the late nineteenth century. There we bring into sharper relief the problem-driven character of the enterprise and trace forward the gradual unraveling of the conception of development that once served to illuminate the problems taken up. Next, in Chapter Three, we undertake a review of the new "historical institutional" literature in APD, a body of recent work in which political institutions themselves serve as the primary reference points of order and change in time. In Chapter Four, we proceed to a definition of political development, one that discards what has been shown as untenable in the idea but retains the problem-driven orientation that has always been the hallmark of APD research. Finally, in our concluding chapter, we address in a preliminary fashion some of the "big" issues raised by our overall formulation of APD, this by way of prodding others to move the conversation forward.

TWO

Unraveling the Premise: The Cultural Critique

We Americans are the peculiar, chosen people – the Israel of our time; we bear the ark of the liberties of the world.... The rest of the nations must soon be in our rear. We are the pioneers...; the advanced guard, sent on through the wilderness of untried things to break a new path in the New World that is ours.... Long enough have we been skeptics with regard to ourselves and doubted whether, indeed, the political Messiah has come. But he has come in *us*, if we would but give utterance to his promptings.

Herman Melville, *White Jacket*

EXAMINING POLITICAL DEVELOPMENT IN THE UNITED STATES is tantamount to interrogating the national premise. Faith in development, with this nation in the vanguard of development, are relentless themes of the culture, inscribed in stories about the origins, common struggles, and higher purposes of the American people. The master narrative of American politics tells of a land set apart by Providence to "bear the ark of the liberties of the world," of a nation released from power relationships accumulated by the "Old World" to "break a new path," of "pioneers" who cleared the way for humankind's advance.

The scholars of the late nineteenth century who first turned American political development into a topic for critical inquiry knew exactly what they were doing. They were the embodiment of Melville's "skeptics with regard to ourselves," avowed in their determination to subject the cornerstones of American national identity to empirical scrutiny. For some, the problem was simply to demonstrate the truth of cultural assumptions; for others, it was to dispel illusions and force a less comfortable reality to the fore. All wanted to treat

33

these assumptions as propositions to be tested against hard evidence and alternative explanations, to gain analytic leverage on popular beliefs about political development in the United States, to reassess the larger significance of the American experience on the world stage.

This critical stance has been a part of APD research ever since. Practitioners are still self-conscious in their scrutiny of the national premise, still intent on reassessing popular understandings of American politics in light of changing circumstances, still attuned to the historical, political, and normative problems presented by a culture that identifies itself so intimately with the concept of development. Their search for the proper diagnostic vantage point, at once independent of the culture but directly engaged in its affairs, has driven some of APD's most important conceptual innovations, and their responses to unfolding events have played out as a kind of counterpoint to common perceptions, illuminating the indigenous ideological themes and cultural patterns that motivate and channel American politics.

In this chapter, we retrace the course of these inquiries. Our aim is to reconstruct the discussion about America's political development that scholars have carried on with each other for more than a century. As a practical matter, our account must be selective. Although historians and others have been a part of this conversation from the beginning, we limit ourselves here to the formulations of political scientists.[1] Moreover, rather than catalogue every influential treatment of APD, we flag major points of reconceptualization. Whatever we miss by forgoing a full inventory, we hope to gain by examining more fully the way in which certain exemplary figures altered the enterprise in the course of addressing new problems and changing times. We have selected individuals who set out new propositions about the historical construction of American politics and about general dynamics at work in American political history, propositions that served to move discussions about political development in the United States to new ground.

Considered each by itself, the various interpretations of American political development that have come and gone over the years read like period pieces. With their central assumptions picked apart and cast aside by later scholarship, they may seem to have more to tell us about the times in which they were written than about political development itself. But the survey we propose here, taking in the grand sweep of these inquiries, reveals more. A review of classic works reminds us that the critics of the 1970s who instigated APD's current resurgence did not operate out of the blue but stood in a venerable tradition of scholarship in American political science, complete with its own mode of argumentation. At the same time, by tracking significant alterations in the critical perspective, our review also points to problems arising within the APD project as it has traditionally been conceived.

In part, these problems stem from an accumulation of questions with which the project must now deal. Beginning with an initial debate between John Burgess and Woodrow Wilson over the developmental status of the American Constitution, scholarly scrutiny of the assumptions of American political culture has steadily expanded the range of issues that bear on the question of development. As is shown, the initial critique of the Constitution's structure led to new thinking about political agency, then to questions about the boundaries of change, and later to a focus on culture as a wellspring of political alternatives. It is not simply that each of these concerns has been carried forward, that each continues to retain a hold on the field; rather, each addressed a new problem discovered in trying to understand the others without it. The result has been a progressive refinement of thinking about all of these issues and a more complicated picture of America's political development as a whole.

These complications only hint at the main problem, however: the erosion of the core concept that has motivated discussions of APD over the years. As our survey picks up the threads of this intellectual history and follows them through their many twists and turns, we begin to see beyond the particulars of interpretations long discredited to the critical thrust of the entire undertaking. The cumulative message of these discussions is delivered through their progressive unraveling of assumptions, an unraveling that drives inexorably from the conceits of the culture toward a confrontation with the premise of political development itself. The original skepticism that initially sought merely to make the discussion of political development in America more rigorous has today all but stripped the concept bare.

It is no small irony that the single most important achievement of this line of inquiry, perhaps of the whole of APD research thus far, has been a stinging indictment of the premise that the field names. The critical mode of argumentation endures, and concerns about structure, agency, boundaries, and creativity abide, but for all intents and purposes the enterprise has shed its common grammar for organizing inquiries, locating problems, and making sense of data. Our review reveals a field that has, in the very course of accumulating new insights, pushed itself back to square one, to a critical examination of its own foundations. To reckon with the unraveling of developmental assumptions as it has proceeded over the years is to discover an enterprise ripe for redirection.

The Constitution: Political Structure as Political Development

As political scientists of the late nineteenth century saw things, claims about the advanced standing of the United States among the governments of the world could no longer be accepted simply as a matter of national faith. They wanted to address head-on doubts produced by civil war and industrialization and to identify America's political trajectory free of the providential assumptions of the American creed. They believed the problem of locating the United States developmentally in relation to the other Western states was central to a proper resolution of the domestic and foreign policy issues of their day, and they devised comparative studies of constitutions to address that problem authoritatively.

Although these scholars argued about just how developed the basic structure of the American polity was, their faith in the developmental character of politics at large was complete. The transition from a providential to a social scientific voice in assessments of APD began with the claim that world history, not the Bible, should serve as the primary source of revelation.[2] These scholars believed that the past offered the more reliable, or at least verifiable, record of the true course of political advancement. They did not question that one might discern in history a line of development encompassing the whole of human experience; their objective was to use the accumulated experience of the West to discover that higher form of regime toward which human civilization aspired and to evaluate American institutions in terms of their advancement toward that ultimate type. Placing America on that line was an intellectual project fully attuned to the nineteenth century's grand historical theorizing about great impersonal forces at work in the modernization of civilization. Hegel's "Reason," Spencer's "fate," Comte's "laws" – each enshrined development as human history's guiding principle. American scholars understood the principle instinctively, and they grasped the opportunity that grand theory afforded to put their own country's developmental pretensions to the test.

Idealism

Anchoring the conservative pole in this early testing was the work of America's German idealists, the most eminent of whom, John Burgess, founded the first graduate program in political science at Columbia University in 1880. Burgess's major treatise, *Political Science and Comparative Constitutional Law* (1891), equated political development with the emergence of a nation-state committed to the idea of civil liberty. A connection of this sort had been standard fare among American intellectuals for some time.[3] Historians looking for origins of the liberal nation-state had pointed to the primeval forests of Germany where an idea of self-rule had allegedly inspired the Teutonic tribes to smash the universalizing authority of imperial Rome. Following the elaboration of this idea in different settings at different times, they identified a "Teutonic chain" of progress, a line of historical advance that led out to England with the promulgation and signing of the Magna Carta and then on to the American Revolution and the ratification of the Constitution.[4]

Burgess's political science updated this view of political development and recast it as a framework that might be applied systematically to the analysis of constitutions.[5] He distilled from history three key features of a modern state – a claim of national sovereignty, protections for civil liberty, and a distribution of sovereign powers among different governmental institutions. Then he examined the referents for each of these features in the constitutions of the United States, Germany, Great Britain, and France. His comparisons indicated that the United States was indeed the most constitutionally advanced of the great states in its grasp of the ideals of civil liberty. Protecting the autonomy of individuals through specific provisions enshrined in fundamental law was, in Burgess's view, "the peculiar product of our own political genius" and our greatest contribution to world progress.

Burgess made a similar though more complicated assessment of the various internal arrangements of governmental power to be found among the great states. He conceded that these arrangements were still very much unsettled, and, given the range of possibilities in play, he found it difficult to determine the ultimate type toward which all were aiming. Still, he thought it clear enough that the United States was "many stages in advance of all the rest in this line of progress" as well. He arrived at this conclusion by projecting that the future lay with republican rather than aristocratic or monarchical forms and by assessing the practical benefits and drawbacks of governing a republic through a separation of powers with a strong presidency. Acknowledging the problems posed by the occasional "deadlock between the executive and legislative branches," he found overriding advantages both in the stability this design offered to republics and in the capacity of the independent executive to act with dispatch in times of emergency.[6]

These findings notwithstanding, it was Burgess's intention to point up problems in American state building. Son of a Tennessee Unionist, Burgess had been traumatized in his youth by firsthand experience of Civil War divisions, and he had turned to political science to discern where Americans had gone wrong as well as what they had done right. Not surprisingly, he found that the most serious of America's developmental problems lay in its approach to the ideal of sovereignty, and he traced those problems directly to the promulgation of the

38

Articles of Confederation in 1777. Burgess charged that the adoption of the Articles denied what the Continental Congress of 1774 had initially apprehended: "that the consciousness of the thirteen colonies...had attained the natural conditions of a sovereignty, a state." By lodging sovereignty in thirteen separate "states," the Confederation submerged the "fact" that Americans had, through their revolutionary act, become "one, whole, separate, and adult nation."[7]

It was plain to Burgess that the Founders recognized the folly of this retreat from the idea of the national state, and he saw the promulgation and ratification of a new constitution in 1789 as an effort to correct the mistake, at least in principle. Nonetheless, his comparisons indicated that America in the early nineteenth century was "lagging in the march of civilization." With remnants of the Confederation's structure carried over into the new one and vestiges of provincial thought from the Confederation era left to fester, the nation's progress on the world stage was thwarted. Remedying this situation was, for Burgess, the project of the Civil War. By finally dispelling the illusion of competing sovereignties and by clearing the way for the abolition of slavery, the Union's victory brought American government more completely into alignment with "the plan of universal history."[8]

Burgess left an estimable legacy. His insistence that American government be understood and evaluated on a comparative grid, his interest in the complex push and pull of ideas and institutions over time, his challenge to the master narrative of unencumbered beginnings, his conclusion that political development in the United States had not always been on the right track – these would leave an indelible mark on the study of American political development. All the more curious, then, that no one of significance followed up on the particulars of his synthesis. One reason was political: World War I led American academics to shun any notion of Germanic origins. But there were intellectual reasons as well. First, Burgess's critique was directed almost exclusively at pre-war America. Taken together, his three criteria for state development served to confirm not only that America in the late nineteenth century was back on the right track but also that it had attained the forward position on the line of progress.

His political science purported to prove that post-Civil War America had gone farther than any other state toward "perfecting the Aryan genius of the Teutonic nations;" its principle conclusion was that the United States had "emancipated" the idea of civil liberty "from the remaining prejudices of European Teutonism" and had become "the cosmopolitan model for the political organization of the world."[9] To those who had turned to political science out of a sense that something was wrong with American government in the late nineteenth century, idealism of this sort was bound to appear misplaced.

Less obvious but equally difficult to swallow was the truncated conception of political change that lay at the heart of Burgess's idealism. Change, as he treated it, was always a matter of advancing on, or retreating from, a fixed standard of development; that is to say, Burgess did not see development occurring through the promulgation of categorically new ideas about government but though a progressive elaboration of a set idea. This was, in its way, a radical claim: here was an American challenging the culturally hallowed notion that the United States had broken from the European pattern of state development to establish "a new order of the ages." But in his efforts to reconnect American political history to European patterns Burgess moved to the opposite extreme: he simply denied that any genuinely new ideals had appeared over the past 1,000 years or that different standards of legitimacy might be applied to political structures over time. The Constitution merely elaborated on this continent the Aryan ideal of order first apprehended in the primeval forests of Germany; the Civil War did nothing to alter fundamentals either but merely elaborated on the clear implications of the Constitution. Burgess recognized the necessity for and importance of reform. He thought that all modern governments remained imperfect expressions of the ideal structure of the liberal nation-state, and thus each, including the American, was open to improvement; but he proceeded from there to judge improvements against a single, unchanging precept. What "developed" in 1774, 1789, and 1865 – and what "failed" to develop in 1777 – were the governmental manifestations of a representative nation-state committed to protecting civil liberties.

And then there was that standard itself. Because Burgess proposed to evaluate the constitutions he found in history against an ideal that he presumed to extrapolate from history, the whole analytic system came to rest on a giant leap of faith in his own historical imagination. Its authority as political science hinged almost entirely on the willingness of others to indulge the rather sweeping assumptions the author was making about world progress and how it was attained, assumptions made all the more suspect by the practical implications he drew from them. Burgess did not simply weigh in against claims that something fundamental was awry in the government of late-nineteenth-century America; he also pressed some rather striking proposals to insure that it would maintain course and capitalize on recent progress. At an institutional level, for instance, he suggested cutting the states out of the amendment process and strengthening national judicial controls over them, this with an eye toward what he saw as their inevitable postwar transformation into administrative units of the national government. At a policy level, he urged Americans to turn their sights outward and assume responsibility for the political organization of the world's less advanced races; at the same time, he urged the Teutonic element in America to "secure its dominance in the balance of power at home," even if that meant excluding others from direct political participation.[10] Burgess's political science was meant to render these proposals uncontroversial. They were to be thought of simply as more of the same, a mere extension of the ideas Americans, indeed the entire civilized world, had already advanced.

Burgess made a deceptively easy target. To challenge his analysis, scholars had only to adopt a different normative standard or an alternative set of historical projections. Far more critical assessments of American government and political culture might be generated simply by substituting other claims about the course of world progress and its relationship to American history. In fact, the true mark of Burgess's influence is that even as studies of American political development became more probing, more empirically demanding, and more culturally revealing – even as scholarly evaluations of the master narrative grew more dissonant – they retained their qualitative character as a test of ideals. As we shall see in the concluding chapter of this book, this remains the case today.

Realism

The leading late-nineteenth-century alternative to Burgess's idealism was "realism," the foremost expression being Woodrow Wilson's *Congressional Government*.[11] Published in 1885, before Burgess's *Political Science, Congressional Government* had already pointedly abandoned the convention of anchoring political analysis in ideals that were thought to inform the structure of constitutions: "The Constitution in operation is manifestly a very different thing from the Constitution of the books."[12] Wilson's call for greater realism in political analysis charged scholars to turn away from "paper descriptions" of governments and to find in their practical workings clearer explanations for contemporary problems. *Congressional Government* itself drew attention to the boss-ridden parochialism of late-century American government and traced these difficulties to a growing disparity between the formal arrangement of American institutions and the actual distribution of political power. The book launched a broadside attack on Constitution worship, with the intent of dispelling the illusion that Americans were the caretakers of some higher dispensation in matters of government.

This was Wilson's first book, and he seemed to spend the rest of his academic career trying to circumvent the devastating implications of its critique.[13] But if his later reflections on American political development are notable for a wider of range of interests and more subtle argumentation, no other statement comes close to *Congressional Government* in its impact on subsequent scholarship.[14] Beginning with the assumption that something fundamental was wrong in American politics in the late nineteenth century, *Congressional Government* conjured an assessment that was the mirror image of that provided by the German idealists. Burgess lauded the Framers for correcting mistakes in the Confederation's design; Wilson pointed to critical flaws in the design of the Framers. Burgess extolled the

United States as a vanguard state; Wilson chided it as a provincial backwater. Burgess promoted the distinctive features of American government as parts of a cosmopolitan model to be emulated; Wilson saw those same arrangements as retrograde and debilitating. Burgess upheld fixed principles as a vital guide to change; Wilson indicted fixed principles for distorting natural processes of change and stifling effective adaptations. At bottom, all these differences could be boiled down to one other: Burgess's analysis drew on an American strain of Whig history, whereas Wilson's drew on the British strain. In Wilson's reading, the Constitution not only had failed to secure the position of the United States at the head of the developmental line, it had also deflected the nation from the proper path it had once traveled.

Inspired by Walter Bagehot's *The English Constitution*, Wilson set the political degradation of American government in the latter half of the nineteenth century against improvements in the government of the mother country being heralded at the time. Looking for the "radical defect" on this side of the Atlantic – the critical design flaw that would explain the very different ways in which these two kindred polities had developed over the course of the nineteenth century – he lighted upon America's adoption of a system of checks and balances, in particular its formal division of executive and legislative responsibilities.[15] The problem at the heart of modern American politics, Wilson argued, lay in the Framers' limited vision. In the grip of revolutionary fervor, they could see little of value in the changes unfolding in British government over the last half of the eighteenth century and understood their task more directly as one of preventing any such developments from taking hold here. Their intervention, though completely understandable given the time and place, threw American political development into the jaws of a grim historical paradox: while the British continued after the American Revolution to transfer power from the national monarch to the national legislature and to advance a modern state design that concentrated decision making and responsibility in a single representative body, the Americans, seeking to recover what they thought Britain had lost, repaired

43

to a model drawn from their happier experience of an earlier day. Their Constitution refortified the system of institutional division and counterbalancing rivalries that the British themselves were in the process of abandoning.[16]

Compounding this "grievous mistake," the Framers froze these divisions in writing and forced future accommodations to change in the nation at large into an increasingly inhospitable frame.[17] The written Constitution thwarted what Wilson saw to be a natural, organic evolution toward a superior type; it could not, as a practical matter, halt political development, but it did distort the inevitable emergence of a single locus of sovereign power. Its failure to provide for the irresistible growth and concentration of power in the Congress was, for Wilson, the cause of America's devolution into a state of national irresponsibility in the post Civil War era. America, as Wilson described it, was a state in which the national legislature had become supremely powerful as a matter of fact but in which the law of the land continued to uphold the fiction of separated, limited and fragmented power.

At the heart of Wilson's realism, and of his understanding of political development generally, was his observation that traditional limits on what government could legislate were fast disappearing. That is what the operational fact of congressional supremacy signaled and what the structure of separated powers denied. Wilson made this a general point in his subsequent comparative study, *The State*: "... *government does now whatever experience permits or the times demand.*"[18] The weakening of traditional restraints on governmental power was, for Wilson, an opening to what would later be called progressive reforms, reforms more fully responsive to "experience" and "the times." But more immediately, and above all else, these new circumstances of governing called into question the executive's function of balancing against the legislature and providing an independent check on its action; they called instead for mutual confidence and cooperation in executive–legislative relations. So long as formal divisions obfuscated the relationship between real power and political responsibility, the American constitutional system could be expected to fall ever farther from meeting the demands of modern government. The Constitution would become, in effect, a shield behind which all-powerful congressional bosses protected themselves from full accountability for the use of their expanding prerogatives. All told, Wilson's analysis suggested that before the United States would be able to act responsibly in these new circumstances, it would have to retrace its steps and correct the basic misconceptions about government and history that it had embraced at its founding.[19]

When Burgess's *Political Science* finally appeared, Wilson was the first to ridicule its projection of a historical ideal onto the formal arrangements of the American Constitution.[20] But Wilson's own projections were hardly less vulnerable, and Burgess deftly returned fire. Defending the modernity of America's separated design against realist charges of backwardness, Burgess pointed out that democratic forms were still evolving within parliamentary governments and that these governments still had to contend with the institutional legacy of monarchy. The United States, in contrast, had discarded monarchical elements from the start and had long since resolved the problem of stabilizing government in their absence (see boxed text). If nothing else, this dispute pointed out just how problematic it was to try to determine with any reliability the developmental status of constitutional forms, to say which arrangements were advanced and which retrograde. In fact, although Wilson's critique of the Constitution would command far more attention than Burgess's defense, the attractions of "Anglomania" as an analytic stance proved to be quite limited.

More important than the particular judgments Wilson had reached about the Constitution, or even the way he had reached them, was his showing that very different judgments could be reached. His argument that American political history was rife with inefficiencies, and that contemporary American politics was caught in a developmental paradox, propelled the interrogation of premises forward. Confidence in "development" as a principle of history generally no longer translated into confidence in the America's political trajectory in particular. The search was on for more reliable standards to apply and a more convincing way to apply them.

The Developmental Status of the Separation of Powers:
Roots of a Classic Debate

Anglophiles in political science criticize [the check and balance] principle as the temporary expedient of a crude political society, and to within the last decade the criticism has been generally accepted as correct. Of course, if it be correct, the American commonwealth is not following the ideal lines of development in this respect; for there is nothing more certain in American history than the facts that the independence of the executive was produced in the progress from Continental and Confederate systems to the Federal system of 1787, and that this independence, from being somewhat timidly asserted for the first forty years of our history under the present constitution, has become the firmly established practice of our government. Shall we be obliged to retrace our steps in this respect in order to put ourselves upon the ideal line of development? I think not. I think that we are upon the right line, and that those nations which have developed parliamentary government are beginning to feel, as suffrage has become more extended, the necessity of greater executive independence. Parliamentary government, *i.e.*, government in which the other departments are subject of legislative control, becomes intensely radical under universal suffrage, and will remain so until the character of the masses becomes so perfect as to make the form of government nearly a matter of indifference. There is no doubt that we sometimes feel embarrassment from a conflict of opinion between the independent executive and the legislature, but this embarrassment must generally result in the adoption of the more conservative course, which is far less dangerous than the course of radical experiments. Means for a better understanding between the executive and the legislature we may indeed discover and apply, but these need in no wise impair the independence of the executive.

I think it far more supposable that parliamentary government, than that the independent executive, is a temporary expedient, – an expedient for avoiding embarrassments of dealing with an hereditary irresponsible executive. When, in states that now have parliamentary government, the hereditary irresponsible executive shall give way to the elected responsible president, holding [office] for a moderate term of years and reentering again the ranks of private citizenship, – and this, I cannot but think, is to be the final result of all Teutonic systems, – I have no question that parliamentary control of the executive will at least be greatly modified. I think we have strong reason to feel that we are on ideal lines in this respect, and that the world will be obliged to come at last upon this point also to the lessons of our experience.

John Burgess: "The Ideal of the American Commonwealth," *Political Science Quarterly* 10 (3), 1895, 420–1.

Democratic Progress: The Agents of Development

No sooner had constitutional criticism become fair game than "realism" shifted its focus. In the 1890s, scholarly thinking about American political development began to take its cues from reform movements that were sweeping the country. Arriving at judgments about whether America was ahead or behind, advanced or retrograde, now seemed less important than evaluating the prospects for something genuinely new arising from within. Attention turned to political action as the source of political change and to the shape of new forms of government that might emerge. Reckoning with the Constitution remained central, but assessments now emphasized how constitutional arrangements affected the pathways of change and the instrumentalities of political transformation.[21] The result was the first of what would become several inward turns in APD's cultural interrogation. Attention to the indigenous resources available for political development in America would, over time, become an increasingly prominent feature of these investigations, with scholars directing attention ever more closely to the peculiar character of the culture itself.

Indicative of the inward turn of the 1890s, Wilson himself set off on a comprehensive reexamination of American political history. Drawing his inspiration now from Frederick Jackson Turner, he examined the synergistic effects that sectional differences had on American national politics, and he employed organic metaphors to describe the course of constitutional change. The problem of American political development, as Wilson now saw it, lay in the uneven pace of political transformation across the different sections of the nation and in the consequent misalignment of their constitutional thinking about new national realities.[22] But at about this same time, a Wilson admirer returned to the arguments of *Congressional Government* and reworked its categorical judgments about America's developmental problems into a more dynamic assessment. In *The Rise and Growth of American Politics* (1898), Henry Jones Ford gave an evolutionary twist to the realist critique of the constitutional structure and, even more than Wilson himself, redirected thinking about American politics toward the actors who change it.

47

The Transformation of the Constitution

Following *Congressional Government*, Ford placed American political development in the stream of British history and asked how it had diverged. Like Wilson, Ford fretted about the separation of powers and its tendency to enshrine petty bossism in the high affairs of state. But Ford's treatment of the Framers marks a critical point of departure. He was less impressed by their limited vision than by their class loyalties, less taken with their misperception of the course of history than with their determination to secure their own interests. In Ford's analysis, the Constitution appeared as a counterrevolution, a reassertion of "class rule" by a conservative gentry against the democratic impulses of the revolutionary "masses."[23] More remarkable still was the fact that Ford refused to treat this conservative reaction as a decisive parting of the ways, a fateful turn down the wrong track in political development. *The Rise and Growth of American Politics* was as much about the regeneration of American democracy as about its defeat in 1789. By identifying the Constitution with class interests Ford had, in effect, underscored its contingent and contestable character, and from there, it was but few short steps to identifying the alternative path of national advancement inadvertently opened up by the Framers' handiwork.

First, Ford pointed out that political developments in England and America continued to move in tandem long after the Constitution was in place. Specifically, he observed that political parties sprung up in both countries to coordinate the activities of executives and legislators and that here, no less than in Britain, party organizers had transformed the social basis of government as well as its mode of operation. The flaw in earlier thinking about political structure and political development was, in Ford's view, a failure to see how structures themselves are altered by surrounding actions. Notwithstanding the fact that the American Constitution was a written document and difficult to change in its formal features, Ford found it to be neither a fixed nor a rigid scheme. His analysis of parties called attention to "development" as it occurred through the grafting of informal, extra-constitutional mechanisms onto the original design, and he showed how transformations of this sort could upend the interests and intentions of those who had designed the Constitution in the first place.

Ford pressed the point. Writing at a time when the American presidency was just beginning to recover from its post-Civil War eclipse, he identified presidential leadership as another potent engine of transformation. Burgess had held up the presidency as a conservative counterweight to the impulses of democratic legislatures; Wilson had dismissed the presidency as an anachronism, an inferior organ in the separated design that could do little more than complicate the proper workings of a supreme legislature. Ford's observation was that the presidency had itself been transformed after the Constitution's ratification into an instrument of democracy and that, as such, it had acquired the potential to become "the master force in the shaping of public policy." In Ford's analysis, American political development had proceeded upon an unintended consequence of the Framers' conservatism: the precautions they had taken to check legislative supremacy and secure the independence of the executive "were so effectual that Congress was made an incurably deficient and inferior organ." Thus, as the nation expanded and the people increased their fitness for self-government, "they lay hold of the presidency as the only organ sufficient for the exercise of their sovereignty." By the time of Andrew Jackson, the chief executive had become "the instrument of the people breaking through the constitutional form," a battering ram for transforming at the level of practical operations the actual meaning of constitutional relationships.[24]

By identifying the constitutionally transforming effects of political parties and a democratized presidency, Ford held out the potential for genuinely new developments to be realized along a distinctly American path. Having observed within American politics a capacity for generating wholly unanticipated forms, he imagined similar advances that might eventually leapfrog the current cosmopolitan standard that he, like Wilson, located in the parliamentary model. Ford granted that, for all their advantages, parliamentary systems were not perfect: acknowledging their aristocratic pedigree, he conceded Burgess's point that they might "turn out to have been after all a transitory phase of political development." From there, however,

Ford went on to suggest the advantages of using the presidential system to resolve the emergent problems that Wilson had identified in his critique of the Constitution. The proper course for America, according to Ford, was neither to follow the parliamentary route by further marginalizing the presidency and rationalizing congressional control over the executive branch nor to insist on the original constitutional design by bolstering presidential restraints on the legislature. The path of development open to American government was toward a higher synthesis: toward a presidential system with Congress in the restraining role, toward an executive-centered government that would have a "parliamentary forum" but stand "independent of parliamentary vicissitudes." Such a government would, he argued, "preserve everything of value in a parliamentary system of government, while avoiding its defects."[25]

Ford's analysis still located American political development on a comparative grid, marking the various positions of the Western states with their different constitutional forms advancing toward the ultimate regime type. But Ford's analysis of contingent settlements and internal transformations loosened the connections between original ideas and future prospects. He showed that preexisting institutional arrangements could have both strengths and weaknesses, that they were neither inherently advanced nor inherently retrograde; his appeal to the presidency as a potent agent of democratic transformations located the solution to seemingly intractable structural problems within the structure itself. The notion that American government, despite its original design flaws, still had the potential to evolve into "the ultimate type" suggested that political development was less an aptitude of constitutions than an aptitude of citizens engaged in reform.[26]

The People and the Interests

For some, Ford's analysis offered a practical program for advancing America's political development. Many political scientists, Wilson foremost among them, seized on his idea of presidency-centered government and promoted it through innovations that could be grafted informally onto America's original constitutional design.[27] For others, however, Ford's analysis merely pointed to the real difficulty: enlightening the people to the path of progress. The next extension of realism eyed the political prospects of America's industrial transformation and saw an even greater demand for empirical rigor and objectivity in political analysis. If political science was to serve democracy as capitalism evolved, developmental analysis would have to strip bare the foundations of government in economic interest and expose all institutions as contingent solutions to democracy's evolving claims.

This new realism was already in place when Charles Beard delivered his lecture on "Politics" at Columbia University in 1908. "... What government does in practice," he reported, "depends not on any theory about its proper functions, but upon the will of the group of persons actually in control at any one time or upon the equilibrium that is established through conflicts among groups seeking to control the government." Just five years earlier, as a graduate student at Columbia, Beard had been instructed in the idealism of John Burgess; now standing before his former mentors, he renounced explanations that merely "gratify national vanity" with "cheap" appeals to the "superior genius of the Anglo-Saxon people." Invoking the realism of Wilson and Ford, he challenged political scientists to undertake an even more radical interrogation of cultural assumptions and to subject American institutions to an even more intense form of scrutiny. Fresh from studies in England and firsthand encounters with the social-democratic movements, he reported that "wherever Hegel... has been dethroned there is a decided tendency to look to economic and material facts rather than to race psychology as the most reliable sources of institutional differences."[28]

Beard's call for a harder-edged materialism in the analysis of American politics informed his whole approach to political development.[29] Though he entertained no thought of proletarian revolution in the United States, Beard was vitally interested in what other forms of political organization would come to dominate in industrial America. He wrote of technological innovation as an irrepressible engine of political change, he pointed to the attendant economic conflicts that held the course of political development in their balance, and he looked to the people acting on their own behalf to carry the day for "industrial democracy."[30] Beard's work was an instrument of his vision, a tool for alerting the people to the developmental challenges at hand. Their objective, as he saw it, should be to tap the expanding potential of capitalism to produce wealth while deploying it in the service of a government that maximized opportunity for all.[31] Historical analysis could help, not only by documenting the economic interests that had constructed the various institutional arrangements of American government but also by exposing the archaic forms of economic and political organization that entrench themselves in law and ideology and become, with the passage of time, impediments to further progress.

For our purposes, the important thing about Beard's work is how this still powerfully developmental conception of politics rendered the line of progress problematic. In pointing out impediments to democracy's advance, Beard was also suggesting something about the difficulty of overcoming them. Later critics who challenged Beard's historical projections in favor of explanations more strictly cultural and less confidently developmental would gloss over this aspect of his work. But just as surely as the Progressives' "revolt" against the formalism of prior institutional analysis had opened wide the discussion of America's regenerative potential, their greater preoccupation with the interest groups contesting the course of institutional change worked to sober things up. Realism of this sort had its own way of magnifying the importance of historical context in the consideration of political possibilities.

Beard's most famous book, *An Economic Interpretation of the Constitution of the United States* (1913), is not generally known for such subtleties; yet, it presents the leading case in point. The basic argument was not new. Some fifteen years before, Ford had claimed that the Constitution was the work of a minority coalition out to protect its class interests, and that argument had been radicalized in subsequent years by the populist historian J. Allen Smith in *The Spirit of American Government* (1907). What distinguished Beard's analysis was his commitment to finding hard evidence

52

to back up this interpretation. Beard went further than Ford or
Smith in specifying the economic interests at issue in the promulgation of the Constitution – "financial, mercantile, and property
interests" against "paper money and agrarian interests" – and he was
more careful in describing how the Constitution's various clauses responded to the material concerns of the first group. At the same
time, he avoided the conclusions reached by other progressive critics.
He did not find the Constitution to be backward looking, a historical mistake waiting to be corrected, a defeat for democracy that
needed to be avenged, or even a victory for class interests over virtu-
ous people. Tying the struggle over the Constitution to the interests
of creditors against debtors, he simply documented the advance of
one coalition of economic interests against another in what would
prove to be an ongoing political struggle to reconcile competing
values.

Beard actively resisted the implication that his work was a de-
bunking of the Constitution. When he permitted himself an assessment of the relationship between the Framers' specific economic
motives and American political development more generally, he insisted instead that he was merely applying the analysis of economic
motivations that James Madison had outlined in "Federalist #10"
to Madison's own achievement. Beard meant to historicize the Constitution, not to indict its Framers; he intended to render the Constitution's solutions to the problems of governing historically contingent,
not to challenge their value in their own time and place. Careful
readers of this and other works will discover that Beard found little
to lament in the governmental arrangements the Framers subverted
and that he found the new equilibrium of interests that produced
the Constitution a clear improvement on the prior state of affairs.
He described the nation's great commercial and financial interests
as "harried" by state legislatures in the years after the Revolution,
and he described the Framers as men driven to action by the "imbe-
cilities of the Confederation."[33] In another passage, he admired the
Framers for "building the new government on the only foundation
that could be stable: fundamental economic interests."[34] Rather than
deride the Constitution as the central problem of American political

development, as previous thinkers had done, Beard saw it as a move to make democracy safe for capitalism.

In fact, Beard's analysis suggested that the Constitution was something of a model for political development. It showed that great and necessary improvements were brought about by groups alert to their material stakes in government, knowledgeable of how to secure them in institutional form, and capable of acting effectively in the political arena. In doing so, the analysis anticipated Beard's rather complicated assessments of the prospects for democratic progress in modern America. The flip side of his admiration for the Framers was his keen sense of the greater difficulties of getting diffuse popular majorities to perceive their interests as clearly and act on them effectively. Economic determinism may have led Beard to anticipate America's advance toward a new industrial order and to promote a new democracy of commensurate scale and power, but his direct observation of democratic politics in the Progressive era and the New Deal left him with a deep appreciation of the problems of getting there. Like other progressives, Beard found impediments to progress in archaic forms of corporate privilege that had come to be accepted by the people as part of the natural order of things. But he worried as well about what he saw as archaic forms of democracy still being defended by small property holders and craft unions.[35] In seeking to hasten America's progress, he flagged interests of all sorts whose attachment to "outmoded" ideas served to complicate the realization of anticipated improvements. Overall, Beard's work pointed to a general tendency for political development to "lag" behind its potential and for the relationship between changes in the economy and changes in the government to get caught up in intricate processes of social and cultural adjustment.[36]

As Beard's later work elaborated on these complications, it cautioned more strongly against the idea of a decisive breakthrough. Writing *The American Party Battle* in 1928, he cast American political development as a long and interconnected struggle in which agrarian and capitalist interests similar to those present at the Founding had periodically realigned themselves to contest the uses of national power.[37] Progress was a sporadic and halting affair, with extended periods of relative stability punctuated by moments of political creativity, moments that were themselves circumscribed by the political resources at hand for analysis and interpretation. The question posed by the book was whether politics as understood within the American tradition – in particular, the lines of conflict drawn by that tradition – could still generate ideas of use for the purpose of advancing democracy in an industrial society. Beard's assessment of the New Deal published in the *American Political Science Review* a few years later struck a similar note. He wrote of prior economic downturns that had awakened the people and spurred them to new thinking about democracy. At each juncture, he observed, reformers had been constrained to draw on their "heritage of ideas and interests" and to "think in terms of some tradition."[38] As Beard now saw it, the heart of the problem of democratic progress lay in constructively applying received ideas to new realities.

This problem had not only made Beard skeptical of the notion that industrial democracy was at hand in the reforms of the New Deal, it had also prompted him to describe developmental processes that were as much cultural as structural or economic.[39] Much about the future direction of the analysis of APD was foretold in these mature assessments. Post-New Deal scholars needed only to sharpen the turn inward on the peculiarities of the American political tradition and more closely scrutinize its "heritage of ideas" to transform Beard's early optimism about the emergence of a new democracy into a profoundly more ambivalent assessment of American political development.

American Liberalism: The Boundaries of Development

The shift toward ambivalence about political development in America was subtle but profound. The facts at the time seemed clear enough: the United States had weathered the Great Depression and World War II without the ideological assaults on capitalism or democracy seen elsewhere; the new forms of social democracy that materialized in America appeared a pale reflection of those found in Western Europe. In this context, the thought dawned that Progressives like

Beard had been patiently agitating for something that was never to be: although America was not decisively ahead or behind other nations in political development, neither was it moving in the mainstream. Beard's suggestion of a political lag in development had presented the United States as a rather ordinary country, fitfully making its own way toward a new kind of democracy under the common pressures of industrialization. In contrast, midcentury scholars began to consider the United States a developmental anachronism blithely spinning out its own peculiar brand of politics on the sidelines of Western history.

The rise of America to world power and the onset of the Cold War magnified concerns about what now appeared to be the highly circumscribed character of American political development. The prospect of such a peculiar polity leading world resistance to communism conjured up all sorts of worries – about American understanding of cultures whose historical experience was fundamentally different, about American paranoia and the ease with which a nation so long insulated fell victim to "red scares," and ultimately about America's hubris in exporting its own ideas of "modernization" to nations where they might not make sense.[40] These anxieties led scholars to consider the cultural boundaries within which American politics had developed and to turn Americans' self-understanding of the "exceptional" character of their political development on its head.

Political Consensus

This new view of APD was put forth most forcefully by Louis Hartz in *The Liberal Tradition in America* (1955). America, Hartz observed, "has always been a place where the common issues of the West have taken a strange and singular shape."[41] Acknowledging all that progressive scholarship had done to cut through the myths of the culture and expose the material bases of conflict and change, Hartz charged that it left obscure the distinctive ways in which class antagonisms played out in the American context. The "pervasive frustration" engendered over the decades by the Progressives' own expectations was, for Hartz, a clear indication that their interest-conflict theory of political development was incomplete.

To account for America's deviation from what more orthodox theories of class antagonism had to say about developmental problems and prospects, Hartz retrieved an insight from Alexis de Tocqueville: Americans had never endured a bourgeois revolution against feudalism but had instead been "born equal." Tocqueville had observed that the Puritans came to America to extricate themselves from their struggle with the English aristocracy; Hartz conjectured that the effect of doing so was to bypass a critical stage in the political development of liberalism. Transplanted from its European origins in a larger contest of worldviews, but already aligned with the political sympathies of their coreligionists, America's Puritan fragment gave rise to a peculiar political culture, one in which the values of individualism, limited government, and equality were so widely shared as to become irresistible to all serious contenders for political power. A "genuine revolutionary tradition" never took hold in this environment, nor did a "genuine tradition of reaction," for there was never any need for American liberals to dislodge an antithetical establishment, to replace one set of ideas with another, or to defend their own creation against anything categorically different. Politics in America would proceed without any consciousness of conflict as a battle over fundamental principles, that is, without true class consciousness, and in the absence of class consciousness, the economic antagonisms routinely produced by capitalist development would be shorn of their potential to generate fundamental changes in social or political aspirations. Having skipped the middle-class revolution against feudalism, Americans became impervious to the idea of a socialist revolution against capitalism.

The consensus thesis identified American "exceptionalism" with a cultural narrowness that constricted political thought, constrained political action, and limited political development. Hartz was not arguing that American politics was devoid of conflict or even that Americans were insensitive to it. His contention was that political conflict in America, though persistent and pervasive, failed to present political alternatives robust enough to yield anything genuinely new or different – that, developmentally speaking, America's political conflicts were "shadows" of the truly momentous struggles being played out elsewhere. This led him to a series of comparisons that exposed the relatively unproductive character of political change in America.

He began by examining the familiar boast that the American Revolution had ushered in a new order of things and asked what exactly the revolutionaries had been out to topple. Compared to their French counterparts, the Americans appeared to Hartz more intent on realizing the ideals with which they had begun than on rejecting them, more determined to preserve a liberal world already in place than on creating something else. Turning then to the framing of the Constitution, Hartz saw a pseudo-aristocracy at work. Fear of the debtors' rebellion led by Daniel Shays had not prompted America's reactionaries to create a government in which they themselves would control things; it had prompted them to create a government in which no single interest could ever hope to control things. A governmental structure riddled with institutional conflicts could succeed, Hartz theorized, only in a polity in which social conflict was far less significant than the Framers imagined, one in which there was little for government to do but manage interests and preserve the underlying consensus on fundamental values. Hartz did not deny that conservative Whigs repeatedly locked horns with radical Democrats in antebellum America, but he pointed out that, in practice, America's conservatives were no more able to resist the claims of democracy than America's radicals could resist the allure of capitalism.

Americans' penchant for exaggerating their conflicts culminated, in Hartz's view, in the writings of Progressives like Beard who, for all their realism, had once again indulged the cultural conceit that the American politics was about to produce something new. This critique echoed and reworked some familiar ideas. Hartz's portrait of American provincialism and self-delusion is, in many ways, reminiscent of Wilson's: like Wilson, Hartz saw in the Framers a desire to escape from history and preserve a prior state of affairs. Importantly, however, Hartz did not assert, as Wilson had, that the Constitution had thrown American development onto the wrong track. If Hartz's

America was anachronistic, it was also manifestly successful. His point was that America's perpetual reassertion of the compatibility of capitalism and democracy was unique and largely irrelevant to politics in the rest of the world. The problem posed was a contemporary one: whether this consensus culture would impede Americans from understanding the very different cultures with which they were now forced to interact.

Hartz's thesis is also reminiscent of Burgess's view of things: like Burgess, Hartz saw political development in the United States as a perpetual elaboration of the same liberal ideas. Burgess, however, had argued that human history had nothing better to offer; Hartz argued that Americans were singularly limited in their ability to conceive of anything better or, for that matter, to conceive of anything else at all. Burgess had urged Americans to reach out to other nations in order to spread their advanced ideas; Hartz hoped that contact with alien cultures might help America "compensate for the uniformity of its domestic life" and overcome the dangers of unreflective dogmatism in the exercise of world power. If there was a bright prospect for Hartz in the Cold War confrontation with communism, it was the thought that grappling with something entirely different might finally awaken Americans to the radical peculiarity of their own experience, imparting to them "that sense of relativity ... which European liberalism acquired through an internal experience of social diversity and social conflict."[42]

Political Realignment

Hartz's response to Beard went far toward rendering the idea of American political development an oxymoron. Scholars might still talk of functional adaptations and incremental advances within American liberalism, but Hartz upped the ante for anyone who would claim more. And yet, if American politics did not develop over time in any meaningful sense, what exactly did it do? Hartz had said more about what economic conflict in America had not produced than about what it had. Taking full account of the culture's most timeless and encompassing features, consensus theory failed to convey any clear sense of what, if anything, distinguished one era from the next. Moreover, though Hartz saw in Marx's theory of development a crucial element of class consciousness missing in American political culture, he was far less attentive to what the Progressives had found most compelling in Marx – an understanding of capitalism itself as an unrelenting engine of social and economic transformation. How exactly could a government fit for nothing so much as the preservation of its original consensus successfully adapt to the rapid pace of change in its economy and society?

These questions led Walter Dean Burnham to the image of punctuated equilibrium as a general description of the dynamic relationship between state and society in America and to a synthesis of mid-twentieth century thinking about American political development in a magisterial theory of liberalism's periodic electoral "realignment." Burnham was not the first scholar to think about American political development in terms of short but decisive moments of mobilization and creativity followed by long periods of stability. Beard had suggested as much in his later writings. Nor was Burnham the first to look to electoral systems and their periodic rearrangement for a general theory of political change in America. That move had been made by V.O. Key in 1955, the same year in which Hartz's *Liberal Tradition* appeared. Burnham, a student at Harvard when both Hartz and Key held sway there, connected Key's idea to Hartz's, and jettisoned the progressive overtones of Beard's analysis in the process.

In his seminal article, "A Theory of Critical Elections," Key had identified certain national elections as more significant than others for the "sharp and durable" shifts they produced in American politics, and he had suggested that these "critical elections" might provide a link between theories that explained the operations of American democracy and theories that explained historic transformations of the American polity. In this initial formulation, the idea of critical elections seemed to run entirely contrary to Hartz's consensus theory: whereas Hartz was observing the uniformity of the American political experience and explaining why apparent breakpoints like the New Deal had changed so little, Key was observing large scale electoral discontinuities like those which had brought FDR to power and searching for an explanation of the decisive political changes that ensued. Burnham, however, saw these two conceptions of American politics as complementary. He proposed that electoral convulsions were the characteristic product of America's exceptional political culture, and with that he set out to resolve Hartz's riddle of political "nondevelopment" in the face of unrelenting social and economic change.

In *The American Party Systems: Stages of Development* (1967) and again in *Critical Elections and the Mainsprings of American Democracy* (1970), Burnham cast electoral realignment as a surrogate for social revolution in a polity culturally immune to social revolutions. At the heart of his analysis was a Hartzian gloss on the "cultural monolith" of American liberalism, evidenced first and foremost by a Constitution designed to preserve the preexisting consensus and deny particular groups the power to change things. Burnham theorized that the new demands on government routinely generated by social and economic change were bound to fester in such a system.[43] As the Constitution worked to intercept and delay adaptations to the changing conditions of governance, relations between state and society were repeatedly left to drift toward moments of extreme national stress. The characteristic expressions of this pent-up tension were periodic electoral upheavals, critical elections or election sequences that realigned the coalitional base of the contending political parties and compelled American government to accommodate new realities, one way or another. These uprisings were momentary and episodic, for constitutional divisions made popular mobilization difficult to sustain, but the return to normalcy would feature a different alignment of interests newly secured through constitutional resistance to further change. The cycle was self-perpetuating.

The orthodox version of this theory highlighted five major breakthroughs coming at intervals of roughly thirty years and centering around the elections of 1800, 1828, 1860, 1896, and 1932. These framed five extended periods of political order or regimes – the Jeffersonian, the Jacksonian, the Republican, the Progressive, and the New Deal. Each of these regimes affirmed in its own way the same basic cultural commitments to democracy and capitalism, but each also framed a distinctive universe of political and institutional action.

The distribution of power among the branches and levels of the government was different in each. So too was the "party system," the competing coalitions of economic, sectional, and ethnoreligious interests. Each brought into government a different mix of policy debates and offered institutional services and supports to different interests. All told, realignments entailed constitutional adjustments of the first order.

This "realignment synthesis" thrust time and change back into the center of the study of America's political development. In Burnham's own words, it showed that "politics as usual in the United States is not politics as always."[44] Widely recognized in the 1970s as the "dominant conceptual picture" of American political history, the projection of coherent liberal regimes periodically reconstructed spawned an enormous literature on the nature and operation of political order in America and on the processes and significance of its transformations.[45] Questions have recently been raised about the historical regularity of major political breakthroughs, about their similarity to one another, about the relevance of electoral realignment to explaining the twisted and halting course of American politics since 1968, about the inability of the theory to accommodate alternative periodizations that seem to apply more readily to so many other aspects of politics. Notwithstanding these many criticisms Burnham's synthesis has yet to find a coherent replacement.[46]

Nor should challenges to the realignment synthesis be allowed to obscure the more circumspect understanding of American political development introduced by the theory itself. Burnham's work severed the connection that was still pervasive between the study of order and change in American political history and the idea of the progress. Though he retrieved Beard's notion of change as punctuated equilibrium, he elaborated it as a complement to Hartz's consensus theory and presented the cycles of realignment as a corollary to the thesis of nondevelopment (see boxed text). Realignment was the peculiar "tension-management" mechanism of a consensus culture and as such a symptom of the anachronistic character of the American polity. In fact, although Burnham allowed for periodic reconstructions of the relationship between democracy and capitalism

The Realignment Synthesis

One may begin . . . with a paradox noted by Louis Hartz: the effective working of the pluralized governmental structures established by the framers of the Constitution has been dependent upon the failure of the social-conflict model which many of them accepted to be relevant to American conditions. Such dispersed structures can function because the Americans who work them share the same broad set of sociopolitical values and because such values have never hitherto been effectively challenged, much less overthrown, by any politically significant group. The reasons for this exceptional state of affairs have been explored at length by cultural historians and need not detain us here. The point is that the overwhelming majority of Americans have accepted bourgeois individualism and its Lockean-liberal political variant as their consensual value system.

In operational terms this has meant the construction of a political system which is – in domestic matters, at any rate – dispersive and fragmented, a political system which is dedicated to the defeat, except temporarily and under pressure of overwhelming crisis, of any attempt to generate domestic sovereignty; a political system whose chief function has been the maintenance of a high wall of separation between political conflict on one side and the socioeconomic system on the other. A deep-seated dialectic has operated over the entire history of the country: while the socioeconomic system has developed and transformed itself from the beginning with an energy and thrust unparalleled in modern history, the political system from parties to policy institutions has remained astonishingly little transformed in its characteristics and methods of operation . . . .

In this context . . . critical realignment emerges as decisively important in the study of the dynamics of American politics. It is as symptomatic of political non-evolution in this country as are the archaic and increasingly rudimentary structures of the political parties themselves. But even more importantly, critical realignment may well be defined as the chief tension-management device available to so peculiar a political system. Historically is has been the chief means through which an underdeveloped political system can be recurrently brought once again into some balanced relationship with the changing socioeconomic system, permitting a restablization of our politics and a redefinition of the dominant Lockean political formulas in terms which gain overwhelming support from the current generation. Granted the inability of our political system to make gradual adjustments along vectors of *emergent* political demand, critical realignments have been as inevitable as they have been necessary to the normal workings of American politics. Thus once again there is a paradox: the conditions which decree that coalitional negotiation, bargaining, and incremental, unplanned, and gradual policy change become the dominant characteristic of American politics in its normal state also decree that it give way to abrupt, disruptive change with considerable potential for violence.

Walter Dean Burnham, *Critical Elections and the Mainsprings of American Politics*, (New York, Norton, 1970), 175–181.

in America, his analyses were even more explicit than Hartz's in raising questions about democracy's advance and even more pointed in
their refutation of Beardian optimism. He dwelled on the realignment
of 1896 in particular because he saw in that starkly sectional division
the demobilization of a once-vibrant democratic politics and the insu-
lation of corporate control over processes of industrial consolidation.
"When the conflict between industrial capitalism and pre-existing
democratic structures came into the open," he charged, "it eventu-
ated in the displacement of democracy, not industrial capitalism."[47]
In realignment theory, then, development became just another word
for change; no longer referring to improvement, it proposed a contingent and uncertain route by which America's liberal political culture
is periodically reconstituted.

Political Invention: America's Alternatives

With the Soviet empire dissolving, with European social democracies
straining to cope with their accumulated burdens, with pundits pro-
claiming the world-historic triumph of something called the "American Idea," the worries that Hartz had expressed about political
development in the United States began to appear in the 1990s about
as relevant as the predictions of Karl Marx. The ghost of Burgess
beckoned, inviting scholars to reassert the vanguard status of American liberalism and to cast the United States once again as "the cosmopolitan model for the political organization of the world." By and
large, however, efforts to push beyond Hartz have moved in the opposite direction. Taking another turn inward in political analysis, the
current cultural critique within APD has revealed still more problems
in trying to understand American politics developmentally.

Rather than greet the Cold War's end as an opportunity to cele-
brate American liberalism's triumph on the world stage, APD scholars
working in the cultural vein embraced it as a final release from all
external standards of evaluation. They debunk Hartz in the same
terms that he himself debunked Beard: now it is consensus theory
that appears too Eurocentric and too economistic.[48] Few of them

today are willing to leap from the absence of feudalism in America to the insignificance of the ideological differences that have divided Americans or of the choices that have shaped their political history.[49] Hartz's portrait of liberal consensus is replaced by a new appreciation for the multiple dimensions of American political culture and for the pivotal struggles this multiplicity has engendered; that "sense of relativity" and "social diversity" Hartz thought Americans could discover only outside their borders is now shown to have been present on the inside all along. More often than not, the alternatives invoked to evaluate America's developmental potential are not those that originated elsewhere, but are distinctly home grown.

This newfound appreciation for the disparate products of American culture signals a revival of interest in indigenous resources available for a reinvention of American politics today. In this work, culture is understood less as something given than as something constantly in the making; interest lies in the sources of new ideas, in how people come to recognize the categories that define them, in how novel connections are made among various ideas to be found in the culture, and in how these allow people to reenvision American politics. As this emphasis on creativity and inventiveness at the level of ideas highlights the political alternatives that have been thrown up by American culture, it does more than explode the claims of consensus theory; it calls into question all forms of analysis that employ preconceived standards to evaluate "development." Whereas Beard evaluated American political development in anticipation of a new form he thought was about to appear and Hartz's evaluation was in terms of forms elsewhere which he thought were unlikely to appear here, this new research undermines all a priori conceptions of the course of change over time, even – perhaps most especially – those that purport to unmask America's cultural deviations from some other course, and insists instead on a polity determined solely by its own historic struggles and choices. Probing the fate of America's alternatives in this way cuts against the concept of "political development" per se, stripping away all its various connotations and leaving behind only the contingencies of the moment.

"Lost" Alternatives

Much of the recent research on "alternatives" has been devoted to a reevaluation of political programs on the losing side of struggles to redirect the course of American politics. A revised narrative of political change in America begins boldly with insurgents pursuing programs for change based on their clear understanding of fundamental issues in dispute; conclusions are proffered with respect for plans that were sidelined and a keen sense of the shortcomings of those that prevailed.[50] In this way, scholars have deepened our appreciation of the New Deal's original radicalism and how it was tamed[51]; of the Progressive's moral vision and how it was lost[52]; of the agrarians' theory of political economy and how it was co-opted[53]; of labor's commonwealth ideals and how they were constricted[54]; of zealous Reconstructists and how they were preempted[55]; of the demands of an incipient urban working class and how they were redirected[56]; of Revolutionary republicanism and how it was transmuted.[57]

More than a vigorous reassertion of the generative capacities of American political culture, this work compels attention for two general propositions it advances about American political development. One is that Americans have actively pursued alternatives that promised to move the nation in directions starkly different from those actually followed; the other is that these alternatives were plausible ones for America to have embraced. The first proposition dispels the illusion of an overarching political consensus within which choices about development are relatively inconsequential; the second challenges the aura of inevitability and progress that history's winners tend to attribute to their own victories. Indeed, by refusing to diminish these "alternative tracks" as intellectually shallow, conceptually inferior, functionally impractical, or hopelessly backward looking – by treating them as coherent, informed, "genuine" – this literature calls into question all claims of special insight into which ideas, groups, or movements represent the authentic forces of progress in history.[58] The effect is not only to displace the consensus view of American political history with fundamental conflict but also to root out teleological projections that earlier scholarship had relied on to judge the worth of the contending ideas.

Note that when external standards of progress in history are abandoned in the analysis of political change – when direction and teleology are discarded as unwarranted ideological valuations of contested ideas – all that is left to consider is the unvarnished history of political choice. This is important, for there remains the irony that by reclaiming the radicalism and the practicality of alternatives that were ultimately frustrated, the contemporary cultural critique leaves us to contemplate outcomes not all that different from ones that Hartz's described.[59] Its partial confirmation of the Hartz's thesis has prompted other scholars to think about America's alternatives differently; nonetheless, pressing forward with the history of political choice reveals its own response, and it is one worth considering. The outcomes of these inquiries may be Hartz-like, but the explanations offered and the implications drawn are quite different.

Finding the alternatives generated in America "from below" to be suitably meaningful and robust, these scholars point to power arrangements "above" to explain why they failed to take hold. Refuting Hartz's charge of a culturally constricted vision, this literature has, in effect, found a gaping disjunction between culturally generated political ideas and institutionally generated responses. For instance, in her analysis of labor in the late nineteenth century, Victoria Hattam documents substantially different political visions motivating sections of the early American labor movement and the distinctive types of union organization they produced. She then goes on to argue that the state played a critical part in selecting which of these would prevail. Although the broader vision of a "producer's alliance" arrayed against finance capital failed to sustain itself, the more restricted model of "pure and simple" craft unions arrayed against employers stuck; in Hattam's account, that is because the former was more dependent on the enactment of a program that the courts would not sustain even when legislators proved responsive.[60] Similar results repeat time and again in studies of quite disparate insurgencies, driving home the notion that alternatives in America are not nipped in the bud for lack of cultural resources but are defeated politically.

This pattern of defeats calls attention to imbalances in the distribution of political resources and to institutional hurdles that stack the deck against certain courses of action. Analysis turns back to the early preoccupations of political scientists with governmental design, but now with the focus on its impact on the outcome of pivotal political contests. The corollary of the claim that meaningful political alternatives in America are not limited by a narrow cultural consensus is the claim that they have been limited instead by governmental arrangements, prevailing political practices, and enduring elite advantage. It is not a failure of ideas that constrains political possibilities in this research but a state apparatus that, for all its divisions and internal conflicts, has variously absorbed, dissolved, and deflected alternative visions with remarkable consistency. As the literature on lost alternatives strengthens the critique of progress, it also points to a way out of the Hartzian box. Historical research of this kind offers instruction not only in the formulation of alternatives but also in strategies for their implementation, anticipating a mobilization that might yet overcome the obstacles that have thwarted past opportunities.

Empowered Alternatives

Contemporary reassessments of American political culture have not been limited to the revaluation of ideas and visions that lost out in past contests. Aware that these efforts to displace Hartz are susceptible to confirming Hartz-like results and to indicting the political system as a whole, J. David Greenstone suggested a different approach. He accepted Hartz's notion of a pervasive consensus on liberal values in America and urged more direct consideration of the possibilities for development that such a culture presents. Echoing progressive critiques of Burgess, Greenstone charged that the central deficiency in Hartz's analysis lay in its inability to account for the promulgation of any genuinely new ideas affecting the practices of American government and politics. By extension, he saw Hartz's theory as prone

68

to understate both the transformative potential and actual impact of the ideas Americans have at their disposal.

In fact, Greenstone observed that Hartz had not provided a causal theory of change; his liberal consensus had merely specified the peculiar political universe within which change in America must occur. Restricting the notion of liberal consensus to a "boundary condition," Greenstone was able to offer amendments to Hartz that would credit ideological shifts in American politics with a potential to offer something more than "more of the same." His search for sturdier supports for meaningful change within a pervasively liberal polity led him to investigate the way in which new ideas are constructed out of the discursive categories of the common culture, that is, of its shared linguistic tools.[61]

Greenstone chose for study a political debate about which Hartz had said next to nothing: the debate in the North over the relationship between "liberty" and "union" before the Civil War. In *The Lincoln Persuasion: Remaking American Liberalism* (1993) he found that political conflict within the North at this time not only worked through these familiar ideas but also produced some new thoughts about them. In particular, he showed that although all parties to the debate invoked both liberty and union as hallowed principles, those concepts admitted multiple meanings and that differences among those meanings were elaborated in the very process of debating their future. Some politicians drew on a secular humanist strand in American liberal thought, with its "negative conception of freedom" – freedom as an absence of constraints – to conceptualize the relationship between these two values; others drew on a Puritan, pietistic strand with strong moralistic and positive entailments. It was Lincoln, Greenstone argued, who found in America's "toolbox" of received ideals and aspirations a combination of meanings that articulated the fundamental clash of values *within* the liberal political culture of antebellum of America, differences that, once articulated, could not be deflected, absorbed, or dissolved.

Greenstone readily granted that when Lincoln conceptualized the Union as a moral force whose ultimate and primary purpose was to facilitate individual self-improvement, he was working wholly within the boundaries of the established culture. At the same time, he insisted that Lincoln had discovered a political alternative, one separate from, and far more expansive than, either the Jacksonian understanding (in which the Union was merely an instrument for maximizing the freedom of white men to do as they chose) or the Whig understanding (in which liberty derived from the Union and had to be regulated in ways consistent with the preservation of the Union). In fact, Lincoln's alternative produced something wholly unaccounted for in Hartz's analysis: a normative revolution that carried a triumphant political revolution in its train.

Though there is much in Greenstone's carefully crafted brief on behalf of liberalism's creative potential that points the way back to a genuinely developmental view of American politics, the claims he made on behalf of that view prove on inspection to be quite modest. His argument was that the stockpile of liberal ideals in America can be, and has been, expanded through interactive processes of debate, that we are not stuck with the ideas with which we began, and that new ideas, once brought to power, are always available for future elaboration and use. He said little, however, about how effectively or closely liberalism's conceptual expansion tracks the course actually taken by American politics. Left unclear is how, if at all, expansive new ideas about liberalism, even those that seize control of the state and change the Constitution, determine the future. Moreover, although Greenstone's friendly amendment to Hartz allows for liberalism's advance, the argument for linguistic inventiveness may just as easily cut the other way. In a culture versatile enough to conceptualize attractive alternatives and see them carried to power, no alternative is really secure; a more generous liberalism may dominate at one moment only to be countered and undermined by a newly constrictive conception in the next.

If there is a single source of disconnection between the elaboration of political inventiveness at the level of ideas and "development" as a premise for political analysis, this is it. The fate of the "Lincoln persuasion" turned out to be a prime case in point, as the vanguard commitments of the Civil War era on behalf of civil and political rights were progressively abandoned through the North's flagging

70

energy for reform and the South's steady reintegration into national politics. Apparently, even alternatives that are empowered can be lost.

Multiple Traditions

As Greenstone scores Hartz for giving too little credit to conflicts within liberalism, Rogers Smith claims that Hartz's analysis was excessively preoccupied with them.[62] In *Civic Ideals: Conflicting Visions of Citizenship in the United States* (1997), Smith mounted a frontal assault on the argument that liberalism has been hegemonic in determining the course of American political development. In his view, America's most potent alternatives have been neither lost nor liberal; nonliberal and downright illiberal traditions are, he observed, prominently displayed in American politics and occasionally ascendant in the high affairs of state.

Civic Ideals documents the persistence in America of cultural values supportive of patriarchy and racism and examines the political effectiveness of advocates of these ideas in competing for the allegiances of the American people with advocates of liberalism's more universalistic principles. Smith argues that, far from displacing these alternatives, liberal advances provoke their reformulation and resurgence, that innovative counterarguments asserted on behalf of these alternatives continually pace liberal reforms and call their guiding assumptions into question. By deeming these alternatives "traditions" in their own right, Smith attributes to them qualities of coherence, distinctiveness, resonance, creativity, and staying power comparable to "the liberal tradition" that Hartz identified with the whole of the American consciousness.

Assaults on liberalism in the late twentieth century are never far off-stage in this analysis, but Smith turns to the late nineteenth century for an illustration of just how potent these other traditions can become in redirecting American politics. The about-face negotiated after Reconstruction on civil and political rights cannot, in Smith's reading, be dismissed as an aberrant loss of cultural bearings or as a time lag in the reconciliation of ideals and reality. He identifies the post-Reconstruction era instead as one of those emblematic moments when competing ideals of ascribed hierarchy reassert themselves and gain the upper hand in American government. Prominent elites, both political and intellectual, responded to the expansion of liberal commitments in the aftermath of the Civil War by reworking illiberal themes with powerful claims on the hearts and minds of the American people. By the turn of the century, Smith shows, these new arguments had achieved dominance in regulating and implementing the rights of citizenship. John Burgess has an important part to play in this story, though his identification of American development with the Teutonic chain and his association of the Constitution with the political genius of the Aryan race cast him here as an advocate of ideals quite at odds with the liberal ones he presumed to espouse.[63] Documenting the success of such arguments in legitimating a substantial reversal of rights formally achieved and exercised in the 1870s, Smith upended the proposition that American political development has been a series of incremental advances on liberal premises.

Smith's critique of Hartz lays bare the vulnerabilities of American liberalism and exposes ungrounded assumptions about linearity in political change (see boxed text). In doing so, it too accelerates the unraveling of developmental premises that Hartz's consensus thesis had already done much to loosen. The distillation of multiple traditions that are fundamentally at cross-purposes shifts the burden of developmental thinking off the stifling hegemony of liberalism in American politics and onto the tentative status of any liberal, or for that matter nonliberal, change that might take place. The specification of illiberal traditions that can be reinvented, inspire potent political movements, and control significant sectors of public policy presents America as a polity given to swings back and forth between competing standards of fundamental value, a polity as fully capable of repealing liberal advances as capitalizing on them, a polity likely to move in opposite directions over time. It is difficult to imagine how one might move further away from the developmental conception of American politics without calling into question the enduring significance of liberal ideals altogether.

Cultural Complexity and Political Development

... [T]he multiple traditions thesis holds that the definitive feature of American political culture has not been its liberal, republican, or "ascriptive Americanist" elements but, rather, [the] more complex pattern of apparently inconsistent combinations of traditions, accompanied by recurring conflicts. Because standard accounts neglect this pattern, they do not explore how and why Americans have tried to uphold aspects of all three of these heterogeneous traditions in combinations that are longer on political and psychological appeal than on intellectual coherence.

A focus on these questions generates an understanding of American politics that differs from Toquevillian ones in four major respects. First, on this view, purely liberal and republican conceptions of civic identity are seen as frequently unsatisfying to many Americans, because they contain elements that threaten, rather than affirm, sincere, reputable beliefs in the propriety of the privileged positions that Whites, Christianity, Anglo-Saxan traditions, and patriarchy have in the United States. At the same time, even Americans deeply attached to those inegalitarian arrangements have also had liberal democratic values. Second, it has therefore been typical, not aberrational, for Americans to embody strikingly opposed beliefs in their institutions, such as that blacks should and should not be full and equal citizens. But though American efforts to blend aspects of opposing views have often been remarkably stable, the resulting tensions have still been important sources of change. Third, when older types of ascriptive inequality, such as slavery, have been rejected as unduly illiberal, it has been normal, not anomalous, for many Americans to embrace new doctrines and institutions that reinvigorate the hierarchies they esteem in modified form. Changes toward greater inequality and exclusion, as well as toward greater equality and inclusiveness, thus can and do occur. Finally, the dynamics of American development cannot simply be seen as a rising tide of liberalizing forces progressively submerging contrary beliefs and practices. The national course has been more serpentine. The economic, political, and moral forces propelling the United States toward liberal democracy have often been heeded by American leaders, especially since World War II. But the currents pulling toward fuller expression of natural and cultural inequalities have also won victories. In some eras, including our own, many Americans have combined their allegiance to liberal democracy with beliefs that the presence of certain groups favored by history, nature, and God has made Americans an intrinsically "special" people. Their adherents have usually regarded such beliefs as benign and intellectually well founded; yet they also have always had more or less harsh discriminatory corollaries.

Rogers Smith, "Beyond Tocqueville, Myrdal, and Hartz: The Multiple Traditions in America," *American Political Science Review*, 87(3) (1993), 552–3.

Redirecting the Inquiry

Over earlier years, scholars confident in some overarching scheme of political development entertained the full range of possibilities for America – America as a vanguard state, a retrograde state, a mainstream state, an anachronistic state. Even into the 1970s, implicitly developmental frames of reference provided leverage for characterizations of the course and meaning of American political history. As it turned out, however, each of these characterizations fell victim to the insights of the next; ultimately, none could withstand critical scrutiny. Meta-narratives of progress have now all been dispelled, and assumptions about direction in political change over time have been thoroughly discredited as unreliable premises for historical research. For all appearances, the analytic program that gave birth to the study of American political development has dissolved in its own insights.

Where to go from here? How to move beyond the collapse of faith in the sufficiency of development as a guiding principle for historical research is a question facing contemporary social science generally, and several responses are already on the table. Trends in political analysis as diverse as postmodernism and rational choice promise to take "the end of history" in stride. What was once unproblematically thought of as "political history" is now open to normative deconstruction as cultural artifice or to theoretical exploitation as a collection of data points. Although both offer ways of sustaining research into America's past, neither substitutes for careful thinking about the historical construction of politics. By the same token, APD is likely either to get absorbed by these approaches or simply lost in the shuffle without some assiduous efforts to rearticulate its program.

A look back at the long line of inquiry reviewed in this chapter points up four possible responses. The first is that APD will continue to elaborate insights into structure, agency, boundaries, and cultural creativity, both individually and in relation to one another, but without any special regard to the concept of development. There is nothing intrinsically wrong with such a course, but none of these topics, by themselves or in their relation to one another, require support by a field of APD; they are of interest in a variety of subfields. It was the concept of development, even if only skepticism about that concept's validity, that brought scholars of these other subjects into a larger conversation. It was the notion that political change over time held meaning and importance of its own that sustained the enterprise.

Saying this, however, points to another possible response: that APD is poised to explore more fully the notion that time itself is an essential constitutive dimension of politics. Not only is this an overriding theme of the literature reviewed in this chapter, it is not one easily taken up elsewhere. As we have seen, the more deeply APD research has probed simple assumptions about progress, the more prominently it has displayed and elaborated the complexities of time in the historical construction of politics. Whereas rational choice scholars, for instance, have reacted to the collapse of the concept of development by moving in the opposite direction, reducing time to iterations and projecting a spare, lockstep movement from one equilibrium to the next, APD scholarship moved from Burgess's historical "mistake," Wilson's paradoxical sequence, Ford's unintended consequence, Beard's "political lags," to Hartz's "boundary condition," Burnham's "critical realignments," Greenstone's expandable "toolbox," Smith's patterned "reversals." In all, APD's cultural critique has done far more than simply undermine the appeal to some idealized notion of progress at work behind political change. It has simultaneously pressed forward the issue of just what ideas about time are most appropriate to the study of politics and served up more interactive, subtle, and multiform possibilities.

A third response to be drawn from this review looks to the unique position of the current generation of scholars, suggesting that we may be the first to actually face development as a question in its own right. The irony of APD research today – of the sustained and growing interest in a field whose guiding premise has unraveled – says a lot about the difference between clearing away unwarranted assumptions about political development and shutting down the discussion of political development altogether. None of the ground clearing that has dominated APD research until now constitutes a straightforward argument that American politics does not develop, and for all that scholars have done to stiffen the challenge of thinking about American politics developmentally, it remains to be seen how far we can get in understanding the cumulative significance of change over time without resort to such a conception. If there is a criticism of the literature to be ventured on this score, it is that the scholars who have done the most to liberate us from the baggage that has hitherto loaded down the study of American political development have not doubled back to consider what of that concept might still remain. To restate a point made at the end of Chapter One, all sense of a definition of development has been lost in critical discussions of the normative aura that surrounds it. Read more constructively, the cultural critique might stand as an open invitation to bracket these issues pending a definition that is more defensible. Doing that would allow us to address these outstanding questions: has anything worthy of the term *development* occurred in American politics? If so, what does that look like, and how did it happen?

A final response to the challenge of recasting APD is to pursue the opening to institutional analysis that is implicit throughout the cultural critique and is especially pronounced in the recent literature on lost alternatives. Though institutions will always need to be explained at least in part by culture, cultural causes of change (or no-change) will always work, at least in part, through institutions. Greenstone, who more than any other contemporary figure in our review sought to rebuild a conception of development through cultural analysis, himself suggested the difficulty of proceeding on cultural ground alone. In the opening sentence of his critique of Hartz, he observed that "connections between ideas of political culture and political development are intrinsically problematic."[64] In their own ways, Burgess, Hartz, Burnham, Greenstone, and Smith all confirmed this; though they reached different conclusions about development in American politics, their analyses all drew on the staying power of ideas. In looking to culture, they addressed the polity's most durable features – liberalism, capitalism, racism. In examining the political visions of reformers they discovered a clarity and coherence of purpose that no up-and-running polity is likely to realize in practice. In this context, a closer look at institutions is attractive at least in part because un-raveling assumptions about development does not seem to translate readily into traction for redirecting our thinking about it.

An institutional turn is appealing because it promises to carry for-ward many of the insights that the cultural critique has offered into the complex temporalities of politics. As is shown in Chapter Three, a redirection of this sort is already proceeding. A field that began with the institutionalism of Burgess and Wilson now plays host to a prolif-eration of "new institutionalisms," each carefully shorn of teleology but more alert than ever to the value of reliable signposts of devel-opment – something built, dismantled, rearranged, retained. Though the importance of cultural ideals and reform visions is confirmed in these analyses, their significance is also modified in ways that seem to bring us closer to something we might defensibly call development. That is to say, though an institutional change prompted by a new idea may not preclude the resurgence of older ideas farther down the road, that resurgence is bound, by the consequences of institutional change itself, to intrude on a polity that is arranged differently, mak-ing reversal in the sense of return to the prior state of affairs unlikely. At issue, in other words, it how institutions hold politics and political change to a discernible path.

THREE

The Institutional Turn: Rethinking Order
and Change over Time

... institutions must advance and keep pace with the times. We may
as well require a man to wear still the coat that fitted him when a
boy as civilized society to remain ever under the regimen of their
barbarous ancestors.

Thomas Jefferson

THE CLAIM OF CONSERVATIVE IDEALISTS LIKE BURGESS, that political
institutions express the aspirations of the civilization they serve, gave
us one view of political development; the claim of progressive scholars
that political institutions reflect economic interests and the balance of
power among them offered another; the claim in some recent studies
in APD that institutions subvert culturally generated alternatives calls
into question the notion of political development itself. What scholars
say about political development turns in good measure on how they
think about political institutions, and the question of how institutions
affect political outcomes currently supports a multifaceted intellectual movement of its own.[1] The claim of the "new institutionalists"
is that institutions do not merely express or reflect or deflect elements
in their political surroundings. Institutions participate actively in politics: they shape interests and motives, configure social and economic
relationships, promote as well as inhibit political change.

For APD scholarship, a "new institutionalism" has several attractions. The more proactive role attributed to institutions in processes
of political change is of obvious interest, but an institutional turn has
a strong instrumental appeal as well. Having discarded a number of
assumptions that guided thinking about political development in the
past – teleology, organic growth, linearity, progress – APD scholars

78

stand in need of a reliable standard by which they can reconceptualize politics over time and track its movement. Institutions promise to fill that bill. Indeed, a more robust platform on which to ground their reassessment would be hard to find. On the one hand, institutions register order; they are important mechanisms through which individuals coordinate their actions and expectations. On the other, institutions are subject to change, and more than that, because of their often highly formalized operations, their creation, transformation, and situation with respect to other features of politics can be readily followed and documented. Scholars who have sought to recast the study of APD along these lines, and whose work we give close attention in this chapter, often call themselves "historical institutionalists": they look at institutional arrangements over time to identify order and change in politics and they search for patterns in successive combinations of old and new elements.[2]

Propositions about how institutions affect politics over time also speak to APD's normative concerns. From the nation's beginnings, democratic theorists have pondered the difficulty of reconciling American government's strong institutional character with principles of self-government. Thomas Jefferson, for instance, was alert to how institutions insinuate themselves into the life of the polity and concerned about how this process would undermine democratic ideals and impede progress. He challenged his compatriot's faith in the reformist bent of representative institutions as insufficient to the tasks of clearing away outmoded forms, and he recommended provisions for a thoroughgoing popular reassessment of governing arrangements every twenty years.[3] How institutions complicate notions of popular control, how they come over time to affect the political perceptions of citizens as well as to constrain their action, is if anything, a more difficult question today because the collapse of the norm of progress has dimmed faith in both the natural instincts of the people out of doors and the innate character of representative government. Our critique of developmental assumptions opens the full two hundred years of piecemeal tinkering with American institutions to new lines of inquiry into the effects of popular politics on government and the processes by which the democracy works its way – or fails to.

The scholarly reassessment currently underway is correspondingly broad in scope. Historical institutionalists want to know more than they do now about the contextual determinants of political choice, more about how changes in political institutions affect changes in the economy and society, more about the cumulative consequences of partial reforms, and more about the constraints on contemporary American democracy imposed by decisions made long ago. They hope to learn these things through detailed historical analyses of interactions between state and society. This work tends to be "polity centered," foregoing explanatory privilege to either social interests or the state and looking instead at what is up and running, which is the full array of organized interactions between the two.[4] In a polity understood in this way, institutions constitute a realm of mutual influence and exchange, one in which the reciprocities of control and volition, structure and agency, authority and resistance work together to motivate events. Rewriting the story of American political development from this vantage point promises to bring a firm empiricism to the observation of different causal elements over time and to demonstrate the practical effects of the historical construction of politics.

The unfortunate note is that gains to date are scattered and particular. In part, this reflects the topical nature of investigations, offering separate treatments of discrete subjects – welfare politics, racial politics, labor politics, party politics, congressional politics, presidential politics, sectional politics, and so on – spread over different decades. These studies are usually intended as windows onto the larger picture, but the substantive material addressed is so different from one study to the next that it is easy to lose sight of common questions asked. Related to this, several versions of the historical-institutional thesis are currently in play, some departing more radically than others from received understandings of how politics changes over time. It is to be expected that institutions will have a variety of things to tell us about the historical construction of politics. But with so many different formulations of the theoretical project on the table – with the alternatives seldom distinguished from one another and often used together in the same work – one is hard pressed to say exactly what the perspective of historical-institutionalism is, let alone what is actually new about it or how it might advance a search for American political development.

We can think of no more beneficial way to proceed than to sort through this literature, distinguishing the major propositions and considering each as they bear on the historical construction of politics. We divide the literature into three groups and consider four examples of research in each. The first group lodges the significance of institutions in the construction of political order *in* time; the second group lodges the significance of institutions in the pathways of political change *over* time; a third lodges the significance of institutions in the operation of multiple, often incongruous, political orderings *at the same time*. These treatments are not necessarily incompatible with one another, nor are the compartments we have put them in air-tight. We separate them to draw out particular points in different research and to show how this literature moves over a range, from more to less familiar conceptions of politics, from simpler to more elaborate conceptions of temporality, and from less to more distinctly developmental conceptions of historical construction.

With these purposes in mind, articulating the rationale for studying political change by way of institutions is especially important. If the progression we see here, toward a clearer specification of the developmental properties of politics, is more than an artifact of our own categories of organization – if it is, as we believe, inherent in following through on an institutional approach – then it is necessary that foundations be carefully spelled out. To this end, we turn first to a brief disquisition on institutions-in-politics.

Institutions-in-Politics

Institutions present themselves in politics in two different modes. The first mode is carrying on with operations on the inside; that is to say, by acting institutionally. This mode includes all of the ways in which institutions organize people and direct their activities for the achievement of particular purposes. In this mode, all institutions, including political institutions, are essentially the same. The second mode in which institutions present themselves in politics is attempting to control the actions of others on the outside; that is to say, by acting politically. Any institution may at times act in this way, though by no means do all institutions always act so. We will reserve the term *"political institution"* for those whose primary purpose is to control persons or other institutions on the outside. These will be taken up in turn.

The attributes of institutions generally are a much-discussed topic in social science. A basic list consistent with our analysis of institutions in the first mode, acting institutionally, can be briefly enumerated. To begin with, institutions have *purposes*, reasons for being, often set out in charters or formal mandates. Purposes are virtually endless in their variety – fraternal, profit making, professional, scientific, honorary, educational, religious, legal. Purposes determine motives, procedures, and techniques; they are standards against which performance is monitored, by insiders and others. Second, institutions establish *norms and rules* for behavior. These may be either customary or codified, but are always set in advance and enforceable through the imposition of discipline. Third, institutions assign *roles*, positions of rank, office, and responsibility, in which appropriate behavior is expected. By assigning roles, institutions also assign identities, affecting the way people think of themselves and are regarded by society. Finally, institutions operate within *boundaries*, either prescribed or self-defined. Boundaries divide persons and activities inside the institution from persons and other institutions outside; boundaries array institutions in society, bringing their activities to bear on one another or keeping them more distant.

Some caveats: though historical institutionalists tend to analyze institutions at the "macro" rather than "micro" level, institutions are not independent of the people who operate them and act within their bounds. Institutions are subject to innovation, redirection, disruption, and to all manner of personal motives of individuals. On the other hand, they are also more than individuals; they motivate a collectivity, their norms and values affect their members, their sanctions guard against unwarranted behavior, and their purposes are sufficiently firm that, barring their complete dismantlement, they can continue on in recognizable form to be worked by new operatives, to the same end, over time. By the same token, institutions are not ideas.[5] That they have purposes means they are often carriers of ideas; their purposes and activities may make them the subject of ideas; a new idea may subvert or alter an established purpose. But it is equally plain that ideas can change without a corresponding change in the purposes of an institution. Ideas arising from a change in leadership or operational exigencies may have no effect on the institution, and whatever effect they do have will be an empirical question. Last, institutions are not, or not only, organizations. Institutions set systematic relations in motion that may extend across society – legal relations, for instance, or the institution of the bar, or the institution of the family. These relations might be expressed wholly or in part within organizational settings, but they are not contained by them.[6]

By doing no more than minding their own business, by simply acting institutionally, institutions have immense political importance. Considered in this mode alone, institutions assert control over individuals within their boundaries and establish relations of authority among them; in these senses they govern and support a political life that is often active and intense. In this respect also, institutions are arguably an important forum for learning behaviors that carry over into political life on the outside; vying for higher position, logrolling, bargaining, and coalition building are behaviors characteristic of institutions ranging from the Congress to the Catholic Church. By ordering individuals for purposeful action and by imposing expected and required behaviors, institutions also contribute to the regularity and stability, the "law and order," sought and relied on by government. Moreover, as dispensers of valued objectives like prestige, wealth, and professional standing, institutions inspire conflict among individuals and social groups, conflict that may be expressed in the wider political arena. Along the same lines, the resources that institutions control, both human and material, are frequently subjects of public policy.

Institutions that present themselves in politics in the second mode have all these same attributes, with the added one that they attempt to control the behavior of persons and institutions outside their boundaries as well as within. The common designation of some but not all institutions in society as political will be seen to be consistent with the distinction that political institutions have control over outsiders as their primary purpose. The most prominent political institutions are the institutions of government. Constitutional branches, government commissions and departments, and offices of all kinds that regularly promulgate and implement laws and regulations are political institutions par excellence in this meaning. But this category also includes extensions of governmental authority deep into society, into the institution of the family, for instance, where husbands have traditionally held enforceable authority over wives, and mothers have enjoyed special legal status in the rearing of children, and to workplaces, where employers have extensive legal controls over employees. Not all political institutions are governmental, of course: political parties, for instance, exist primarily to mobilize electorates and control government institutions. Still other political institutions combine both government and nongovernmental elements: the institution of lobbying, for instance, encompasses private organizations that seek to influence lawmakers and the laws by which they operate. Moreover, institutions with purposes that are not primarily political may at times act politically; that is, they may attempt to influence the behavior of others outside their churches, business corporations, mass media companies, professional associations, and so on, to serve their primary (or other) purposes.

Among political institutions, government institutions are distinctive for the mandates under which they operate, authorizing them to make rules for society at large, including for other institutions, both outside government and within. This means that government controls over outsiders are often wider in scope and more continuous in their effect than those of nongovernmental institutions. Government institutions can also utilize force, including violence, in controlling others, in addition to the money, mass communications, and similar resources that other institutions deploy; in the United States, government has come to exercise a near-monopoly of legitimate violence. All of these things place government institutions center stage in the institutional analysis of politics. When nongovernmental institutions attempt to exert control over others they often appeal to government;

this is true also of individuals and social movements. When institutions that are not primarily political in their purposes act to control government, that is to say, when they act politically, it is often in reaction to ongoing or prospective government controls.

The two modes of institutions-in-politics are closely connected in their operations. As just suggested, the extent to which institutions not primarily political in their purposes will devote resources to controlling outsiders may be reactive: business corporations, for instance, devote far more resources to this task than was the case before they were so extensively regulated by government and before they were singled out for direct pressure by environmental and civil rights activists. In other cases, nonpolitical institutions may be inhibited by their purposes and rules: in the United States, fundamentalist churches were constrained by tradition and doctrine from participating in electoral politics. In the case of government institutions, for which controlling others is ongoing, activities on their interface with outsiders may determine internal operations and reform. The contemporary presidency's preoccupation with public opinion coincides with the proliferation and dominance of mass media and their investigative bent; another example is the establishment of standing committees in Congress in early decades, which were a response, at least in part, to the informational resources and threatened intrusion of executive branch officials. For an example in a political but nongovernmental institution, competition between the two political parties for control of voters has brought about the development of new techniques of fundraising and new cadres of political professionals in both of them.

What is important in this way of looking at things is the picture of the polity it pushes onto the page. What appears is the polity as an aggregation of outward-reaching, interactive, mutually impinging institutions and the reactions it provokes. Foreign relations, as it were, animate the scene, as political institutions assert control over outsiders and respond to outsiders with adjustments in their own internal operations. The picture is not complete. Even in its own terms, ambitious leaders might want sketching in, and the clash of institutional mandates (it is said that there are more than eighty thousand government authorities in the United States and sixty thousand have the authority to tax[7]) will convey even more tension. If a single premise unifies the disparate strands of historical-institutional research, and much of the rest of the "new institutionalism" as well, it is that coordination problems are endemic and pervasive in the operations of government. Some of these tensions might be technical in nature, arising from incomplete information, perhaps, or signaling problems; others will indicate deeper strains – cross-purposes of mandates, or the incompatibility of old and new procedures.

In such a view, what needs highlighting now is order. Order may be found within an institution's boundaries, suggesting regularity of its internal operations; it may be found in a political institution's larger domain, that is in the (relative) consistency of interactions with outsiders it seeks to control; finally, it might be found across political institutions, where different controls are asserted in different domains. The interesting thing is that once the various aspects of political order are disaggregated in this way, the dimension of time pops up, so to speak, all on its own. In Chapter One, order was defined as a constellation – practices, ideas, institutions – that hangs together while other things continue to change. Order sustained inside a particular political institution, then, will over time likely complicate the realization of order within in its larger domain; order sustained between insiders and outsiders in a particular domain will over time likely complicate the realization of order in the polity as a whole. As political institutions carry on through time under existing mandates, they will over time likely riddle the political world with obsolescent and incongruous controls. All current versions of historical institutionalism contemplate this paradox.

To students of politics in the United States, these contingencies of order will be second nature, for they are built into the design of the Constitution. Federalism and the separation of powers multiply the points of tension among agencies of control; checks and balances induce contests among them; provisions for representation and elections hold officeholders in suspended relations with those they are mandated to control; their staggered terms of office accentuate incongruities and abrasions. To all appearances this is a "system" of government purposefully designed to keep order provisional, to insure it is routinely contested and off-balance. We have argued here that this state of affairs only replicates the larger model, applicable to other aspects of the American polity and to polities generally. When individual interests and motives are understood with reference to their institutional settings, when political institutions are understood in terms of controlling outsiders, when government's capacities to bring order to the polity are understood to be limited by its own institutional composition, the political analysis of institutional effects naturally leapfrogs to wider interactions, extending over lengthening time horizons.

Ordering Mechanisms

Our first sampling of the historical-institutional literature is concerned with the institutional construction of political order. The four studies illustrate various ways in which government officials, singly or collectively, bring about stable arrangements of control, both outside their own institutions and within. Here again we encounter a proposition about institutions and politics that echoes classic American themes. James Madison employed this idea in his argument that the design of representative institutions could control interest groups seeking their favor.[8] So did Martin Van Buren, when he argued for parties constructed and arranged in a manner that would make it possible to at once mobilize citizens into politics and temper their antagonisms.[9] One way or another, all the disparate strands of the "new institutionalist" movement in political science today are trying to figure out how, and with what impact, such ordering mechanisms work. As we move through this particular sample, we see the answers grow increasingly circumspect, qualified by the multiple sources of movement and change.

Example 1: In a study of politics in antebellum America, Barry Weingast singles out Congress's "balance rule" for granting statehood – the admission of one free state paired with the admission of one slave state – as crucial to the maintenance of comity between rival sectional interests.[10] Documenting the potential for the empowerment of a free-state majority long before it actually occurred, Weingast observes that "nothing inherent in the antebellum era inevitably preserved rights in slaves." More to the point, he argues that with the rapid expansion of the North in both population and territory, neither the arrangements of the Constitution nor the intersectional design of the two major party organizations were sufficient by themselves to give southern states the assurance they needed to hold them in the Union. Because statehood automatically conferred two seats in the Senate, the "balance rule" gave the South a veto in that chamber over the enactment of any national policy that might impinge on its regional economic interests.

Important to Weingast's analysis is that the rule of sectional balance was devised early on. It was the product of a time when economic prospects in the two regions were evenly matched and representatives of the North perceived themselves no less vulnerable to economic policies than those of the South. Incorporated into the Missouri Compromise of 1820, before the institutionalization of national two-party competition, the rule became increasingly important to southerners as a sign that the North would not press its growing political advantages, even in the face of rising public outcry against slavery. Given these circumstances, the antebellum order was increasingly susceptible to misapprehensions and miscalculations; still, legislators adhered to the rule long after the circumstance that initially gave rise to it had changed. The effects went beyond the rule's immediate purposes to set basic parameters of the antebellum political economy, including a limited role for the national government in economic affairs and a radically decentralized pattern of economic development.

Example 2: In his study of the late-nineteenth century American political economy, Richard Bensel shows a direct relationship between rapid industrialization and the policies of the federal government, and explains how these were sustained while under constant siege by politically powerful interests armed with opposing legislative proposals.[11] The political architecture of these years is revealed through a series of contingent alignments. Three policies were critical to the outcome: maintenance of an unencumbered national market, maintenance of the protective tariff, and maintenance of the gold standard. Throughtout the period, these critical policies were contested by three principal interest-group antagonists: cotton exporters, yeoman settlers, and financial capitalists. The antithetical designs of these interests were grounded on and bolstered politically by their geographic concentration in three distinct regions: respectively, the South, the West, and the Northeast.

This tripartite organization of the late-nineteenth-century economy interacted with the peculiar tripartite structure of American government to produce an outcome that by itself claimed no social or political consensus. As Bensel explains it, each of the branches of American government took the lead in successfully protecting one critical policy against alternatives championed by the South and the West, even though these regions together sometimes enjoyed institutional majorities. The Supreme Court worked to maintain open markets against regulation-prone southern and western representatives and populist state legislatures; the justices owed their appointments to Republican party power in the Senate and to conservative Democratic Senators tied to the New York financial community. Congress protected the tariff, twice defeating reduction plans offered by President Cleveland in an effort to unite southern and western Democrats with the party's more conservative eastern wing; congressional leaders structured logrolls putting northern labor and select agricultural commodity groups on the side of northern industry to maintain trade protection. Presidents supported the gold standard against potentially inflationary schemes in Congress; they were responsible for the workings of the Treasury and mindful of an electoral college in which New York and the financial interests of the Empire state played a pivotal role. Rapid industrialization emerges in this analysis as an effect mediated by multiple institutional arrangements. Though decisive in foreclosing popular alternatives, this effect was not planned, agreed upon, or coordinated by the branches of government; it was produced by interactions among institutions that were differently structured and motivated to deal with the interests that pressed most directly upon them from the outside.

Example 3: Terry Moe's study of the National Labor Relations Board explains how, from the 1950s through the 1970s,

89

representatives of business and labor coexisted peacefully in stable equilibrium.[12] Moe attributes this equilibrium to two factors. The first was the passing of the electoral volatility of the 1930s and 1940s. A new partisan alignment within and across the institutions of the national government made it unlikely that either business or labor could prevail in altering the regulatory regime established during the preceding decades, and freed politicians in the executive and legislative branches to turn their attention to other priorities. The second factor was the addition to the National Labor Relations Board (NLRB) of a competent agency staff. Taking advantage of the prevailing political stalemate, the NLRB hired lawyers recently trained in the new law of labor and industrial relations, and greater professionalism at the agency provided assurance to usually contending economic interests of the integrity and predictability of the regulatory process itself. After the 1950s, then, a stable regulatory order emerged through a combination of administrative competence and political indifference.

Moe points out that whenever one of the political conditions supporting peaceful coexistence during this period gave way, the threat was deflected by other institutions with interests in system maintenance. But in 1981, with the election of an ideologically charged president and a reinforcing change in political control of the Senate, a major political offensive was opened against the interests of organized labor on the board. Moe stresses that the NLRB's business clientele did not lead the charge. Traditional sources of business influence in Republican administrations put forward nominees to the Board who could be expected to support business interests within the established framework, but President Reagan passed these over, choosing appointees likely to wage a frontal assault on prevailing institutional norms. Moe's analysis suggests both that the institutional arrangements of government might over time affect the preferences of the economic interests contending within them and that government actors, eyeing the strategic environment with their own purposes in mind, might press radical action independent of the express preferences of their economic allies.

Example 4: In his study of the "forging of bureaucratic autonomy" Daniel Carpenter examines how, in the late nineteenth and early twentieth century, middle-level administrators redefined agency missions, garnered political support, secured the acquiescence of legislators, presidents, and political parties ostensibly in charge, and created political order anew.[13] The key strategy of these "bureaucratic entrepreneurs" was to turn each of their agencies into an "organizational nexus" for bringing social interests and reformers together and devising new programs of action. To this end, they cultivated extensive contacts among those who might value the services they were creating, they employed their reputations as leaders in their field to mobilize outside interests on their behalf, and they used their newfound clout to influence lawmakers. Through programmatic innovation, interest enlistment, and political organization, these bureaucrats not only inverted traditional lines of control between themselves and their "principals" in elected office but did so in ways that fundamentally recast the way in which societal interests related to the state.

Carpenter shows that this reordering of authority did not occur across the board in American government but only in pockets. The transformation of controls achieved at Department of Agriculture's Forest Service, for example, stood in contrast to the persistence of traditional lines of control at Interior Department's Bureau of Reclamations. The reordering effect was associated with particular agency characteristics, occurring where a bureaucratic culture had developed over the long haul to identify a clear mission, where control over the recruitment of personnel was largely internal and new recruits were instilled with the faith. It helped as well when agency heads were known among networks of social reformers as leading spokesmen for new ideas, for this enhanced their legitimacy among other politicians. In all, authority relations were transformed by a confluence of circumstances brought into focus by leadership efforts within the bureaus themselves.

Discussion: Before turning to the differences that distinguish these four studies from one another – and distinguish historical institutional analyses generally from other currents of "new institutionalist" research – certain shared points of departure deserve mention. Most obvious perhaps is that each of these studies weighs in against the notion that political orderings of social interest in history can be subsumed by larger cultural or sociological processes. Institutions of government are at the center of each explanation, and actively so. Each study rejects the image of government as a "black box," so many parts and gears processing social inputs. None posits an "American political order" of fixed and interconnected authority, operating seamlessly to produce optimal effects from interest conflicts. Rather, their shared finding is that political order is circumstantial, something that officials within government institutions will create or not, sustain or not, depending on their own interests, on the available resources, and on the obstacles to change. Finally, the orderings observed here are not only contingent and purposeful, they are constructions of broad consequence. Weingast claims that the balance rule for admitting slave and free states determined the character of the antebellum political economy; Bensel argues that economic policy making at the end of the nineteenth century catalyzed a shift toward forms of industrial development desired by only one section of the country.

Depictions of order as the formative constructions of politicians in power carry a powerful argument for returning political history to its earlier position at the center of social science research. The effects observed politicize history by directing attention to how purposes within and among government institutions shape social and economic organization; at the same time, they historicize politics by directing attention to the conditions that give rise to particular orderings in time. What makes this return to political history especially interesting, however, are the points of divergence among these studies, for these indicate revisionist ambitions of different extent. Moving from one study to the next, a progressively wider range of institutional actions is brought into view, the sources of movement and change become more varied, and the mechanisms that produce order are correspondingly less straightforward. This openness to more complex and intricate formulations is, we think, a defining feature of the historical-institutional strand of the new institutionalism. Not coincidently, the willingness to depart decisively from received assumptions about order and change in politics invites us to reconceptualize politics overall in distinctly developmental terms.

One point of divergence among the four studies concerns the specific nature of relations between state and society, and in particular between governmental officers and social interests. Although all describe top down effects of government on society and each challenges bottom up treatments, there is considerable variation among them in what kind of action occurs at the top. For Weingast and Bensel, the actions of politicians inside institutions remain closely tied to the outside interests they represent. Weingast's southern congressmen act on behalf of the slaveholders that elected them. Bensel's Supreme Court justices decide cases according to the political coalitions responsible for their appointments. The processes of mediation they describe would be familiar to Madison: government institutions structure interactions among economic groups and filter them through the political calculations of the officers who represent them. If these calculations are not reducible to the interests of outside groups, neither are government officers very far removed in their purposes from those pressuring them for action.

By contrast, officials in the Carpenter and Moe analyses are far more independent; they are creative actors pursuing substantive political projects of their own. Moe writes of ideologies that prompt elected politicians like Ronald Reagan to act in ways that depart from the preferences of their interest-group backers and of labor lawyers motivated by their professional standards to act differently from the unions, corporations, and public officials they deal with on a regular basis. He points also to how the interests of economic groups are affected over time by their interactions with others within the government. The mutually constitutive relationship between state and society is demonstrated directly in Moe's analysis through the independent actions of the institutional incumbents themselves. Going farther, Carpenter has government actors selecting, shaping, and mobilizing social interests for their own purposes; entrepreneurs in the full sense of the term, they compel others, in government and relevant social groups, to follow their lead and enact their vision. The institutional construction of order here goes far beyond the mediation of interests in the two former examples; government institutions and the officials who operate them appear now as interest makers as well as interest takers.

These stronger claims on behalf of government institutions permit stronger claims on behalf of development as a central feature of politics. The revisionist thrust of Weingast and Bensel attach APD to the agenda of the political historian; both propose to tell us more than we knew before about what went on in a particular period. Weingast casts his study of the balance rule in terms of a dispute between "traditional" political historians and "new" political historians over the centrality of slavery in antebellum politics.[14] Bensel casts his as a refutation of both cultural historians, who treat popular politics in the late nineteenth century as if it was detached from the economic choices of the day, and of economic historians, who dismiss the importance of government in the transformation of the economy during this period.[15] Carpenter and Moe are not indifferent to the ways in which closer attention to institutions might resolve historical disputes or correct imbalances in historical interpretation, but their work anticipates a more thoroughgoing reassessment of politics in time. They are at pains to describe causal arrows that reverse directions in different times and places and, in so doing, anticipate a study of politics in which institutions and interests do not simply come into alignment at certain times but push and pull one another through time.

A different issue raised by these studies concerns the existence of a "prime mover" or master synchronizing mechanism that drives a larger construction of order by government. Looked at one to the next, these studies might convey the impression that ordering processes have grown more complicated over the course of American political development. Weingast's analysis of the antebellum period is Congress-centered; Bensel, Carpenter, and Moe, dealing with politics in later periods, look to wider interactions to explain outcomes. On reflection, however, it is implausible that slavery and the related sectional issues that surrounded it in the antebellum years were less complicated than labor relations in the midtwentieth century. Weingast's assertion that Congress' balance rule trumped other rules operating at the same time – party rules for nominating candidates, constitutional rules protecting property, even the Senate's own rules of debate – is a simplifying assumption, which, though common in certain strands of new institutional research, does not invite the broad reconsideration of institutional construction implied by the operation at once of several different ordering mechanisms.[16] Of our four studies, Weingast's is the most intent on searching out a prime mover and the strongest in its programmatic directive to think about ordering mechanisms in terms of prime movers.[17]

The ambivalence on this point apparent in our other studies reflects their readiness to think about ordering mechanisms differently. No single institution of government functions as prime mover in Bensel's analysis of rapid industrialization. His presentation seems to attribute that role to the Republican party, but on inspection, the different ordering elements he identifies among the constitutional branches operate at a considerable distance from the assumption of that institution's dominance. There is bipartisan complicity, for instance, in prompting a judicial defense of open markets, at least insofar as conservative Democrats were instrumental in appointments to the Court. Moreover, successive presidents' defense of the gold standard clearly did not hinge on the incumbent being a Republican (the crucial test came under Grover Cleveland); it turned instead on the national structure of electoral college competition which, in this era, made New York crucial to a Democratic presidential victory. Notwithstanding Republican party intentions, Bensel's evidence suggests that rapid industrialization was the aggregated effect of actors from both parties who were motivated differently, depending on their institutional locale.

Carpenter directly refutes Congress-centered models of institutional ordering, and though he offers a bureaucracy-centered explanation of certain outcomes, he resists the implication that he is just substituting one prime mover for another.[18] In fact, his central finding – that bureaucrats in some agencies get elected officials to do their bidding but not in others – suggests not only that the role of principle actor might vary across policy arenas but also that government exhibits different arrangements of control operating at the same time. Furthermore, Carpenter argues that the administratively driven reorderings he does observe cannot be explained as products of any overarching "strategic design," for "many of the core properties of turn-of-the-century bureaucracies – career systems, administrative organization, agency culture, capacity, and bureau chief's access to multiple networks" – were themselves historically evolved configurations with different sources.[19]

Moe is the most explicit on this score. He proposes that scholars reject "the tendency to assume that any particular institution is the prime-mover." The program of institutional study he outlines would anchor explanations of order in how different institutions, each harboring its own roles, interests, and perspectives, fall into and out of alignment over time.[20] Moe does not dispute that human agency is at the heart of the equilbrium he observes between labor and management in the setting of the NLRB. His thesis is that order is achieved in time through the juxtaposition of controlling agents – parties, presidents, senators, bureaucrats – rather than through controls exerted by any one of them separately. This said, it is the potential for each part to move independently of the others that lends his description of order an intrinsically dynamic character.

These efforts to move away from simplifying assumptions in the study of political order are important ones for APD research. Assumptions about black boxes, bottom-up constructions, and prime movers are being replaced by the discovery of more elaborate ordering mechanisms that take into account the mutually constitutive interactions between state and society and the operation of relatively independent institutions moving in and out of alignment with one another. Whether there is any general rationale available for thinking that the institutional construction of order proceeds by these elaborate pathways remains to be seen. To a large extent, that is the burden of institutional research concerned with other types of historical effects.

Pathways of Change

The four studies in our second group are concerned with how different political formations, often separated by broad spans of history, are connected to one another. Each recognizes the ordering capacities of institutions, but their focus is less on order achieved *in* time than with the course of politics as it threads its way *through* time and negotiates period boundaries. Outcomes are tied to constraints imposed by institutional settlements arrived at long ago in political decisions often far removed from the issues that come to be posed down the line. Explanations draw out the political consequences of previously established governing arrangements, the way choices made earlier are reinforced over time, how alternatives are eliminated and political changes channeled along a particular route. In the parlance of historical institutionalism, they explore the "path-dependent" attributes of political change.

Example 1: Stephen Skowronek begins his study of twentieth-century American state building with reference to a sequence of political development unique among Western nations: democracy before bureaucracy.[21] Skowronek traces problems encountered by efforts to expand national administrative capacities to the fact that the early American state made little provision for a national administrative arm, relying instead on an arrangement of governing instruments that evolved over the nineteenth century as "a state of courts and parties."[22] Breaking away from this arrangement meant breaking it down, and to the extent that reformers succeeded at that, their new forms were caught in extended struggles over the reorganization of constitutional authority at large, struggles that had to be pursued through the twists and turns of politics in an already well-developed electoral democracy. Overcoming the limitations of a civil service based on party patronage implicated bonds forged between president and Congress; overcoming the limitations of a state-based militia implicated the authority of state governors and the patronage networks riddling the War Department's bureaus of supply; overcoming the limitations of court-based regulation of business implicated the prerogatives and constitutional deference enjoyed by judges.

Skowronek shows that in the decades immediately following Reconstruction administrative reformers were foiled by parties and by justices aggressively exercising their own prerogatives to fashion responses to the problems of the day. A shift in electoral conditions

around the turn of the century gave reformers an opening to promote their administrative designs, but an extended struggle to rearrange authority throughout the state apparatus insinuated itself into
the structure of new forms as they emerged. Between 1900 and 1920
the continuous vying between president and Congress for control
over civil administration left new forms of oversight locked in a
standoff between the competing branches; a similar struggle over
new forms of railroad regulation ended in the creation of a singularly powerful Interstate Commerce Commission, "independent" of
effective overseers in either branch. The struggle over the Army ended
with a War Department reorganized to meet new national objectives
but laced with tangled lines of control, from the executive and legislative branches and local authorities as well. All told, the process
of "building a new American state" replaced the arrangement of
courts and parties with bureaucratic arrangements organized around
a series of constitutional stalemates, raising serious questions about
how these new concentrations of governing authority could be made
democratically accountable.

Example 2: In her study of social provision in the late nineteenth
and early twentieth century, Theda Skocpol disputes the idea that
the United States was a laggard among Western nations in welfare
state development.[23] Challenging the identification of the welfare
state with the enactment of policies targeted at working class men,
she analyzes social provision in all of its variety and at different
times in American history. Skocpol shows that the nineteenth-century
patronage-based state was a precocious social spender: even as it
resisted demands by working-class men, it ably supported a generous and patronage-friendly system of pensions for Union veterans
of the Civil War. The Progressives' reaction against patronage in the
early twentieth century likewise did little for working-class men. Instead of extending the up-and-running system of soldiers' pensions
to workers, reformers built on the efforts of middle-class women to
gain government support for mothers and children and constructed
a "maternalist welfare state" outside established political channels.

Welfare state development is not smooth or evolutionary in
Skocpol's telling, but proceeds in fits and starts.[24] Each American

variant was a political construct of its own time: in the nineteenth century catering to the interests of Union veterans, in the early twentieth, to the interests of middle class women. Beyond the study's time frame but still always in view, the New Deal would respond to the demands of working-class men with policies resembling those of other countries. Although residues of earlier arrangements can be found later on (thus the continuance of womens' benefits in the New Deal), Skocpol's study is not about the origins of modern forms.[25] On the contrary, her point is that states can respond to similar problems in radically different ways over time. Moving across periods, welfare provision changed its form in accordance with changes negotiated in other parts of the state apparatus; within periods, the conception of welfare privileged at that moment either fit the designs of institutional actors engaged in breaking down older forms of governance or it fit a niche in existing institutional arrangements. Mothers' pensions were successful in the 1910s and 1920s in part because no agency or coalition in government had a large stake in them one way or the other.

Example 3: In his study of race and welfare policy, Robert Lieberman compares the history of Old Age Insurance (OAI) and Aid to Dependent Children (ADC), programs enacted during the Depression in a single legislative package in 1935 but with very different administrative designs.[26] Anticipating transfers of support between generations, OAI was a contributory scheme, centrally administered by the federal government. Benefits were distributed according to a standard actuarial formula by a single agency insulated from political control. To secure passage in a Congress with many prosegregationist southerners in positions of power, the program excluded agricultural workers and domestics, occupations where large numbers of African Americans were concentrated. By contrast, ADC was built on the financially starved but still existing system of widows' pensions, with its administration still lodged in the several states. Coverage was inclusive – a national standard for poor relief could not easily have discriminated by race; but the federal government provided only minimal guidelines and partial funding for its operation, leaving to the discretion of local lawmakers and administrators the level and distribution of benefits.[27]

Lieberman asks how these initial choices in program design informed the subsequent development of policy and politics in each area. The contributory nature of OAS created a large and powerful national constituency able to defend and expand program benefits; at the same time, federal administrators were given leeway to devise strategies for meeting the growing political pressures on the program. Over time, initial exclusions of recipient groups were eliminated. Recipients under ADC, however, were left to the shifting fortunes of localities. In response to increasing numbers of African Americans in northern cities, Lyndon Johnson's War on Poverty sought to channel federal funds directly to ghetto residents, but these efforts were thwarted by a coalition of big-city mayors and southern congressmen. Urban unrest in the meantime made poor relief more controversial, and the steady migration of whites to the suburbs diminished the political clout of core urban areas. The devolution of power to the localities in the initial design of federal poor relief continued in this way to determine the program's course, right down to its dismantling in the 1990s.

Example 4: In a study of the emergence of national health insurance in the United States, Great Britain, and Canada, Jacob Hacker explores why the United States is the glaring exception to the pattern of universal coverage found in other economically advanced nation-states.[28] In fact, national health insurance was a live proposal in the United States in the 1910s, 1930s, and 1940s, but in each period it failed to gain necessary support, something Hacker attributes to constitutional fragmentation and structural impediments to third-party movements peculiar to American government. What developed instead were networks of private provision, often with government endorsement and support. Over time these private systems became so elaborate and extensive and so ideologically weighted against governmental control that when the federal government did finally intervene in the 1960s its participation amounted to paying the bill for the residual high-cost populations – the old and poor – that private insurers would not cover, an approach that only deepened the attachment of crucial interests like organized labor to employer-based insurance.[29] Government interventions in Great Britain and Canada were also limited initially to the working class and to selected provinces, respectively; but these early successes, Hacker shows, altered political relations in the health sector, vesting strategic interests with leverage to expand the program at opportune junctures later on.

In this analysis, foregoing state intervention in private sector arrangements becomes as consequential as positive state action, and the timing of state intervention in relation to private sector growth is shown to affect both the substance and future course of policy development. America's comparatively late entry into government health care created neither the impetus nor the platform for more comprehensive provision down the road. Instead, government became more responsible for supporting the private system and solving problems that had grown up around it. Hacker argues that President Clinton's proposal for universal coverage in the 1990s was doomed in part by the complicated political and policy imperatives of trying to accommodate the byzantine system in place. He concludes that reform in the United States is not destined to culminate in European-style national health insurance, that the vision of stepwise progression toward universal coverage is illusory, that incremental approaches are unlikely to evolve into anything fundamentally different.[30]

Discussion: These studies cast the United States in a comparative frame, as one country among others making its way (or not) through problems like state building and social provision. Different historically evolved configurations of interest politics and state power within each country are shown to explain divergent outcomes. They determine paths – national trajectories – along which alternatives for change in the future are limited by changes made in the past. In this way, historical-institutional research is tied to issues of development per se, examining them in particular national settings, including the United States.[31]

This literature has roots in diverse currents of historical theorizing. It draws on Marxist and Weberian traditions; it follows work in APD from John Burgess to Louis Hartz, where the American case was always located on a comparative grid; it is influenced strongly by research on American public policy. Much of the recent work on path dependence takes its point of departure from an insight had in the 1930s by E. E. Schattschneider and elaborated in the 1960s by Theodore Lowi: "new government policies create new politics."[32] By reversing the more familiar causal arrow of politics-causes-policy, this move enabled scholars to step back in time and consider causes sequentially, from both sides of the state/society divide, as they move the polity forward. All of the authors in our sample see governmental institutions and their social supports in mutually constitutive relationships that are reinforced or undermined over time, here too placing historical movement and nonrandom change at the center of theorizing about politics.

The affinity between this line of research and APD's own core program is captured by a leading advocate when he states that path dependence lays aside the "snapshot" view of politics in favor of the "moving picture view."[33] Theorizing along these lines has in recent years taken on a degree of formality, aligning path dependency with other theoretical projects and presenting its own analytic vocabulary: "start-up costs," "sunk costs," "increasing returns," from models of investment; "feedback loops" from systems theory; "fit" from ecology and evolutionary biology. In principle, this language also advances APD's programmatic interests, providing a substitute for the older, more normatively tinged discourse of development. It is precisely because the attractions of moving down this road seem so compelling that the basic formulations deserve to be scrutinized closely with an eye to their potential for sustaining a research program about political development. To this end, we will avoid, so far as possible, the technical apparatus that has grown up around research of this kind and concentrate instead on questions about political change over time that can be drawn from our four cases.

Let us first consider the overall description of political change that occurs in these accounts. In its essentials, change is described in terms of the relationship between two stages: first, paths, along which politics proceeds according to existing political arrangements and ideological commitments; second, junctures, those points at which politics in some aspect changes by moving off in a new direction. It is clear in all of the examples that orderings observed along a path are not static but dynamic constructions, reinforced and channeled as they go. Even under attack from reformers, Skowronek's state of courts and parties was not helpless in the face of late-century governing demands but active in spinning out solutions, sometimes scooping the proposals of administrative reformers and bending them to its own ends, and sometimes discarding them altogether in favor of solutions of its own.

What is less clear is whether, and to what extent, the explanations offered are limited to these reinforcement effects, to explaining movements along paths, and what constitutes a new direction. If junctures are simply exogenous shocks that disrupt established patterns and place politics on a new path, then the notion of path dependence loses much of its interest, reduced to the idea that politics follows a particular course until something happens that changes the course. The stronger argument for political development is that responses to exogenous shocks are themselves informed by structures, identities, cleavages, programs, agendas present in the prior period, that what happens at critical junctures is also to some degree "path dependent." But if this is the case, the problem becomes how to distinguish between paths and junctures, between the kind of change that counts as reinforcing and the kind that counts as redirecting.

In fact, all of the studies in our sample connect paths across junctures. Skowronek and Skocpol describe a reflexive or "dialectical" relationship in which the prior path prompts a political reaction, directing reformers to root out the previously established mode of governmental operations. Thus, reform in the Progressive era was defined against the structures and mores of the patronage-based state, the choice of new governing instruments caught up in a larger programmatic determination to displace the old. For Skocpol, a maternalist welfare state recommended itself to authorities as much for what it was not, an extension of the old patronage politics, as for what it was, a new vision of welfare. For Skowronek, the overweening power of courts and parties in the early American state explains the lack of judicial discipline and the weakened conditions of parties in the bureaucratic state that replaced it.

This formulation of the relationship between periods captures both the idea of a disjuncture in history, of a break with the past, and the historical nature of the new construction that ensues. But does this relationship hold as a general proposition and how far does it extend beyond the ideological thrust of reform and into the politics of institutional construction itself? Nothing of this sort appears in the Hacker or Lieberman studies; on the contrary, both describe the important moments of departure as extended negotiations with arrangements of the past. Lieberman shows how ADC, a program spurred by the Great Depression, was absorbed into older interest conflicts and shaped by established ways of doing things, even to the extent of reviving and extending the largely moribund administrative structure of widows' pensions. Hacker goes further. He speaks of early junctures in the history of American health care policy as moments when redirection seemed possible but failed to materialize and of federal action on health insurance in the 1960s as a critical intervention that reinforced the path of private provision. So, too, in Skowronek's analysis of state building where, notwithstanding the Progressive-era reaction against the old arrangements of courts and parties, new administrative forms are shown to bear the imprint of accommodating in new arrangements the constitutional institutions carried over from the past. The connections between periods drawn in these studies call attention to governing arrangements from the past that persist through the critical periods of change and to new forms that are powerfully affected by what remained in place.

The issue raised is not simply a matter of nomenclature. Even if we assume that health-care policy in Hacker's telling admits of no critical junctures, that the history in this policy arena has been about the reinforcement of a single linear path, relationships of order and change, of continuity and breakpoints, remain undertheorized and hard to disentangle. In this literature, we know little about when and in what sense junctures overtake paths, about when and in what sense they reinforce them, about their variability in redirecting politics – in general, about the relationship between the two paths they separate in time. Knowing more is essential if the notion of path dependence is to provide a sturdy platform for the study of political development.

A related set of issues concerns the concept of reinforcement itself, especially as these bear on the institutional construction of interest-group influence. In path-dependence research, success in gaining access to state resources is often structured by the correspondence between governmental arrangements existing at the time and the goals of interest groups seeking influence. Interests promising to bolster, or at least not to disturb, relations among government elites are the ones who receive the government's largess, and this bias in selection locks the two sides into a relationship that is mutually reinforcing into the future. Thus, Skocpol explains social provision in the late nineteenth century in terms of the fit between patronage-oriented politicians and the interests of Union soldiers in pensions; she explains social provision in the early twentieth century in terms of the fit between the antipatronage agenda of Progressive politicians and the interests of middle-class women. The institution of mothers' pensions was attractive because women stood outside of patronage politics, they mobilized on behalf of progressive good government values, and they stepped on few bureaucratic toes. Likewise, reinforcement of this kind crowds out interests that are not similarly compatible with state dispositions, as, in Skocpol's analysis, the politics of the progressive era crowded out the demands of industrial workers for pensions.

On inspection, however, the concept of fit offers a rather narrow view of the politics of access, at least insofar as political development is to be considered a long-term, cross-period proposition. Social interests that thrive by filling a niche within established institutional forms or by discovering a channel for action made available by them have little interest in seeking major changes in the governing arrangements that favor them; on the contrary, they can be expected to hold politics to the present path, pressing only for those adaptations that promise to maintain the current relationship between institutional politics and public policy. Moreover, as Skocpol's study implies, a "fit" that is too neat at the start may leave the social interests served extremely vulnerable to any substantial alteration in politics elsewhere down the line. In this regard, consider how welfare services to soldiers in the late nineteenth century and to middle-class women in the early twentieth century might have been limited by their fit with prevailing institutional mores: because neither interest actually recast surrounding institutional arrangements, neither ever "locked" the government into a program for servicing them. Both of these welfare systems remained highly susceptible to shifts in the political climate affecting others around them, and in the end, both became mere historical curiosities. On Skocpol's own telling, the interests that fit exhibit limitations and dependencies that make them poor conduits for "development" over the long haul.

Perhaps then it is the interests that don't fit, not those that do, that are pivotal in political development. No doubt incongruous interests, those whose demands directly challenge prevailing institutional arrangements, will have a hard time getting a hearing from those in power; but they are also the interests most likely to elaborate programmatic interests in substantial institutional change, to hammer at established forms of governance, and to throw their support to those who promise to alter them.[34] On occasion, if they play the breaks correctly, the misfits may succeed in transforming institutional relationships, making the government fit them rather than visa versa. At the very least, it seems plain that the developmental conception of politics implicit in the idea of path dependence will be incomplete without a fuller exploration of the dynamics of fit and misfit in relations between interests and institutions. Recent studies of the institutional designs of the Farm Bloc and the labor movement in the 1920s have been suggestive in this regard, for they tie the emergence of the most durable forms of modern American politics to interests that persistently challenged the established forms.[35] The greater staying power of the welfare state built in the New Deal may itself be attributed to substantial adjustments in surrounding authorities that had to be made to accommodate the interests of working men; security for this system as opposed to the earlier welfare systems Skocpol identified was underwritten by the rearrangement of governing institutions around new policies and the political interests behind them. In this way, two very different forms of political feedback have come into view. One is mutually reinforcing: interests able to thrive in the niches and channels provided by the existing institutional environment will serve to bolster the governing arrangements that sustain them over time.[36] The second is mutually threatening: those excluded or repressed develop their own sense of interest with reference to the limitations of prevailing channels of action.

As we have suggested, the question raised here about path dependence has less to do with its description of an essential attribute of politics than with its adequacy as the foundation for new thinking about political development. This research has gone far in readdressing the developmental character of politics without succumbing to the old normative baggage of progress, but by its very nature, the historical connectedness of politics lends itself to a seamless web of construction. The instinct behind path dependence – to move political analysis backward in time in order to locate the institutional arrangements channeling politics through time – is a good one, but it falls easy prey to the dangers of infinite regress: policy can explain politics and politics can explain policy until everything is connected one way or another to everything else. The downside prospect of these proceedings is that the more we learn about these connections, the harder it is to say what elements are fundamental; that for all the substantive insights generated, the study of political development will simply spin around the initial insights that policy choices have political consequences and that history matters.

For these reasons, we are inclined to think of path dependence as an important way station on the historical institutional road to the revival of a theory of political development, not as the end of the search, and we would therefore caution against getting sidetracked by problems that are probably an expression of something else, analytically deeper. The appeal to metaphors of economics and ecology for theoretical grounding may itself indicate that we have not yet followed the logic of historical institutionalism itself far enough. In our view, the upside potential for capitalizing on the very real gains that research into path dependence has made, and, more generally, for securing what is most distinctive about a historical institutional analysis of politics, now turns on the elaboration of concepts that join institutions, history, and politics more directly. We have in mind concepts that can account for the composition and operation of the polity in terms that are strictly historical and institutional, and from which other general properties of politics – path dependence among them – can be derived.

Multiple Orders and Intercurrence

The studies in our third sample describe institutions, and the larger governing arrangements they comprise, as historical composites, carrying a number of different purposes forward from the past. Each study incorporates some of what the research already discussed has brought into view, in particular the ordering capacities of institutions and the path dependent attributes of politics. However, they do so with special reference to the partial and uneven character of political change over time. Each study is interested in what occurs when institutional purposes ingrained in an earlier era encounter new and antithetical purposes later on; each attributes to the presence of prior institutional arrangements the fact that political reform is often incomplete, that adverse principles and methods of operation remain in place. The claim here is that insofar as all political change, even at critical junctures, is accompanied by the accumulation and persistence of competing controls within the institutions of government, the normal condition of the polity will be that of multiple, incongruous authorities operating simultaneously.

Example 1: In his study of the American presidency, Jeffrey Tulis identifies problems of constitutional legitimacy that result when new rules and expectations of presidential performance are layered on older ones.[37] By examining the rhetorical practices of presidents over different eras – their messages and modes of address – he finds two distinct patterns. One, dominant throughout most of the nineteenth century, is congruent with the original design of the Constitution, reflecting its purpose of fostering deliberation among independent government branches. Acting accordingly, incumbents spoke rarely in public, spoke mainly on ceremonial occasions, and employed highly ritualized forms of address; communications were usually written, addressed to the Congress, and limited to the president's constitutionally prescribed duties. The second pattern, evident throughout the twentieth century, is responsive to the critique of the Constitution by progressive reformers and incorporates their more participatory idea of politics. Here, incumbents speak in public freely and often on whatever issues concern the national interest. By talking frequently and directly to the public at large, over the heads of congressional representatives, presidents aim to mobilize public opinion behind their policy goals and use it against Congress through constituency pressure to enact administration programs.

The newer rules of speech were well adapted to the growing prominence of Washington, D.C. in the federal system and to the availability of new technologies of communication. What Tulis demonstrates, however, is that these rules, and their associated agencies and personnel, never displaced the governing arrangements on which the old rules were based. As a consequence, the modern "rhetorical president" sits uneasily on top of the constitutional one, each engaging competing standards and compromising the authority that can be claimed on behalf of the other. Modern rhetorical practices subvert the integrity of interbranch deliberation on public issues, and older forms of governance dictating interbranch deliberation frustrate issue leadership by presidents. Occupying an office that is neither wholly modern nor wholly traditional, modern presidents regularly invoke their standing in public opinion polls to overrun constitutional constraints, while at the same time promising the public more than they can ever hope constitutionally to deliver.[38]

Example 2: Andrew Polsky narrates the "odyssey" of the juvenile court system, a form of local government that has persisted for decades despite perpetual controversy, internal disarray, and failure to achieve key objectives.[39] The institution differs from other tribunals by modifying the traditional legal goal of discovering individual guilt and innocence in favor of remedying social injustices that expose children to harm. The juvenile court was inspired at the turn of the twentieth century by newly professionalized social workers who thought juvenile law offenders ought to be treated in a less adversarial, more therapeutic manner than common criminals. The court was staffed accordingly. Polsky argues that combining the goals of the legal professionals with the goals of social-work professionals has produced an institution constantly torn by the competing missions its operatives bring to the table. Involving lawyers in social work and social workers in law enforcement has kept the juvenile court suspended in turmoil, turning this institution into an endless source of conflict among interested groups and political authorities at the local level.

Polsky's point, however, is not simply that the juvenile court has been torn by internal divisions and beset from outside, or even that the court has persisted in spite of all this, but that the court's internal divisions are what explains its tenacity. Polsky shows how charges of failure leveled by both public and private critics have been deflected time and again through a reformulation of institutional norms competing for dominance. Notions of therapy and punishment, of compensating for social injustice and law enforcement, have been combined and recombined over time; and while none of these amalgams has made for a more internally coherent or capable institution, each has solved some political problem of the moment thrown at it from the outside. Though the court was from the beginning an institution at cross-purposes, it has survived, and even flourished, by endlessly recycling goals that it cannot reconcile.

Example 3: Kenneth Finegold and Theda Skocpol compare two emergency agencies, the Agricultural Adjustment Administration (AAA) and the National Recovery Administration (NRA), both instituted during the Great Depression, in the aftermath of the electoral upheaval that brought Franklin Roosevelt and the Democrats to power.[40] With one aimed at farmers and one aimed at businessmen, both agencies were backed by the same coalition in Congress and both had the goal of raising incomes in their respective sectors through collective price-setting and production controls. Such a comparison would seem well calculated to hold historical variance at bay. In fact, however, Finegold and Skocpol find that the AAA and the NRA had very different success, with results exactly contrary to what purely sectoral, nonhistorical understandings might have predicted. Whereas the farmers, many more in number and individually scattered throughout the country, should have presented a more difficult problem of coordination than businessmen, the results were the opposite. Farm programs flourished; the industrial program collapsed.

The authors explain this outcome by contrasting the administrative histories of the two domains. The AAA operated within an established policy network, extending back to smaller-scale farm programs in the Civil War and the Progressive era. This provided a supply of administrators already schooled in lessons of these earlier initiatives, connected by education and experience to their counterparts in the private cooperatives and land grant colleges, and well acquainted with the proposed solutions to the problems facing them now. The NIRA, by contrast, proceeded on a terrain pitted by irresolute regulation, antitrust prosecutions and industrial warfare; it also lacked a similarly professionalized staff. The disparate effects of prior history were reinforced later in the New Deal, as liberals moved to replace their failed partnership with business by a closer partnership with labor. For decades to come, the government would engage in cooperative relationships with unions and farmers' groups while projecting an adversarial stance toward business.

Example 4: In her study of American labor politics, Karen Orren details a rigidly hierarchical legal system in control over the nineteenth and early twentieth century workplace, one dating back to feudal England and operating alongside liberal-democratic forms prevalent elsewhere in the United States.[41] Being common law, and incorporated as such into American constitutions, this order of master-and-servant was enforced by the judiciary according to changing doctrines – vested rights, enticement, common law conspiracy, freedom of contract – that kept employment relations apart from the parallel world of legislation and free bargaining inhabited by businessmen in their commercial affairs. Beginning after the Civil War, a prolonged and often violent campaign of organizing and collective action by workingmen assaulted this system of controls, giving lie to the proposition that it was essential to maintain industrial "order" and demanding equal rights to compete and bargain with their employers. To stem this tide, the judiciary enjoined labor activity and overruled prolabor legislation in an assertion of its authority unprecedented in American history for its aggressiveness, continuing up until the Court's losing battle with the New Deal in 1937.

Orren explains the master-and-servant law's demise in terms of its deterioration on several fronts. One was the workplace itself, where labor literally battered away at employers' prerogatives. A second was the courtroom, where workers' strategies outreached the logic of judges' increasingly convoluted decisions and made it all but impossible for juries to decide the cases before them. A third was industrial, functional, due to the sheer impracticality of maintaining strict separation between the law regulating labor and the law regulating business in the face of increasing economic dislocations and the public outcry for the government to step in. In that sense, the Wagner Act of the 1930s was a successor to public policies, especially railroad regulation, that were largely indifferent to labor's interests but were required by their mandates to grapple with industrial reality. The collapse of the old labor law took the common-law barrier between constitutional branches down with it, ushering in Congress' untroubled reign over social policy for the next half-century.

Discussion: Each of the above examples is a study of conflict and contradictions within a particular institutional setting: within a constitutional office, within a local agency, under the same New Deal mandate, under the same Constitution. Each provides a specifically historical explanation for what it finds: rules evolved in separate centuries, purposes pursued within different professional traditions, experience drawn from separate policy legacies, coexisting laws with separate lineages. If we seek a single explanation that unites all four, it is this: the institutions of a polity are not created or recreated all at once, in accordance with a single ordering principle; they are created instead at different times, in the light of different experiences, and often for quite contrary purposes. As these studies suggest, politics in the United States, like politics elsewhere, consists, in large part at least, in acting out the consequences.

As a general proposition about the historical construction of politics, nonsimultaneity in institutional creation speaks to all those out-of-synch governing arrangements on display not just in these studies but in studies with different theoretical underpinnings presented throughout this chapter. The same thing can be seen in Weingast's argument that a balance rule was necessary to protect the free and slave states from one another, in Carpenter's finding of bureaucratic autonomy achieved here and there amid older forms of control operative elsewhere, in Skowronek's description of new administrative agencies struggling for authority against a state of courts and parties, in Lieberman's analysis of efforts to prevent new welfare provisions from interfering with established race relations. The effects of non-simultaneity in institutional creation are pervasive and inescapable, creating an overall picture of political institutions quite different from that found in more conventional analyses. One scholar, alerted to the multiple orderings of authority found within Congress, summarizes the implications as follows: "Rather than providing stability and coherence, as the metaphor of institutions as equilibria suggests, institutions embody contradictory purposes, which provide for an ongoing, churning process of development."[42]

In previous work, we have given the phenomenon of multiple-orders-in-action a name: intercurrence.[43] None of the research discussed, not even in this last sample, uses that word and none extends its implications as far as we do here. But the fact that these authors and others have stumbled onto this common ground without any apparent guidance from prior theory, but simply in the course of investigating how institutions impact politics over time, is suggestive in itself. Intercurrence depicts the organization of the polity seen strictly from a historical institutional point of view. It directs researchers to locate the historical construction of politics in the simultaneous operation of older and newer instruments of governance, in controls asserted through multiple orderings of authority whose coordination with one another cannot be assumed and whose outward reach and impingements, including on one another, are inherently problematic.

Though this may be the least familiar of the concepts floating around in the historical-institutional literature today, we think intercurrence is the purest expression of historical-institutional reasoning about politics produced by that literature to date. It connects history and institutions in a single, general statement about organization of the polity and anchors political analysis in terms that are irreducibly historical and institutional. It is, at once, a descriptive statement of the normal state of the political universe – of multiple orders arranged uncertainly in relationship to one another; a statement of *the* historical-institutional problem – the operation of asymmetric standards of control and incongruous rules of action; and a standard template from which the familiar themes of historical institutional research – the contingencies of order, the multiplicity of authorities, the particularity of path trajectories, the significance of redirecting junctures – may all be derived. As such, intercurrence recommends itself as a foundational concept on which the other historical-institutional constructions of politics in this literature may be said to rest and around which historical-institutional theories of politics may be more securely built.

The four studies in our sample derive intercurrence in equal parts from the fragmented, incomplete character of political change and the mutual impingements of the different political elements in place. Tulis observes that the new rules of the modern presidency did not eliminate constraints on the presidency put in place by the Constitution; old and new shaped the politics of the future by locking horns. Polsky observes that the new juvenile courts brought social workers into the criminal justice system without displacing the lawyers; the institution used its conflicting principles of action in chameleon-like fashion to protect itself against attacks on each. Skocpol and Finegold describe new forms of cooperation taking hold in agricultural and labor relations amid the failure of a similar change in business relations. But how far do these insights extend? Is there any reason to believe that these are general features of the organization of the political universe? The claim that political change is partial, that it never transforms all governing relations at once in accordance with the same organizing principles, should present few problems in the context of an up-and-running polity; constitutional democracies, in particular, are valued for their reformist tendencies. The claim is tested at extreme points of rupture, most especially during revolutions, when the deepest and most comprehensive of political transformations occur.

Orren's work speaks directly to this point.[44] The radicalism of the American Revolution was manifested institutionally in the outright dismantling of previously established governing arrangements and their replacement with alternatives that operated according to very different principles. Hereditary titles were abolished. Legislative and executive institutions were purged of their ties to separate orders of society – commoners, lords, and king. Representation was reconstructed along liberal lines, ultimately taking shape as a set of coequal institutions of government all beholden to the same people. Notwithstanding these sweeping and portentous changes, however, it is clear on the historical record that the achievement was neither holistic nor synthetic. Other governing arrangements were carried over from the past, and they continued to operate on their own institutional supports as authoritative elements in the new scheme. Some, like the institutions of slavery, were incorporated into the new government quite deliberately; others, like the common law of master-and-servant and the legal foundations of patriarchal family, were incorporated with less apparent concern for the incongruous rules and standards of legitimacy on which they rested. All told, the "new" order of the ages, the liberal order, was one of several that America's new government would actively enforce.

The point may be extended to account as well for familiar curiosities of American constitutional design. In some arenas of governance, previously established institutional arrangements were neither discarded nor carried over intact but modified by the addition of new elements, much as Polsky describes the formation of the juvenile court and Tulis describes the formation of a "modern presidency" in the twentieth century. The Framers' efforts to create an independent national government led them to modify the prior system of state-based sovereignties and produced the contentious interfaces of American federalism. Their efforts to create an independent national executive led them to modify the preexisting supremacy of the legislative branch and produced the contentious interfaces of checks and balances. Notwithstanding the elaborate theoretical justifications for these arrangements found in *The Federalist Papers*, the delegates to the constitutional convention dealt with a practical problem – how to relate the new institutional authority desired to that already in place; after ratification, political struggle gravitated naturally to their handiwork's ragged seams.[45]

Here we encounter the other central tenet supporting the thesis of politics as intercurrence, as the impingement of controlling authorities on one another. Whether this be observed in the narrow setting of a juvenile court, on the broad canvas of New Deal reform, or at the level of constitutional organization at large, the omnipresent characteristic of impingement indicates both the outward reach of political institutions and the plenary nature of authority. Intercurrence addresses a polity permeated by authority relations that have been constructed historically, a polity caught up in their contradictions and animated to seek their resolution. Politics takes shape around challenges to authority in place and becomes more radical as more authority is challenged.

For these reasons, intercurrence enters political analysis not only as a description of the political universe but also as a central part of the explanation for its change, especially as it produces contradictions for agents, entrepreneurs, and leaders to exploit and alternatives for them to imagine.[46] At the level of action, it is not simply that governing arrangements of one sort or another inform behavior in all spheres throughout the state's domain but that their variety and incongruity are not easily concealed for long, that, on the contrary, these incongruities become conspicuous over time, prompting political conflict. Whether the political initiatives and institutional innovations to resolve conflicts are limited deliberately, unconsciously, or out of practical necessity, the effect is to juxtapose new controls against existing ones, introducing new disparities into the exercise of governmental authority. Controlling authorities at any given historical juncture will be, as a result, a mixed bag of coercive instruments, with future political conflict all but guaranteed given their asymmetries and mutual impingements.

Intercurrence in this light may be regarded as the point of departure for theorizing about what elsewhere we have called "politics in the fullness of time."[47] Partial transformations of plenary authority impart to governance the organizational form of a temporal matrix of intercurrent controls.[48] The vertical axis of this matrix arrays governance *in* time. It indicates the limits of order that stem from the simultaneous operation of institutional instruments of different origin, each of which seeks both to control outsiders and to defend its own authority against potential incursions from competing authorities. Moving down the vertical axis we would observe for instance the current status of the constitutional presidency, of the law of labor relations, of authority over the agricultural and business sector. At the higher, more rarefied levels of the matrix, we might find arrangements – like the balance rule – invented by politicians to mitigate tensions below, contingent solutions designed with greater or lesser effect to prevent the various ordering mechanisms that compose the whole from colliding into one another.[49]

The horizontal axis of this matrix identifies governance as a historical composite moving *through* time. It equates significant changes or "critical junctures" with the addition and subtraction of controlling instruments and locates pathways of change in the always-limited openings created for new authority to take hold. An authoritative instrument added or subtracted will always have some developmental significance; how much will be determined by how extensively the change rearranges authority relations up and down the matrix. Authority may be added without dislodging completely the alternatives in place as Tulis and Polsky indicate, or it may be displaced altogether as slavery and common law of master-and-servant were ultimately displaced. Either way, political junctures can be identified as more "critical" to the extent that more of existing authority is disrupted, and established "paths" are redirected as more authority is rearranged.

Though this image of government as a matrix of intercurrent authority relations may seem abstract, it facilitates an analysis of political change that is rigorously empirical. It targets the essential complexity of organized political life not as a problem for analysts to overcome but as a source of knowledge to be unpacked. That is to say, it facilitates just the sort of analyses that historical-institutional investigations routinely produce. The problem of proceeding without such a foundational concept is that the originality and analytic bite of historical-institutional analysis remains obscure, lost in thick descriptions of entangled relationships. The concept of intercurrence helps pull historical-institutionalism out the shadows of other theoretical traditions and bring forward an understanding of politics that is its own.

New terms ought not be introduced without some reference to others to which they have a family resemblance. Like the familiar idea of "pluralism," for example, intercurrence evokes the political dynamism inherent in multiplicity. Also like pluralism, intercurrence points to ongoing, open-ended conflicts structured by rules, and it identifies problems of accommodating conflict. But there are also important differences. Pluralism has traditionally referred to competition among interests structured by "rules of the game" upon which all parties agree; it is, at base, a description of order amid conflict. Intercurrence, by contrast, refers to the simultaneous operation of different sets of rules, to a politics structured by irresolution in the basic principles of social organization and governmental control, and it describes the disorder inherent in a multiplicity of ordering rules. A similar distinction might be drawn between the idea of intercurrence and the idea of "multiple traditions" in contemporary renderings of American political culture. Intercurrence, like multiple traditions, entails different principles of control, but it identifies these in the operation of specific institutional forms; it is not the historical juxtaposition of different ideas or traditions that is critical but the historical juxtaposition of differently constituted governing authorities, which may be created, modified, and displaced without any discernible effect on traditions.

The Institutional Turn in APD Research

Each of the different strands of historical-institutional research we have identified and discussed in this chapter contributes something arguably slighted by others, and there is no reason to suspect that any will soon exhaust its utility. The point of this exercise is not to foreclose options; it is to show that historical-institutional analyses move logically toward more distinctive and development-friendly conceptions of politics itself. Institutional investigations of the historical constructions of politics have exposed government as a set of controls made up of disparate and impinging parts, an arrangement of authority riddled with uncertainty at its many interfaces. From this insight, the intricate temporal structure of governance has been exposed in greater detail than ever before, and the study of political order has been brought more directly to bear on the dynamics of political change.

Historical-institutionalism, then, is perhaps after all an awkward appellation for a line of inquiry that has been so effective in unearthing sources of contingency, movement, and turmoil in politics. It has, however, lent APD some much-needed traction, allowing it to advance in the face of the unraveling of developmental assumptions about politics on other fronts. The various propositions we have found percolating through this literature seem to point the way toward a new and more productive search for development in politics. But they take us only so far. Sorting out different propositions about historical construction and political development from ideas found here and there in existing historical-institutional studies may lend a certain coherence to the present state of the enterprise, and identifying certain essential characteristics of political institutions may indicate where this is leading, but the common program remains implicit. We still have some work to do before we can say with confidence exactly what political development is, why it should be studied, and what it can tell us about the polity we inhabit.

FOUR

Political Development: The Definition

...although laws may be changed according to circumstances and events, yet it is seldom or never that the constitution itself is changed; and for this reason the new laws do not suffice, for they are not in harmony with the constitution that has remained intact.

Niccolò Machiavelli

TOGETHER, THE CULTURAL CRITIQUE OF DEVELOPMENTAL THINKING, recounted in Chapter Two, and the institutional turn in historical research, recounted in Chapter Three, leave APD spinning around a wobbly center. Neither provides a ready response to a disarmingly simple question: What is political development? With the concept purged of teleology, the leading formulation so far is the inconclusive metaphor of "path." In this chapter, we set these literatures aside for the purpose of offering a definition that identifies political development as a distinguishable event, one that can be established empirically and is a phenomenon worth study in its own right.

That a definition of this sort is desirable may not be self-evident. No one has complained that the topics addressed so far by APD scholars are misguided or that the substantive payoff on particular historical questions of broad interest has been inadequate. In fact, the flip side to APD's current lack of focus is the growing attachment of historical researchers to other areas of political science with well-established protocols of their own – political economy, for instance, or public law, or comparative government. Under these circumstances, why look for trouble? Why rehabilitate a concept already stripped of its currency when there are so many other choices?

What is to be gained at this point by drawing lines between political development and political change or, for that matter, between political development and all manner of other political or politically relevant activity in American history?

The answer as we see it is that development remains a central concern, albeit one addressed largely by indirection. There is indirection in the cultural critique, which confronts developmental thinking through an assault on the idea of progress; there is indirection in historical-institutionalist studies that harbor several variations on development themes without converging on anything firm. Clearly in APD research today there is more at stake than political change in the past and strategic interactions in historical context. Questions about continuity in politics, about whether and to what degree past changes bind future politics, about whether changes show a discernible trajectory over time: these are still positive motivators of inquiry. If they are not to be declared off-limits, and if answers are not to be left to unfold haphazardly in the setting of diverse individual studies, then it is necessary to pin things down and to at least clarify the standards by which the historical record may be assessed.

On APD's theoretical side, the prospect is to organize the current discussion of order and change in time. As our inventory in previous chapters suggests, nothing has more effectively transformed historical study of American politics than impatience with conventional demarcations of time. By disaggregating "eras" and allowing parts of the whole – institutions, policies, ideologies, parties – to signal their own beginnings and ends, researchers have uncovered greater dimensionality, texture, and specificity in the historical construction of politics. But disaggregation also runs a risk, which is of an increasingly fragmented canvas, a collection of disparate time lines with no clues as to how the pieces might relate to one another. A definition, then, will serve to direct findings back to common interests in order and change and to foster debate on a shared intellectual program. The debate might be joined on how particular events in history are connected to one another, on the larger patterns of seemingly disparate episodes, or on the terms the definition itself.

Similarly, on APD's substantive side greater clarity about development in politics will help to cut through many of the interpretive debates that have accumulated in the literature and left students of American political history at an impasse. Some of these fall under the rubric of "old wine in new bottles": did the Wagner Act liberate labor in industrial relations or merely exchange one system of subordination for another? Others thrive on "contradictions": Progressive-era reform as populist revenge *and* corporatist consolidation, political demobilization *and* middle-class democracy. Although debates such as these are unlikely to be resolved by a definition, laying out in general terms exactly what is of critical interest in the historical material at hand can move the discussion constructively beyond them. A definition that can distinguish between a political development and a political change, and between political development and developments in the culture or the economy, should at least sharpen these episodes, what they did or did not achieve, and whether and in what sense they made a difference for what would follow.

Two arguments stand against defining political development. The first is the inescapable Whiggish pedigree of the concept, with its a priori assumption of progress in the relationship between past and present. This argument is easily overstated; between predetermining the answer and begging the question, there is ample room for an approach that facilitates discussion. We agree that those who would argue that American politics does, in fact, develop must bear the burden of proof. Our way of meeting this challenge includes detaching the concept of development itself from its more sweeping applications and working with a definition that has less normative baggage. The second argument, perhaps more serious, is that definitions are by their nature imperious, that in an enterprise as freewheeling as APD, codification would be premature and likely counterproductive. We do not claim our definition is neutral with respect to existing choices or styles in current APD scholarship or that it does not set out its own priorities. Largely for reasons just mentioned – of bearing the burden of proof – we have taken our cues from historical-institutional work, picking up where our discussion left off in Chapter Three. We believe, however, that the definition we offer not only carries APD's cultural explorations along but also underscores their importance.

The Definition

We propose the following: political development is a durable shift in governing authority. By "governing authority" we mean the exercise of control over persons or things that is designated and enforceable by the state. By "shift" we have in mind a change in the locus or direction of control, resulting in a new distribution of authority among persons or organizations within the polity at large or between them and their counterparts outside. Political scientists have a natural and keen interest in changes of this sort. Liberalism, free speech, free markets, citizenship, family and gender relations, popular sovereignty, representative government, federalism, the separation of powers, checks and balances, globalization – all build and turn on the distribution of authority. The term *durable* acknowledges that the distribution of authority is not fixed, and that its stability or change in any given historical instance must be regarded as contingent. Shifts in governing authority are important in historical inquiry, because they are a constant object of political conflict and they set the conditions for subsequent politics, especially when shifts are durable.

By examining the historical record for evidence of a specific kind of political change – or its absence – we mean to indicate what it is that the study of APD ultimately needs to explain. The study of durable shifts in governing authority is well suited to APD as a theory-building enterprise: it is open to the promulgation of generalizations, it is portable in time and place, it is sufficiently pointed to set up comparisons, it engages separate pieces of the polity, it is capable of arraying a wide range of historical information. Likewise, this definition of political development promotes APD as a substantive enterprise as well. To ask where and when shifts in authority occur, why and by what processes, and to inquire into their consequences is to place exacting demands on the description of change in governance over time, on the identification of causes and the weighing of their relative significance, and on the accurate portrayal of the new historical patterns they produce. In all of these ways, it encourages scholars to sidestep a priori logics of development, to question stylized treatments of history, and to anchor theory building more firmly in empirical evidence.

The focus on governing authority, designated and enforced through state institutions, should not be misconstrued as a return to a political analysis of an overly legalistic kind. The purpose is not to diminish the significance of noninstitutional aspects of politics but to highlight what seems most characteristic of political development. The definition takes in *all* activities and events in which the distribution of governing authority is at issue, including those that fail ultimately to produce any discernible shift. If our definition resists equating political development with the appearance of a new idea, the actions of a new movement, or the election of new leader, it also calls attention to these and all other factors that inform, promote, inhibit, or limit changes of the sort we have specified. The point is not to exclude political leadership, social movements, or wars from their role *in* political development or to deny economic and cultural changes as important influences *on* political development. It is to locate development and nondevelopment as it occurs, to identify changes and continuities in an ongoing organization of authority. Political development thus understood is a historical variable to be registered against the constancy of political conflict and the swirl of persons and movements bent on different outcomes.

Authority: "Authority" is the key term in our definition: it is authority that needs to shift to produce political development. The word calls attention to resources for influencing the behavior of others, but that by itself is does not distinguish it politically. So too does "power," a concept also likely to figure prominently in the explanation of any given shift in authority: questions are asked routinely about the relative influence of corporations and labor in the formation of the American welfare state, about the relative influence of populists and progressives in the emergence of business regulation at the turn of the twentieth century, or, more generally, about political events like landslide elections that rout one coalition and install another. These are questions about power. We use the term authority because of its stronger connotation of governance. If power is the means, authority is frequently the objective.

Authority may be distinguished from power by several of its attributes. First, authority is something designated in advance. It is not about the influence of those trying to change the terms of control; it is about the terms of control themselves as they are set out and known by those to whom they apply. Second, authority works through institutions. It boasts continuity and dependability, resistance to mere shifts in the political winds, persistence until its agents are directed otherwise. Third, authority works through mandates that are enforceable; in the American polity, this often means enforceable through courts of law. Authority in this sense is not simply coercive; it implies protection for those who carry out its dictates and sanctions against those who do not. Fourth, authority works through perceptions. It is strengthened by legitimacy, by the perceptions of all concerned that those formally in control are acting appropriately; as authority loses legitimacy, it becomes more vulnerable to being shifted.

Each of these attributes points to authority as the permanent locus of development in politics. But as we have observed in Chapter Three the organization of authority relations at large is riddled by complications that produce, at the level of practical operations, arrangements that are inherently dynamic and impermanent. In political history, governing authority in any given period presents itself as a complex web of relations, a composite of controls gotten up at different times for different purposes and, as we have argued, for this reason likely to engage conflicting institutional mandates and methods of execution. Often the asymmetries of authority signal adherence to inconsistent standards of legitimacy, inconsistencies that individuals or movements may themselves use to challenge specific authorities on the scene: slavery was highly institutionalized in the South in the antebellum period and politically destabilizing nationwide.

These contradictions attend authority's actual exercise at any historical point. Authority cannot accomplish its purposes simply by formal declarations of intent. In particular, for our purposes, authority does not shift – political development does not occur – because

a court or president or some other high officer or agency de-
clares that it should. President George W. Bush declared home-
land security a top national priority and Congress created a new
federal department to coordinate control at the border and beef
up surveillance of internal affairs, but this ambition immediately
highlighted the difficulty of rearranging jurisdictions among previously scattered agencies and, beyond that, it called into question
the authority of others throughout the federal establishment. In
the 1890s, the Supreme Court endorsed a radically prohibitive interpretation of business practices outlawed by Congress under the
Sherman Anti-Trust Act, but neither the Act nor the Court's interpretation stemmed the tide of corporate consolidation; as Martin
Sklar and others have indicated, the Act merely created a glaring incongruity between the law as interpreted by the Court and actual
practices supported by the rest of the national government.[1] The
historical-institutional literature is, as we have seen, full of examples
of policies in which the government accepted major commitments
or responsibilities with arrangements designed expressly to minimize
significant disruptions of existing institutional prerogatives. The federal government's landmark Aid to Families with Dependent Children
(ADC), for instance, was, as Lieberman shows, purposefully crafted
to protect and preserve local discretion, and therein lay many of the
problems associated with the "development" of the American welfare
state.[2]

Notice that stipulating that it is authority that must shift identifies development as a structural event. As growing discontent with
established authority is not in itself a political development, neither
is a statistical trend. Rising GDP per capita may indicate economic
development, but not changing relations of government. Within the
institutions of government, federal outlays, tax revenues, and public
employment climb upward throughout American history, with points
of leveling and surge; so do judicial case loads, numbers of statutes,
and immigration levels; presidential vetoes and tariff levels, on the
other hand, ebb and flow. These are all indicators of political change,
and changes like these may burden or embolden particular institutions, but there is a difference between the growth and abatement of

existing historical-institutional patterns and a change in relationships among governing authorities. The impact of the former on political development remains an open question, pending evidence of what if any authority was transferred and how governing relationships were altered.

Shift: The importance of "shift" in our definition builds upon a proposition advanced in Chapter One with regard to "sites," namely, that authority is plenary; that even when it is contested, its terms are always and everywhere complete. Extending the idea of plenary authority to the polity at large means that political development is, in effect, zero-sum: for politics to develop, it is necessary that authority be moved from one location to another. "Shift," in our definition, implies *re*arrangement, *re*direction, *re*construction. Significant shifts in authority are highly charged, inherently controversial events; in a polity as thoroughly institutionalized as the United States, they are likely to incite extended negotiations among several surrounding agencies, each with its own mandates, its own resources, and its own history. Cast in these terms, the analysis of development operates at a considerable distance from conceptions associated with "germ" theories or "organic" theories of politics. Rather than assume that origins are imprinted with a natural order of growth or that change follows a course or a blueprint implicit in earlier forms, our definition assumes the resistance of established authority to political development, it anticipates a clash of purposes among governing institutions, and it illuminates political contests of greater or lesser scope.

"Shift" presumes all the various processes by which authority may be transferred. The authority of an institution, for instance, may simply be allowed to expire. Sunset provisions, in which the legislature specifies a time limit on the exercise of authority by others, cause shifts of this sort; similarly, the charter of the national bank granted in 1791 was not renewed at the end of its term in 1811. Another process is dismantling – institutional disassembly in whole or in part. The Jeffersonians abolished internal taxes; the Thirteenth Amendment abolished slavery. Neither expirations nor dismantlings necessarily anticipate where the authority eliminated will relocate; in other processes, transfers are explicit. "Displacements" remove authority from institutions through circumvention or transfer to other mechanisms: Andrew Jackson sought to preempt the rechartering of the second national bank in 1830s by taking the government's deposits out of the existing bank and transferring them to politically friendly state banks. From the 1970s through the mid-1990s, AFDC was substantially "displaced" by an alternative form of welfare targeted at the working poor, the Earned Income Tax Credit.[3] In Chapter Three, we talked as well about "layering," the placement of new forms of authority atop old ones left in place. Layering, though common, is an incomplete transfer of authority, a change likely to perpetuate controversies over exactly how much authority has shifted, over who gets to control what and how.

Shifts take varying lengths of time. The Pendleton Act of 1883, the measure creating the Civil Service Commission, anticipated a shift of authority in control over civil administration away from parties, but its bearing on other authorities remained doubtful for decades as party competition waxed and waned, the financing of party campaigns changed, and presidents, legislators, and labor unions jockeyed for control over the newly created domain of merit administration. Shifts that appear abrupt and categorical on their face often leave open important questions about the scope of the prerogatives curtailed. After World War II, the United States entered into several mutual security agreements obligating it to come to the defense of other nations, but Congress was careful to serve notice that it was not prepared to abdicate its constitutional authority over future decisions to go to war, and events triggered prolonged debate over the precise extent of the delegation implied.[4] Shifts in authority that cut more deeply through existing social and political relationships – the ones that are most developmentally significant – are likely to occur over longer periods of time. The displacement of slavery and its attendant institutional legacy of apartheid shifted more authority than the extension of the franchise to 18-year-olds by the Twenty-sixth Amendment, and the conflict over new forms of controlling race relations has been correspondingly more sustained.

A central analytic question raised by shifts in authority is "how much?" Is the rearrangement at issue limited or extensive? Is it adequate to the purposes contemplated? How does it the bear on surrounding authorities, and how do surrounding authorities deal with it? These questions bring us to the final element in our definition, which is durability.

Durability: Durable means "lasting"; it refers to the span of years that any shift holds on, into the future. Shifts in authority that hold on for a half-century, in the same polity, and within some broader context of years, without getting reversed or deflected by other events, are, prima facie, durable in a way that shifts that hold for a decade or less are not. For instance, in Chapter Three we referenced the shift of authority under the New Deal from the judiciary to the legislature; this resulted in Congress' sovereignty over social policy that lasted without serious disturbance for a half-century. This shift was durable in a way that, let us say, the shift associated with the Eighteenth Amendment installing prohibition was not. The problem with this approach, however, arises with shifts in authority that are observable for considerable periods of time but are manifestly not durable. Take an example important in America's early colonization: the assumption by the Stuart monarchs of power over the Parliament in the name of divine right. This was a shift in that it bore fruit in public policy and had great consequences of a kind. But neither was it seen in its own time by central players – Parliament, judges, the Exchequer, the army, and others – as more than tentative;[5] nor is it regarded as durable by historians today.

In our framework, the key difference among comparable spans of years is the extent to which shifts had the effect of bringing surrounding arrangements of authority into line with the new state of affairs; this happened under the New Deal – acts reorganizing executive, legislative, judicial, and administrative relations accommodated the welfare state – but not under the Stuart monarchy. Durable shifts have this effect, and it is evident to participants in politics at the time. They form and build on alliances in adjacent institutions; they successfully over time preempt naysayers in positions of authority nearby; they engage ideologies, whether grand or localized, that declare the rightness of what has occurred. We propose that shifts that fail to become durable do not do these things and that shifts that result in back-and-forth – as, for example, the on-again/off-again experiments with national banking in antebellum America – do not do them sufficiently. Within the same polity, a wide variety of factors will influence the result. One, across centuries, might be the "pace of change": fifty years was arguably a shorter period in the seventeenth century than it was in the twentieth, because of the entrenchment and strong interconnectedness of traditional institutions. More generally, durability must depend on the ambitions and abilities of opposing leaders and their resources, the availability of ideologies, the state of public opinion, and so forth. In any given instance of political development, the explanation of durability comes closest to the way conventional political analysis explains outcomes.

Durability and development would seem to work at cross-purposes. The more durable the shift, the more resistant the arrangements it reconstructs should be to subsequent alteration; all other things being equal, this should hold for any particular corner of the polity. But because the conception of the polity-at-large endorsed here is one of multiple orders, mutually impinging institutional arrangements and different patterns of change, the relationship between durability and development is varied and complex. The establishment of the New Deal was a durable shift, and its very solidity was a platform for major political developments elsewhere, for instance, the "rights revolution." The circumstances that accompany political development may be important in this regard: after the disruptions of the Civil War, Republicans could build their new order of recently empowered national institutions under cover of "the bloody shirt." The nature of the institutions involved may also make a difference: durable shifts to legislatures would seem to augur further change, as under the New Deal; shifts to courts and bureaucracies less so.

In this perspective, our understanding of durability, in terms of the rearrangement of surrounding authority, recasts thinking about the constitution of government. Polities at large may be presumed to have different dispositions toward political development, and democracies in particular to be biased against durable shifts in authority. Toqueville remarked on the "mutability of the law" in democracies, suggesting that law was observed in America by virtue of its being "a self-imposed evil...of transient duration."[6] We know that changeability and reversibility of laws enacted by elected majorities are moderated by many constitutional constraints: federalism, bicameralism, judicial review, checks and balances, and differently configured elections, complete with a written text and an arduous method of amendment. These obstacles to full empowerment of majorities may, somewhat surprisingly, suggest a Constitution on behalf of development; barriers against majorities supportive of new proposals are also barriers against the will of majorities who would come along and undo their predecessors handiwork. The problem with this conceit, however, is in the evidence: whether the example is national banking in the nineteenth century or Prohibition in the twentieth, majorities have repeatedly overcome the constitutional obstacle course and in both directions – a situation that takes us developmentally speaking, back to square one.

By contemplating something more than a simple marking of time, we believe our formulation of durability offers a stronger rationale for development in politics. It does so by placing the seemingly fixed and rigid structural constraints associated with the Constitution within the context of a fuller array of authority relations and by lending greater significance to the alteration of arrangements among the parts. When authorities surrounding an innovation are rearranged, when they take the innovation into account in their own operations, the constitution of government itself is changed; a new platform for political action is established and, with that, the premises for any future political opposition that might form. The more extensive the rearrangement prompted by an innovation, the more durable we would expect that innovation to be.

Consider now the broad program of study encompassed by our definition. First, a search for American political development directed to the study of shifts in authority will sort political history into nonevents, failed events, indecisive events, prolonged events, and events of varying degrees of significance. In doing so, it will bring into a common frame much of what the APD literature now investigates topic by topic. Shifts in authority are at the heart of recent studies dealing with changing definitions of citizenship and civil rights;

with the ambiguous status of "the modern presidency"; with state building and bureaucratic autonomy; with the differential impact of the New Deal realignment on business, agriculture, and labor; with the failures and achievements of the populists; with the decline and resurgence of party organizations.

Our definition also aligns much of what the literature is exploring theoretically – junctures, path dependence, and intercurrence. Junctures will be seen as shifts of varying depth and significance registered against a matrix of authority relations that carries other governing arrangements forward from the past; intercurrence is the normal structure of politics created by these partial and incomplete rearrangements of authority; paths are openings for change as they are delimited by extant arrangements. Finally, when the analysis of discrete governing arrangements is placed within these wider political scenes, the study of development as defined should effectively address important historical debates. Did the Supreme Court's holding in *Plessy v. Fergusson* (1896), that for constitutional purposes separate could be equal, shift authority in any way or did it merely confirm and justify the status quo? Did the Reagan administration mark a political about-face or a failed revolution? Answers hinge on identifying the relevant institutions and the distribution of controls among them before, during, and after the changes in question.

Applications

The usefulness of any such definition must ultimately be demonstrated in original research. Still, we can do more here than give scattered examples invoked in the course of explaining our terms. In the remainder of this chapter, we provide three applications that indicate what political development looks like and how our definition organizes history for developmental study. Each account is a sketch, not intended to exhaust the developmental questions that might be posed. Moreover, in describing our cases and examining the political problems presented, we rely mainly on what is already well known. If our framework brings fresh and cogent readings to familiar material, analytically consistent across episodes, prospects for aligning and directing original research should be bolstered accordingly. To suggest our definition's versatility, we have picked examples that are very different from one another. The first, Reconstruction, was chosen as a singular episode whose developmental status is a continuing point of dispute. The second, church and state, was chosen because of all the arrangements of multiple orders in the American polity, this is perhaps the most well-known. The third, federal land management, is offered as a typical application to the politics of public policy.

Though these accounts were not stylized to illustrate other concepts introduced in this book, it would be surprising if we did not stumble upon examples of these as we proceed. Our foundational concept, intercurrence, appears quite naturally in all these episodes of political development once its presence is appreciated for what it is. We see it at work in the limits placed on political development during Reconstruction, in the political fallout of disrupting long-established relations between church and state, and in the accumulation of purposes in federal land policy. In each sketch, the historical construction of politics appears in junctures where elements are transformed, establishing to a greater or lesser extent a new platform for future actions.

Each application foregrounds political institutions, in particular their outward reach and their mandates to control other persons and agencies. For that reason, it is impressive how closely tied to ideas in the wider culture each example turns out to be. As institutionally pure as these narratives could have been structured, it is difficult to see how emancipation or voluntarism or ecology could have been filtered out as motivating concepts altogether. In this sense, these applications argue strongly for our position that an emphasis on institutions in studying political development does not turn away from culture or ideas, but instead locates them in the setting where, politically speaking, they count most.

Reconstruction

Reconstruction, the dozen years after the Civil War, presents an interesting challenge for developmental analysis. On the one hand,

Reconstruction is the outstanding example in United States history of dismantling an entrenched political order. A legal relation that confined four million individuals to servitude, one wound tightly into relations of authority ranging from federalism and checks and balances to the administration of justice and the family, was pronounced terminated, unenforceable under the Constitution; those who had been subjugated were declared to be free citizens. On the other hand, Reconstruction is also the outstanding example in American political history of developmental misfire: when the dust settled, those freed were isolated, impoverished, denied equal rights, and left without means for collective or personal advancement. The long view from the twentieth-first century has only compounded the curiosity of the whole affair. Constitutional changes that were all but dead-on-arrival, their paper persistence a mockery of democratic pretension, became important vehicles of transformation a century later, while leaving Reconstruction's own legacy no less unclear.

Exactly what happened has vexed the most searching of scholars.[7] Early interpretations of Reconstruction resolved this developmental paradox with allusions to congressional excess, political redemption, and constitutional restoration; later work countered with a language of advances and reversals, of rights derailed and promises delayed. The impulse to choose up sides in these debates is understandable, but it has left the analysis of change in time steeped in normative spin. We propose to tackle Reconstruction as our definition would any other developmental event, through the generic problem of shifting authority. A single, clear-cut question is presented: how much political authority needed to shift to end the relation of slavery? Words like "end" and "the relation of slavery" were not less ambiguous during the 1860s and 1870s than today, but for all the twists and turns, this was the question argued by participants at the time, the one that coherently aligns for developmental analysis what is safely on the historical record, and the one that adheres to what is still Reconstruction's unfinished business.

Given slavery's long reach into American institutions, the answer to the "how much" question would ultimately be determined by the willingness of those in authority to throw the rest of American government into contention. In this light, a review of the prewar debates about slavery reveals that, for all their intensity, none of the parties on either side showed much of an inclination to think deeply or comprehensively about a redistribution of constitutional authority. The major proposals – the Missouri Compromise, the Wilmot Proviso, popular sovereignty, colonization, Kansas–Nebraska, the Crittenden plan, compensation – dealt with race relations as a problem that could be solved by tinkering with received understandings of states rights and national powers; minimizing collateral damage to other governing relationships was the chief selling point of the various plans for restriction, expansion, and extraction. The radical abolitionists who most deeply probed the institutional reach of slavery and who, unlike William Lloyd Garrison, did not wish to trash the Constitution altogether, professed that the Framers' design, looked at hard enough, supported the antislavery cause.[8] Among the thousands of pages written on the Constitution in the 1840s and 1850s, the only plan that contemplated a serious reconfiguration of American government was offered by slavery's most prominent advocate, John C. Calhoun[9]; the only institutional innovation of constitutional significance to come out of the antebellum Congresses was the creation of non-Article III judges to enforce the Fugitive Slave Act.

The removal of slaveholders' authority calls attention to the unique institutional character of slavery. Slavery was situated at the interface of state and personal relations, one of a larger set of special statuses governing the workplace and the family. Slaves were bought and sold, controlled by others in their every action and association, unable to earn or possess property. The status of black persons generally was unleavened by the status of citizenship. In southern states, even blacks freed by their masters were, without specific legislative provision to the contrary, unable to marry, testify in court, serve on a jury, be educated, or vote. In northern states, free black persons did not enjoy the legal privileges of whites; Chancellor Kent, in his treatise on American law, described African Americans, even when free, as a "degraded caste."[10] Shortly before the Civil War, Arkansas, Iowa, Illinois, Oregon, and Indiana banned immigration by escaped or manumitted slaves.

All this made manifest the potentially revolutionary implications of slavery's dismantling; the scope of the change implied by emancipation was anyone's guess. The future status of former slaves would turn on how the governing arrangements in which slavery had been embedded adjusted to its end. By the same token, these baseline circumstances caution against invoking the limits of Reconstruction to discount the significance of emancipation as a political development. No other single act in American history changed so many lives so profoundly as did the Thirteenth Amendment. Notwithstanding the instincts of those who sought to limit the consequences, or the success of those who sought all along to frustrate the interests of the freedmen, the termination of the master-slave relationship was political development of the first magnitude.

At the center of the controversy over how far Reconstruction would reach was the shift in constitutional authority to Congress. Authority to protect those persons who had been freed was expressly given to Congress in the Thirteenth Amendment, the first amendment adopted since the generation of the Framers. This change was second only to emancipation itself in constitutional importance, for unlike earlier shifts that had established Congress' authority to regulate bankruptcy or immigrant ships, this one curtailed the states' hitherto undisputed jurisdiction over domestic relations. The grant to Congress was essential, if for no other reason than because the prerogatives of the several states with regard to matters other than emancipation would remain unimpaired. All of the measures that followed – the Civil Rights Act of 1866, the reauthorization of the Freedman's Bureau, the Fourteenth Amendment, the Reconstruction Act, the Fifteenth Amendment, the Ku Klux Klan Act, the Civil Rights Act of 1875 – were a gloss on section 2 of the original authorization: "Congress shall have the power to enforce this article by appropriate legislation."

From the start, Congress embraced its role as Reconstruction's institutional protagonist by advancing a more rather than less expansive interpretation of what the shift in authority entailed and by impressing all those affected with the revolutionary implications of its mandate. It refused immediate restoration of the rebellious states,

thereby buying time and protecting the strength of a political majority favorable to a more extensive shift; it held an occupying army in
place in the states which it wanted most immediately to transform;
and it empowered its military agents to carry out its objectives. Developmentally speaking, legislators would either rearrange the authority
of others or lose it themselves. In this respect, the situation ahead was
eminently practical and deeply impacted.

The key developmental issues presented may be seen to line up
along a single divide that runs from the persons most directly affected in their daily lives by emancipation to the highest levels of
government. On the side of the former masters, what occurred was
a massive violation of legal rights, ruinous by any interpretation but
still uncertain as to its full extent; on the side of the former slaves,
legal bondage was ended, but overcoming the disabilities of slavery
had only just begun. The circumstance of the former masters most
directly implicated the authority of the judiciary; under the Constitution, the judiciary was assigned the prior duty of protecting rights of
record and scrutinizing incursions on existing rules and boundaries.
The circumstance of the former slaves most directly implicated the
authority of Congress; Congress had to establish rules and arrangements that would give effect to the Thirteenth Amendment. Former
masters against former slaves, existing rights and rules against new
rights and rules, legality against politics, conservatives against radicals, Court against Congress – these were the systemic components
of the conflict over "how much."

Other institutions aligned according to how Congress' new authority bore on their own prospects: the states and the Democratic
party were pulled to the side of the former masters by their own
imminent loss of prerogatives and political resources; the Republican party was pulled to side of the freedmen by closer association
with the war effort and concern for its national coalition in the postwar era, though the latter calculation would be subject to a host
of strong cross-pressures. Where interests were less clear-cut, institutions ran a greater risk of being pulled apart. Presidents, for instance, involved as they were in both lawmaking and preserving the
Constitution, in both military command and civil law enforcement,

straddled the central fault line, and for them, wait-and-see was not an option. Lincoln, Johnson, and Grant each risked the authority of the presidency against Congress' determination to reconstruct, the second squandering all in a desperate bid to block it.

Repeatedly, Congress was prompted by the institutional resistance it encountered to claim more authority for Reconstruction: southern states passed the Black Codes, President Johnson turned obstructive, and northern states proved reluctant to enfranchise blacks. At first, the Supreme Court seemed the least of its problems. A Lincoln-appointed majority not only eased congressional fears of judicial obstruction, it prompted legislators to try to enlist the Court as its agent in breaking through obstacles encountered on other fronts. The hard facts were that Congress had no civilian apparatus of its own to carry out its will in the South and the administration of its laws through local courts, juries, and lawyers promised to stymie the desired outcome. Its remedy was twofold. First, it legislated to bring disputes into federal courtrooms and to ease the procedural route that inhibited other constitutional claims. Second, it enlisted the military, in particular the military courts, as its principal tool for reconstructing the South.

Using military courts presented problems of its own. Military personnel were not prepared for such work, and military government was hard for democratically elected representatives to defend, but there were no alternatives readily available at the time. Moreover, examined together, Congress's instruments for shifting authority compounded its predicament. The tactic of breaking local authority through the ease of access by freedmen and allies to the Supreme Court could not but magnify the importance of the Court's own institutional instincts, including its preference for civil over military authority. This difficulty was signaled early, when the justices unanimously invalidated a military court proceeding that had occurred during the war in a northern location where the civil courts were open.[11] It took on heat when they voided a federal provision that all attorneys practicing in federal court must swear they had never supported the Confederacy.[12] The boiling point was reached in

January of 1868, when the Court agreed to hear a direct challenge to military detention in the South, based on the unconstitutionality of the Reconstruction Act.[13] Congress' response was swift. Within three weeks of the case being filed, the House voted 116–39 (33 not voting) to require from then onward a two-thirds majority of members of the Supreme Court, then 6 of 8, to invalidate any congressional act.

This remarkable measure was actually less severe than another introduced earlier that year, which would have required the justices' unanimity for such a holding. When the two-thirds bill reached the Senate, the Judiciary committee in charge laid it aside in favor of a still more draconian proposal, a measure declaring Reconstruction to be "political" in nature and therefore outside the Court's jurisdiction altogether. In March, with that bill still in committee, time running out on the legislative session, and a Court decision overturning the Reconstruction Act imminent, Congress opted for expediency: it revoked the habeas corpus authority under which the Court was hearing the case in question, an authority only recently extended in the legislature's efforts to remove civil rights suits from hostile state judges. This bill sailed through both houses without debate and was passed again over the President's veto.

The judiciary's role in Reconstruction has hardly gone unnoticed.[14] But for other than legal scholars, the Court's actions in this instance have been overshadowed by Congress' impeachment of President Johnson that occurred during these same weeks.[15] From the standpoint of political development, conflict with the Court presents the central issues of Reconstruction in a more starkly institutional way than does the partisan engagement with President Johnson. The Court proved more adept at maneuvering than the embattled President. Its majority was not fired by political antagonism to Congress, and the congressional majority was not anti-Court. The developmental problem was that after the Civil War, Congress' authority in the nation at large had changed, whereas the Court's, with respect to Congress, continued to function as before; indeed, it was the Court's adherence to time-honored rules for interpreting statutes that alerted Reconstruction's opponents to the judiciary's potential value as an instrument of resistance. Still, it was neither the substance of the Court's decisions nor its usual practice of splitting hairs that posed the greatest difficulty; it was the historical presence of the Court itself, its insistence on its own hard-won authority, its enduring sense of purpose in adjudicating constitutional relationships that Congress was out to reconstruct by new lights.

Had the Court launched a direct assault on Congress' program, it would have been flirting with its own extinction. Judicial review of the decisions of democracy's representatives, a traditional sore spot with populist politicians from Thomas Jefferson to Andrew Johnson, had recently drawn the fire of Republican insurgents outraged by judicial negation of the Missouri Compromise in *Dred Scott* (1857). Now faced with a greater threat than would later be posed by Congress under the New Deal, the judges punted, delaying their decision until after the 1868 elections, by which time the radicals had narrowly lost President Johnson's impeachment trial and with it precious time and momentum. When the Court returned to the case, it acknowledged that Congress had revoked the authority under which it was proceeding and dismissed the plaintiff's grievance. In a telling rejoinder to the question of "how much," however, the chief justice announced that Congress could not possibly have meant to revoke the Court's habeas corpus authority in full and determined to hear other cases of this sort under the jurisdiction it held prior to the recent extension.[16] Congress too returned to the business it had set aside, but when the bill to declare Reconstruction outside the Court's jurisdiction was reintroduced into the Senate, western Republicans defected. The window of opportunity for political development had begun to close.

Notice the gain in an account focused on shifts in authority. Against this assessment, the old saw of congressional excess – the charge that the Congress was possessed by radicals hell-bent on the destruction of the Constitution – misses the point, for it assumes a Constitution that the Thirteenth Amendment had thrown into question. Considering its new constitutional mandate and the pervasive resistance it encountered, Congress' assault on old institutional defenses becomes all but predictable. It made sense rhetorically: the cause of emancipation had flourished on the manna of "higher law." It made sense institutionally, at the level of principle, where the rub was the common-law legalism at the Constitution's foundation. More surprising perhaps is how Congress' own attachment to legalism hampered the Reconstruction campaign at its source. The disconnection between the speeches of radicals like Brigham and Sumner, ringing with natural law, and the dry, negative formulas agreed on in the Civil War amendments is as striking as it is instructive.

Equally so is the chasm between the rhetoric of Republicans and their party organization. If little before the war suggested that American government would comprehensively reorganize itself to sustain black freedom, nothing during or after the war suggested that the Republican party would centralize itself sufficiently to single-mindedly carry out that project. With the sole exception of the habeas corpus controversy, Republican representatives continuously expanded the jurisdiction of federal courts during this period, looking not just for favorable civil rights rulings but also for favorable conditions of commerce and trade. Reluctant to antagonize the legal profession, they failed to overturn the Court's opinion on loyalty oaths. Congress reacted against the Court only when its core program of military administration was directly threatened. As Republican congressmen were pulled toward competing concerns, they left Republican justices leeway to speak to the question of "how much" without again broaching the legitimacy of military administration.[17]

In this account, it is not just the charges of congressional (or Republican) excess that fall wide of the mark, but the newer language of developmental "reversals" as well. Exhibit Number One is the Fifteenth Amendment. The "reversals" narrative, eminently plausible on its face, casts the constitutional ban on race discrimination in suffrage as the pinnacle of national commitment to equal rights in the nineteenth century. The voting of freed slaves was accomplished in the first instance by military force, but a majority of black citizens in most Southern states continued to vote through the 1880s, after Reconstruction's official end.[18] Drastic disenfranchisement thereafter, though technically not on racial grounds, bespeaks a turnabout, a reversal. In Rogers Smiths' recent interpretation, the wartime dominance of a liberal tradition conducive to equality and human rights was eclipsed by a resurgent hierarchical tradition, sympathetic to old ascriptive distinctions, including distinctions of race.[19]

Perhaps; but for black disenfranchisement in the South in the 1890s to stand as proof positive that American political development has no reliable direction, it needs to be established that there was political development in the South in first place.[20] Black suffrage "fit" an extraordinary, precarious, and fleeting circumstance: military occupation. It remained throughout highly vulnerable to the removal of its fragile political supports. With the army gone, most white Republicans were soon converted or forced to become Democrats, and the "right" to vote was left to the creative manipulations of those with superior resources on the scene. An ideological advance for American liberalism well may have been reversed by these methods. A reversal of political development, however, requires plausible evidence that the arrangements undone were ever secured through the adjustment of other institutions or acceptance of their legitimacy, in this case evidence that black voting in the South had become self-sustaining, independent of contrivances imposed through military force.

The weakness of the Fifteenth Amendment as a foundation for political development in the South is indicated by the circumstances of its passage. The amendment was a congressional response to Republicans' embarrassment that blacks were not yet enfranchised in the North. Between 1863 and 1870 proposals to give blacks the vote were defeated in fifteen northern states and territories.[21] The amendment was proposed in 1869, in the now-or-never atmosphere of the waning 40th Congress, when Republicans could already see their hold on national power starting to slip. Its passage through the Congress and the country occurred in a single year, more through bobbing and weaving and avoiding land mines than through hand-to-hand combat; in the House, it received virtually no Democratic support. It emerged from the joint conference committee in a watered-down version that infuriated its strongest supporters. When it reached the states, it still had not gained broad public acceptance. For fear it would empower Chinese residents, no western state except Nevada supported ratification. It prevailed easily only in New England, where blacks already voted, and in the South, where the military supervised elections; in the four southern states where black voting was not already imposed, Congress made it a condition for rejoining the Union.

Against this patchwork, the amendment achieved its aim. It shifted authority to persons who had none before, which is to say blacks in the North; and in North, the change stuck. It is this enduring impact that provides our most solid clues to the developmental significance of Reconstruction over the longer haul. In the decidedly northern bent of its effect, the amendment exemplifies the fragmented, uneven quality of change that, we have argued, political development regularly produces and that constructs politics through time. No one will doubt that that the disjoint movement of authority negotiated North and South in this period figured prominently in the construction of future struggles; certainly civil rights in the 1960s cannot be separated from the power of black voting in the North.

Church-State Relations

Reconstruction was an extraordinary political event by any standard. What makes it remarkable by ours is that so extensive a system of authority was forcibly dislodged by actors so firmly committed to the governing arrangements in which it was embedded and, as a consequence, a revolution decisively authorized was at the same time authoritatively stymied. Analyzed through the intercurrence of its parts, however, Reconstruction reiterates political development as we anticipate it generally. Through the removal of one plank in the constitutional frame, emancipation exposed the rest. Reconstruction politics tested the extent to which what was new would be made to conform to what had been carried forward. In the end, authority relations, though partially transformed, were no less disjointed than before. New rules laid down by Congress, designed to reorder states and their citizens, met resistance from older rules protected by the Court, designed to preserve federalism against national authority. When the Fifteenth Amendment passed, neither federalism in its essentials nor the incentives of the Republican party had changed; that was the Amendment's difficulty.

Our second application is American church-state relations. Somewhat outside the core APD literature,[22] it is broadly familiar as an arrangement of coexisting or "multiple" orders. Our analysis departs slightly by identifying three critical orders rather than two. Corresponding to "church" is the order of religion, made up of the extensive and diverse array of houses of worship, denominational groupings, and interdenominational bodies and movements. Corresponding to "state" is what we refer to as the free-exercise order, those government institutions that regulate religion, including constitutional and statutory provisions as these are applied by different government agencies. In between these two we have added the order of political parties, operating here as elsewhere to connect citizens and groups, including religious citizens and groups, to the institutions of government. These orders are animated by different, often contradictory, rules and principles and have different structures. The analytic task consists in understanding how each order changes and relates to the others over time. Of particular interest will be the long stretch of time when authority among the three is essentially unchanged. For that period, the intercurrence of these orders worked to bring about political development within each, while maintaining the status quo overall. In more recent decades, in contrast, changes within each order have carried church-state relations to the brink of realignment. To account for both results, we need to double back several times, conveying the fugue-like motion of stops, starts, and repetitions that is typical of politics in time.

In a framework that sees politics in terms of contradictory rules and structures, it is fitting that an analysis highlighting church-state separation begin with a historical episode of church-state consolidation, to wit, the consolidation of the Catholic church into the English state, accomplished by Henry VIII in the sixteenth century. This was political development on the grandest scale, shifting all priestly authority in society to a position subordinate to the King. The Calvinist resistance that followed on this event and roiled England for over a century was decisive for both the structure and style of church-state relations in the United States. Institutionally, it resulted in two church establishments in the American colonies, one Calvinist (in New

England) and one Anglican (in Virginia), a situation that persisted into the nineteenth century. This division effectively ruled out the possibility, if only on pragmatic grounds, that the framers who drew up the Constitution would establish a national church. Also, against this background, the dominant principle of American religion, voluntarism, often portrayed in cultural and social-movement terms, may be seen as a technique of political authority. Absent a national church establishment, with its coercive religious regulations and support of ministers' salaries, and soon absent state-level church establishment as well, American religious organizations would attract and govern their members voluntarily or not at all.[23]

As an active force in politics, voluntarism expresses itself in the propagandistic, outward reach of Protestant denominations, determined to thrive on collective rebirth and good works instead of state patronage. It also includes their offshoots, the loosely connected, interdenominational figures and organizations seeking to control personal and political behavior in ever-widening circles, and quick to adopt innovative techniques to this end. The "benevolent empire" of the antebellum period is the prototype, a vast network of churches, Sunday schools, denominational colleges, publishers, orphanages, poor houses, asylums for the physically and mentally impaired, and all manner of groups promoting abolition, anti-Catholicism, temperance, women's suffrage, and Sabbath observance. These networks appear repeatedly throughout American history: the urban ministries, YMCAs, and foreign missions of Gilded Age; the radio broadcasters and bible institutes of the 1920s; the Federal Council of Churches and youth organizations of the Cold War era; the Moral Majority, the Christian Coalition, and the National Right to Life Committees of today. At intervals, such activity has been associated with the experience or hope of "revival," personal religious awakening on a national scale, intensifying concern among participants for the policies of American government.[24]

This pattern of organization has given religious authority in America an inverted, fragile structure, united at the top in inverse ratio to its distance from the churches that recruit members, pay the bills, and divide and redivide over doctrine. Still, authority, with its full political

connotation, is the appropriate word, and no less for its being formally "private." Leaving aside the controls churches exercise over
their members, for which until recently they were not answerable in
secular courts: throughout the better part of their history, American
clergy and churches have exercised all-but-complete control in diverse settings over nonmembers. This was true, for instance, in the
custodial institutions mentioned above – in orphanages, for example,
and asylums; also on Indian reservations. But of all these, religion's
most important nonecclesiastical jurisdiction was America's public
schools. Beginning with the common schools movement in the 1820s,
straight through the building of the system of public higher education, it was all but taken for granted that Protestant morality would
be taught, that Protestant prayers and hymns would be a daily exercise, that Protestant ministers would serve as college presidents and
trustees. Insofar as this authority depended on express law, it was,
ironically, on those statutes and constitutional provisions that prohibited public aid to "sectarian" schools, sectarian meaning Catholic;
these remain in place in most American states today.

Intercurrence between the order of religion as described above
and the order of political parties that followed in its wake can be
observed even before both orders take on their characteristic forms.
In early-nineteenth-century New England, for instance, Congrega-
tional ministers watched Federalist elites abandon the enforcement
of anti-gambling and anti-fornication laws in campaigns against Jeffersonian opponents (in response, ministers organized interdenominational "moral societies" statewide).[25] By the 1820s, the effect on
national political development is unmistakable. The Jacksonian party
originated, at least in part, to protect government against the popular
energies released by the religious revival of the period and especially
the Revival's condemnation of slavery. Chief architect Martin Van
Buren writes he was motivated above all by fear that the balances
of the Constitution would not survive grandstanding by ambitious
congressmen occasioned by the antislavery controversy. To select the
type of leaders American democracy required for its continuance,
another vehicle was needed, outside the government and anchored
securely in local interests and negotiated upward from there.[26] To be

sure, this did not preclude religious methods, as the mass meetings, marathon speaking, and torchlight parades pioneered by the Revival became characteristic techniques of party campaigns.

Looking back on this history, one might imagine party development – political development – spurred by some issue other than slavery – temperance, perhaps, or nativism; these too were projects of the Revival. It may also be relevant that Van Buren was a politician in New York when the rural regions of that state ("the burned-over district") were rocked by fervent revivalism. In any case, by 1840, when the new Whig party established itself on the same Jacksonian model, the order of parties was set on the course, parallel to the order of religion, it would follow for the next 150 years. If it seems counterintuitive for two such internally contentious instruments of popular mobilization to move in an essentially continuous pattern of stable relations for so long, that is the finding of a multiple-orders analysis. On closer inspection, their minimal collision can be explained by their different structures. The thrusting, interlocking character of American religion positioned against the interest-based, locally disciplined order of American political parties allowed officers in each to tend to their business in studied disregard of activities by the other.

This depiction by no means implies smooth sailing. On the contrary, the party order was regularly buffeted by party-building efforts closely attuned to the purposes of the churches and sometimes moving in loose affiliation with them: Conscience Whigs, Know-nothings, Civil War Republicans from 1856, Prohibitionists, Bryanites in 1896, Progressives in 1912, Goldwaterites in 1964. Far from campaigning on local issues, these insurgencies embraced higher laws, constitutional amendments, and self-described extremism. They enjoyed notable successes: abolition, civil service reform, prohibition, anti-immigration, anti-abortion. But the pattern also includes the politicians in these campaign-crusades regularly backing off the moral high ground and returning to their parties' purpose of being moderate, interest-based electoral machines. By the same token, despite the prominence of religiously loaded issues in political campaigns throughout American history, no national party has ever challenged religious authority head-on; no major-party candidates for higher office have ever professed their personal detachment from religious belief.

Equally striking is the degree to which the order of religion changed without upsetting its relations with the order of political parties. By 1900, it included many more Catholics and Jews; it contained proportionally fewer churches of the old establishment denominations, Episcopal and Congregational-Presbyterian, and more evangelicals, Methodists, and Baptists, and homegrown religions – Mormon, Christian Scientists, Seventh-Day Adventist, Pentecostals.[27] The party order absorbed and deftly managed these changes: at that time, Republicans held the Protestant core in the North and picked up the majority of Jews; Democrats held evangelicals in the South and Catholics and picked up members among the homegrowns. Secularism grew apace with government; still, the church-state status quo continued to impress itself on the polity through the prosecution of gamblers, bootleggers, prostitutes, and other offenders against Christian morals, through generous tax exemptions, and in public rituals of all kinds. This happened in part through statutes and in part through common law and always imperfectly in that religious and political party obligations were never completely the same.

This brings us to the third order important in church-state relations, the order of free exercise within the government. The many rules of the free-exercise order that affect religion belie any too-rigorous commitment in any quarter to church-state separation. Consider legislation at the federal level: after the Civil War, Congress passed laws regulating religious matters in the territories, the military, and in Indian affairs; in the 1880s and 1890s, it forbid the practice of polygamy; in 1921, it sanctioned the waiving of civil service rules so that Prohibition might be enforced by properly moral persons, that is to say Protestants.[28] When challenged, these laws were upheld by the Supreme Court.[29] States were likewise active. In addition to their support of religious expression in public schools at all levels, they underwrote the distribution of Bibles to the poor, granted the churches property, enacted special criminal laws for clergy and religious services, endorsed religious symbols and ceremonies, and otherwise took

steps unacceptable today. By 1940, when the Supreme Court determined that state actions respecting religion under the First Amendment were protected by the Fourteenth Amendment, it had already
heard seventeen challenges on grounds of due process.[30]

In general, then, the free-exercise order was united in its support
and sanction of the order of religion. There is no disputing the privileged position of Protestantism in this accord. However, an examination of the cases that finally reached the Supreme Court suggests
that if there was any bias it was in favor of religion over irreligion,
or what the justices regarded as such. Churches won on their continuing rights under English charters and common law (1815), over
donated property against heirs and departing members (1852, 1856),
and over control of internal discipline (1872).[31] Catholics won in
their refusal to swear military oaths (1866), on receiving federal support for Catholic hospitals (1899), on educating Indians (1908), and
on the right to operate their parochial schools against state laws to
the contrary (1925).[32] Jehovah's Witnesses won on public soliciting
(1943) and on flag salute (1943); they lost on the employment of child
labor (1944).[33] Conscientious objectors who were not members of
well-recognized pacifist sects lost when they refused military service
in World War I (1918).[34] Mormons lost on polygamy (1879 through
1890).[35] The point here is, again, not that the free-exercise order was
less respectful of separation than government is today, which it was,
or that it was even-handed, but that throughout the nineteenth century and the first half of the twentieth the free-exercise order carried
on, without serious eruptions, intercurrence-as-usual.

The same may be said of church-state relations considered as a
whole. Here too, patterns across the three orders reinforced each
other, even as they engaged opposing principles of control. Legally,
justices extolled the First Amendment in the same breath they announced "this is a Christian nation;" commentators from Story and
Kent onward said Christianity was part of the common law.[36] Struc-
turally, the fragmented order of religion anchored and stabilized the
allegiances of the citizenry. Instrumentally, the principle of separation removed entailments of political affiliation, fostering church

membership and allowing politicians to align openly with religion and its benefits, whatever their own affiliations or beliefs. Stylistically, the emotionalism and experimentation of religion complemented the routines of the parties and of the free-exercise order, alternately renewing and resettling American politics. When a religious campaign was victorious, for instance, in the aftermath of the Civil War, and ministers went home to resume earning their salaries, party politicians were there to reconsolidate electoral organizations, which in turn served as essential bulwarks for the order of free exercise.

But not forever. Beginning in the 1960s, and at an accelerating pace thereafter, the Supreme Court has acted on its own. In 1962, with no statute before it and citing no precedents, it held that public schools could not require students to recite a prayer, even if it was nondenominational and students could be excused on a parent's request; the following year the Court decided the same for readings from the Bible.[37] Similar rulings had been made based on five state constitutions but not more recently than 1929, and twice as many state courts had found otherwise; several large cities, mainly in the Northeast, prohibited prayer and Bible readings, but these too were by far the minority.[38] As a prominent politician suggested at the time, excluding these options raised the question of whether the Court had held that God himself was unconstitutional; indicative of the widespread surprise and furor, more mail was received by the Court on school prayer than on any decision before or after.[39] The Court soon made it clear this was not an isolated move, ruling steadily and adversely to the religious position in several other areas: contraception (1965), pornography (1965), science teaching (1968), abortion (1973). By 1979 its decisions had begun to apply standards of due process to internal church governance. Among its school prayer decisions, in 1985 it voided Alabama's provision for silent and voluntary prayer and in 1992 it prohibited religious exercises at school graduation.[40]

To account for the Court's actions, it is necessary to refer back to political development within the free-exercise order almost three decades before, when in the aftermath of assuming a posture of deference to Congress' judgments on the constitutionality of economic matters, the Court suggested that in the future it would apply a higher standard of scrutiny to legislation affecting noneconomic rights, including rights associated with religion.[41] Put in terms of our analysis: having shifted to Congress authority over economic matters that throughout its history the Court had vigorously exercised itself, the Court would attempt to shift to itself authority over noneconomic matters, including religion, that throughout its history had been relegated to the Congress and to the states. The Court's saying this did not permanently settle things; but as far as church-state relations were concerned, it opened the way for institutional independence where before there had been institutional convergence – if not on every detail, certainly on fundamental principles. In the earlier example of Reconstruction, the question of political development presented was "how much" authority needed to be shifted to Congress to protect the freedmen. In church-state relations, the questions now became whether the Court's assumption of authority would hold against resistance from its surroundings, and if so, how the Court's breaking ranks would reshape authority in this domain.

Despite the initial uproar, organized resistance by the order of religion was delayed several years. Not that there were no warnings of things to come. Compare reactions in 1947, when, in a decision upholding the constitutionality of publicly funded transportation to parochial schools, the Court for the first time uncovered a "wall of separation" between church and state. The lineup of reactions was predictable: Catholic leaders united in praise of the result; Protestants leaders united in praise of the rhetoric.[42] By contrast, reactions to the decisions on school prayer and Bible reading divided liberal and conservative religionists – Catholics, Protestants, and to some extent, Jews. Equally important, evangelical Protestants now were aligned against mainline churches, a division that would become a feature of later years, perhaps best symbolized by the decade-long bitter struggle within the 145-year old Southern Baptist Convention and its takeover in 1991 by fundamentalists. Indeed, a reason for the delay in organizing against the Court was an inbred religious disposition against organizing for politics – the fundamentalists, based a resignation to "end-times"; all Baptists, based on a historic commitment to church-state separation; and virtually all conservative denominations, based on fierce traditions of independence and rivalries among ministers and churches.

Overcoming these obstacles required yet another blow from the order of free exercise, in 1978, in the form of new rules issued by the Carter administration's IRS to rescind federal tax exemptions of the Christian academies churches set up during the years of court-ordered school integration. Tax exemptions are a privilege that American churches have enjoyed since the colonies; their denial here, moreover, threatened the stability of schools that were already a refuge from earlier defeats. Within months of the IRS decision, a group of ministers had formed the National Christian Action Committee, a loose confederation of Protestant churches that in 1979 would evolve into the Moral Majority. The Moral Majority was in many respects the standard-model sprawling, interdenominational, well-financed, media-savvy religious organization – now including Catholic and orthodox Jewish members alongside evangelical Protestants and focused on political organizing and campaigns. As such, it foreshadowed the politics of the Christian Right in the decades to follow.

The role of the Christian academies, and the prominence of southerners in conservative Christian politics generally, suggests the idea that race rather than religion might lay at the root of these events. Although neither Christian academies nor racially inspired politics are limited to the South, it is also likely the case that growth of Republican Party strength since 1964 in that intensely religious region, spurred apparently by racial resentment among white voters, greatly enhanced the prospects for Christian political influence, both there and in the nation at large.[43] That said, the timing of events indicates that evangelicals' entry into politics was an independent surge. Jimmy Carter had met an enthusiastic reception from them in his 1976 campaign, and as late as 1980 the largest number of Southern Baptist ministers continued to identify themselves as Democrats.[44] By 1979, in fact, Christian academies had begun to integrate their student bodies, albeit slowly.

If religious alignment was still tentative in 1980, the response of the party order to religious indignation was unambiguous. That year the Reagan campaign endorsed school prayer, the end of abortion on demand, and support for the Christian academies. Since that time, there is growing evidence of a Republican-Democratic divide over questions of religious authority, as well as clear signs that the disruption of older patterns will prove permanent. Of special significance is development within the order of political parties. By the early 1980s, both parties had shifted authority to their national committees to help select candidates, undertake strategic planning, conduct polling and voter registration, and provide staff and financial backing for campaigns; in this, Republicans led, with far more staff and more sophisticated methods of finance. Convinced that a too-overt alliance with conservative Christians would prove a net negative among voters, Republican managers constructed a dual system, with, on the one side, mass media ads aimed at the general public and, on the other, targeted mailings, solicitation of conservative ministers, and new techniques for getting out the vote. In later years, ties with conservative Christians have grown stronger: in the 1996 campaign, for instance, the Republican National Committee funneled $650,000 to the National Right to Life Committee to undertake efforts on its behalf.[45]

These structural changes must, in turn, be set alongside others, more distant from religion but just as likely to change the role of parties as the shock absorbers for America's religious crusades. Doubling back, we see that the party convention, the key vehicle by which local chieftains of the old party order brokered political compromises and produced appropriate candidates, has given way to increasingly nationalized primary contests, "candidate-centered" politics, and campaigns organized around the positions of individual leaders, both in and out of office. These shifts raise the possibility that American parties today may be less effective as moderators and buffers and more likely to transmit political conflict along the lines of conservative and liberal religion. For instance, of the 33 new Republicans elected to the House from all regions in 2002, at least 31 were on record as opposing abortion.[46] Party identification, too, is in flux. Whereas until recently the longest-lived, strongest predictor of party allegiance in the United States was Protestant versus Catholic, today some scholars claim this is being replaced by conservative versus liberal religionist, across denominations, Christian and non-Christian.[47]

Political development in the party order necessarily implicates the order of free exercise, although to what effect remains to be seen. Over the decades, church-state politics have come to increasingly mirror the lopsided support for the Republican party given by the Christian Right and vice versa. For instance, constitutional amendments to permit school prayer of various kinds have been introduced in committee and, less often, on the floor in both houses of Congress, beginning within a month after the Court issued its decision on this matter in 1962. Votes in support of these measures proceeded through the 1970s with Republicans increasingly prominent, but they always included sizable Democratic support and considerable Republican opposition. By contrast, in 1998, votes in the House Judiciary Committee to send the so-called Istook amendment to the floor were on a strict party line; when the amendment reached the floor, nearly 90 percent of representatives voted, for or against, with members of their own party.[48] So far none of these proposals has passed either house, but they can be expected to keep coming.

Amendments aside, the harder question for the free-exercise order, and for church-state relations, concerns what will happen if Republicans in Congress are able to pass statutes on religiously charged issues that bring about a direct confrontation with the Court – on abortion, for instance, or homosexuality, on which the Court has adopted a secular stance. A dress rehearsal along these lines occurred in 1997, when the Court overturned the Religious Freedom Restoration Act (RFRA) of 1994 as it pertained to the states. The RFRA, which received close-to-unanimous congressional support and was signed into law by President Clinton, required federal courts to exercise strict scrutiny of state laws that imposed disadvantages on religious practices or groups. Congress passed it under its constitutional authority to regulate the federal judiciary, in direct response to the Court having ruled a few years earlier that legitimate secular purposes would justify overriding religious rights. The Court's RFRA opinion, signed by the five most conservative justices plus Justice Ginsburg, was stunning for the statement of its intention to preserve and protect its own authority to determine rules under the First Amendment.[49] The lineup of justices is significant, for it suggests that even under a reconstructed party order able to change the makeup of the Court to suit evangelicals, reasons of institutional authority might well still prevail.

At this point in the process of rearrangement, it is far from clear how exactly authority will realign; nonetheless, RFRA also signals a shift from the order of religion to the order of free exercise that augers to be durable. For all appearances, the once-broad controls that religious denominations exercised within all manner of public projects now regularly rely on the political process for endorsement, negotiated and painstakingly defined in each instance: witness, for instance, the labored course of George W. Bush's faith-based initiative. This circumstance is not remediable by the appointment of a new Court more like the Court before 1962 or before 1937. Even if a majority on the Court had been willing to uphold RFRA, it would have involved the Court subsequently in more intensive regulation, in "strict scrutiny" of the balance between religious and secular concerns in individual cases. Moreover, with divisions on religious issues being conveyed into the government by a now-reconstructed order of political parties, the former independence enjoyed by the order of religion seems gone for good.

As we have said earlier, the durability of any shift in authority is determined by the changes it brings about in its larger field of operations (what in Chapter One we called its "site"). Internal division within the order of religion is not unprecedented of course; but formerly, with important localized exceptions, a continuing consensus on Protestantism's religious authority dominated national politics through the sheer number of Protestant voters. By contrast, the current split, among liberal and conservative Protestants as well as other religionists, opens to nationally orchestrated contests on core issues, a situation in which the new breed of candidate and professional party operative are only too happy to assist. This is not consolidation in the manner of Henry VIII, but it arguably portends a subordination of religion to the workings of politics not seen for centuries on this continent.

Federal Land Management

The reader may observe that the two sketches we have presented thus far, though very different from one another, are not devoid of similarities. Both refer to orderings of authority – slavery and church establishment – operative in America long before the Constitution was written, both scout out governing arrangements that accommodated hierarchies within those orderings for a long time afterwards, and both locate later shifts in authority toward stronger claims on behalf of individual self-determination. Notwithstanding the different issues and outcomes, these sketches, then, describe assaults on historical encumbrances in favor of a more liberal-democratic relationship between state and society.

Whatever might be said of these findings, they remain independent of the definition of development employed in their analysis. In our concluding chapter, we will consider how our definition addresses the issue of an overarching direction in American political development. The point to underscore here is that no particular direction is implied by the definition itself. Our third application is in part a caution against premature conjectures of this sort, for it is as different from the other two as they are alike. Here we examine political development in a domain of public policy, in which alternative orderings of authority had largely fallen away before the time the Constitution was written. Freedom of contract had its "first and most dramatic victory" in matters of real property, and liberalism took hold of land management in the United States with few of the historical trappings of authority prominently displayed elsewhere.[50]

The point should not be overstated, especially not in an analysis asserting the primacy of historical construction and intercurrence in political affairs. Even a relatively unencumbered case like early-American land policy is not free of other orderings of authority on the scene. Notwithstanding England's own advances with regard to the commodification of land, ancient restrictions like the quitrent, a feudal tribute recognizing the superior ownership of land by higher authorities, and primogeniture, the regulation of inheritance to keep estates intact, carried over to the colonies, and remnants of these practices, along with their attendant conflicts with newer alternatives, persisted into the nineteenth century in Maryland, Pennsylvania, and New York.[51] Controversy over the legal status of the tribal lands of Native Americans and of their rights to hunt and fish continue to this day, as does the legacy of other European occupations, for example, of the Spanish land grants in New Mexico. But following up these complications here would obscure the novel features of the case and their value in illustrating the range of our analytic proposal. In early America, land was abundant, the labor to work it was scarce, and barriers to full individual ownership by new settlers were relatively weak. By the time of the Revolution, the rights of title holders to buy, use, sell, and bequeath their land at will were widely established, and great events – the confiscation and sale of Tory estates, British recognition of America's claim to territory stretching west to the Mississippi, the decision of the former colonies to relinquish to the national government claims to land outside their borders – served to limit the national significance of local variations. Heavily in debt and holding a public domain the size of France, the Confederation Congress enacted ordinances that fostered public land sales to private parties and led to the creation of new states even less attached to Old World practices than the originals.[52]

Looking forward from this vantage point, the outstanding questions of political development are informed less by the operation of older forms of authority than by the capacities of the new form sweeping the field, the leading characteristics of which were dynamism and malleability.[53] Formally, state and federal governments retained full control over their own extensive land holdings; they also held a reservoir of authority over private lands through their powers to impose taxes, to take property for public purposes, and to regulate activities such as the building of fences, hunting, and fishing. By and large, however, they sought to foster settlement and to promote individual entrepreneurship, supporting the further commodification of land, creating a more rational private market, extending the scope of the public domain, and aiding in the construction of an infrastructure for travel and commerce.[54] To say that there was a national consensus on early-American land policy would be an exaggeration: debates over whether to sell off large or small tracts, to a large or small number of buyers, in favor of revenue or yeoman ideals, figured prominently in national party development, as did debates after 1820 about what do with the surplus income generated by the first great land rush.[55] But these were political questions wholly within the purview of the liberal-democratic forms of decision making in American government.

The dictionary lists "a lack of strictness or rigor" as the first definition of liberalism; that meaning is nicely conveyed in the responsive character of authority over land in early American history. In comparison to the other cases we have examined, the uses of authority in this domain appear wholly instrumental. Courts could have employed common law strictures to inhibit land's commodification, and they faced early pressure on this point from codification campaigns to limit judges' discretion and subordinate their authority to the legislature. But the courts took the offensive almost immediately, aggressively manipulating the common law to promote productive use and entrepreneurial innovation. Judges, like legislators, treated the law in this area as a tool of policy.[56]

Manipulations by the political arms of the state – elected officials, bureaucrats, and statutory law – were hardly less innovative. The story of federal land policy is often told by a standard periodization around the succession of politically promulgated national purposes – acquisition and disposal, reservation and conservation, and environmental protection. Our concern in this sketch is less with the causes of these shifts than with their successive negotiation and changing shape, but the broad correspondence between mandates of public policy and stages of economic development suggests nothing so much as the adaptability of authority in liberal government to changing national conditions. Acquisition and disposal dominated the era of agrarian settlement; reservation and conservation rose to prominence in the era of the industrial economy; environmental protection became a pervasive concern of the suburban, consumer economy.[57] The history of federal land management appears on this broad canvas as the normal politics of liberal democracy, a politics driven by changing interest pressures, public opinion, political coalitions, and, on occasion, swept up in the ideas of popular movements – Manifest Destiny, the conservation "crusade," the *Silent Spring*.

It is when the changing purposes of government are aligned with the agencies designed to carry them out that the value added by our definition of political development becomes clear. Problems of dislodging and rearranging authority take center stage here, with political development becoming increasingly hampered by the proliferation of institutional mandates. Confrontation with existing authority was, of course, present at the outset, part and parcel of the desire to acquire land. Authority over land in question was claimed variously by Native Americans, Spain, Britain, France, Mexico, and Russia; for U.S. authority to be extended, these others needed to be removed. Outward-reaching ambitions were vented by the most elemental instruments of state power, the War Department and the State Department; the authority of others was dislodged by armed force, diplomatic negotiation, or often, some combination of the two. These displacements through acquisition would leave in their wake considerably more local variation than among the original colonies, but whatever their limitations, they were more extensive than anything that occurred later on.[58] The acquisition of land between the Treaty of Paris in 1783 and the Gadsden purchase of 1853, along with the displacement of Native American claims, created a public domain under the authority of the federal government that at one time or another accounted for three-quarters of the land mass of the contiguous forty-eight states. The Purchase of Alaska in 1867 brought the last major additions, as later acquisitions involved lands in which the federal government recognized private land titles already held.[59]

Disposal, shifting authority out of the public domain into private hands, was no less impressive in scope. Over the course of the nineteenth century the United States disposed of nearly two-thirds of the public domain, about half of the land area of the fifty states. Direct transfers were made through preemption laws, homestead laws, land grants to states and railroads. Administrative means were also used: the army offered land bounties,[60] the State Department issued land patents, and the Treasury oversaw land sales. When the Census of 1800 exposed extensive pockets of tenancy in Eastern states,

Congress created public land districts with local offices to facilitate sale. These offices were consolidated in 1812 under a General Land Office (GLO), which became a principle unit of the new Department of the Interior at its formation in 1849. Disposal through the GLO continued through the New Deal, after which the agency was abolished and replaced by the Bureau of Land Management.[61]

These early shifts were not only massive in scale, they were relatively freewheeling in operation. Transferring authority into the public domain and then to private ownership, the American state played fast and loose with restraints on the exercise of its power. In acquisition, for instance, President Jefferson's reluctance to make "blank paper" of the Constitution by purchase of the Louisiana Territory ultimately gave way to an appeal to public opinion. President Monroe capitalized on Andrew Jackson's "unauthorized seizure" of a Spanish military post in Florida to press Spain into negotiating the Transcontinental Treaty of 1819. President Polk's message of 1845 informing Congress that a "war existed" by virtue of Mexican incursion onto American soil – a war that all suspected would justify American seizure of California and the greater Southwest – was no less pretentious for his careful orchestration of the facts.

Disposal was likewise loosely bound.[62] Despite the national system of federal land offices in place at the local level by the 1830s, local interests were empowered by the reliance on small, patronage-based staffs, and on private finance and surveys. Corruption and mismanagement in the local land offices were infamous and not always a subterfuge of political intent; Congress spent time and energy on special legislation exempting individuals from the standards it put in place. When, in the mid-1880s, President Cleveland gave control of the GLO to a reformer bent on cleaning up operations, Congress made certain his tenure was short lived. Moving authority in and out of the national domain, the American approach was no-holds-barred, as the development question – "how much" – ran up against weak rules and porous boundaries. The law was an instrument that facilitated "more," to an achievement with few rivals in the annals of history.

Reservation and conservation in land policy can be traced to 1869, when President Grant set aside breeding grounds for the northern fur seal in the Pribilof Islands off the Alaskan mainland. The budding idea behind that action was that active federal management of public lands could enhance and extend the economic value of their important natural resources. Fostering human uses remained the priority, but expansion of national industrial capacity and the closing of the frontier raised new concerns about resource scarcity and unregulated private exploitation, and these lent currency to new strategies for employing government authority.

The instruments fashioned for proactive land management were quite unlike the form-processing and record-keeping land offices of the era of disposal. The Fish Commission and Biological Survey (forerunners of the Fish and Wildlife Service), the Geological Survey, the Bureau of Reclamations, the Forest Service, the Bureau of Mines, the National Park Service, and, later, the Bureau of Land Management were knowledge-based agencies charged to apply scientific, technical, and planning expertise to problems of land use. Huge tracts of land were to be withheld from private sale and placed under the authority of one or another of the new land management agencies. In effect, the state began to divide authority over its lands among different discretionary agencies according to their primary uses: forest lands were managed primarily to meet the demand for timber and water resources, park lands were managed to meet the demand for recreation, reclamation lands were managed to meet the demand for irrigation, land remnants were managed to meet the demand for grazing. At times, as in the creation of eastern forest reserves, private land was purchased by the federal government to extend management capabilities, but with nearly a third of the land in the United States still held by the federal government, the change in priorities from quick disposal to active management had ample room in which to make itself felt on its own.

The development problem at this stage was not in conceiving new tasks for goverment, but in shifting authority to new agencies, distributing it within and among them according to new purposes and resolving conflicts over its redistribution. The entrepreneurial initiative for these shifts came from different sources, not least of which was the future managers of the new agencies themselves; but a different mix of interest behind each shift meant considerable variation from agency to agency in how much authority actually changed hands and to whose advantage.[63] Moreover, the disruptions and displacements in the most extensive of these shifts were not clean, single-jolt affairs but repeated offensives that reverberated back and forth across agencies, building intercurrent tensions into everyday operations.

As in the first stage, the courts proved a willing partner in these shifts. Notwithstanding the formative role they played in other areas of economic regulation, courts had relatively little to say about how the federal government used its own lands, and although they were occasionally drawn into the fray to settle delegation and federalism issues, they did little to impede and much to facilitate the shift toward bureaucratic autonomy.[64] The harder part was wresting administrative discretion from Congress; that was accomplished catch-as-catch-can. One early measure of the outer limits of Congress's tolerance was the elimination of self-financing schemes hatched by bureaucrat entrepreneurs in the Forest Service and the Bureau of Reclamations that would have removed their agencies from political control through the annual appropriations process. Even within these limits, Congress could prove a fickle ally, for discretion once delegated and exercised provoked counterpressures that elected politicians were hard pressed to ignore. A famous case in point was the vast expansion of the national forest system that occurred in 1907. Early that year, Congress moved to rescind the blanket discretion it had given to the presidency in 1891 to create forest reserves out of the public domain. The rescission, which applied specifically to public lands in the northwestern states, was a clear signal of congressional discomfort with the Roosevelt administration's relentless campaign to shift government policy away from land sales by the General Land Office of the Department of the Interior to land management by the Forestry Division of the Department of Agriculture. As it happened, Congress's restriction was effectively nullified by Roosevelt, who, acting on a plan provided by Chief Forester Gifford Pinchot, withheld his signature from the rescission bill until he had reserved forty-three million additional acres of northwestern forest land, creating twenty-one new national forests and expanding eleven others in the states specified in the bill.[65]

The shifts in authority that occurred during this period were often displacements of a quite literal sort: the General Land Office was displaced in its authority over certain public lands by the Forest Service; the Forest Service was displaced in its authority over certain public land by the Park Service. But as Congress had no intention of sacrificing land sales for managed forests or managed forests for national parks, the proliferation of agencies with stronger rule-making authority than those of the earlier era was only one hallmark of political development in this arena. Another was increased competition among agencies as Congress parceled authority out and divided it up among more specialized units. Congress's sensitivity to charges of shifting "too much" to any one purpose perpetuated the struggle over "how much" authority each agency could claim for itself.

Stiff resistance came in the first instance from old-line agencies that were as adept as new advocates in applying constituency influence and garnering congressional support. One of these, the Army Corps of Engineers, limited the advance of others, principally the Geological Survey, the Bureau of Reclamations, and the Forest Service, pressing for national water policies that looked beyond its own traditional concerns with navigation and transport.[66] The struggle between Interior and Agriculture proved especially explosive. The transfer in 1905 of control over the forest reserves, from the old-line General Land Office in Interior, to the new-light, science-friendly Division of Forestry in Agriculture was one of the signal triumphs of institution building during the Progressive era. But as already seen, Congress rescinded presidential discretion over further expansion of the forest system within two years. Two years after that, President Taft supported his Interior Secretary, former GLO chief Richard Ballinger, in initiatives that threatened to reverse the transfer altogether. Fearing the worse, Gifford Pinchot determined to save his agency by wrecking Taft's governing coalition. As chief architect of TR's conservation program and a leading symbol of Taft's commitment to Roosevelt-style progressive reform, Pinchot openly defied Taft by personally relaying to the Senate charges of corruption against Ballinger that the president had already dismissed. Not surprisingly, this blatant insubordination prompted Taft to fire the chief forester, but Pinchot's accusations and Taft's response fueled the progressive insurgency in Congress against the administration, and Ballinger himself resigned within the year. Pinchot's parting gift to the agency he had forged was to discredit its main rival in land management and secure its own survival.[67]

The shift to new authorities did not end with these partial displacements of the old but continued as authority hemorrhaged from new forms themselves. Again, the Forest Service is the leading case in point. Though its legislative mandate to manage forest reserves directed attention specifically to timber and water supplies, top forest administrators extended their authority to cover all the uses of their lands – grazing uses, wildlife and forage uses, mineral uses, and recreation uses. Their research orientation and their ideas for "multiple use" and "cooperative forestry" also drew them into close relations with state governments and politics.[68] These were bold management concepts, but they left the Forest Service vulnerable to a wider range of constituencies, any one of which might become disaffected by its choices and priorities. Disaffection by recreation users and naturalists crystallized early. Pinchot had initially reached out to them for political support, but his commitment to multiple-use left him adamantly opposed to the creation of any national park that would be closed to logging. He antagonized naturalists further by supporting the construction of a reservoir in Yosemite National Park to serve as a water supply for San Franscico, by campaigning to head off the creation of a separate parks bureau within the Interior Department, and by promoting the transfer of control of the existing national parks to the Department of Agriculture.

In the wake of the Ballinger controversy, Pinchot's successor, Henry Graves, sought to repair damaged relations with disaffected groups. But with Pinchot out of office, continuing to agitate for the Yosemite reservoir, President Wilson's Interior Secretary Franklin Lane pushed through a National Parks Act in 1916, securing for naturalists a separate park administration service in Interior beyond the Forest Service's reach. With a new rival now threatening to strip the Forest Service of political support, not to say of land to manage, and with Interior reclaiming the ideological offensive, later Forest Service chiefs sought to limit future transfers to the park service by designating primitive and recreational areas within the forest lands. Nonetheless, the pattern of creating national parks at Forest Service expense continued; after the Depression, it accelerated. Highway development spurred public interest in the creation of new parks and other recreation outlets; at the same time, an increase in demand for lumber prompted the Forest Service to move closer to the timber industry and to loosen its standards for "sustained yield" logging.[69]

The proliferation of separate authorities awkwardly balanced against one another during the first half of the twentieth century set the stage for the most recent policy developments in federal land management, the shift toward "environmental protection." The environmental movement traces antecedents back to the American transcendentalists and to naturalists at the turn of the century, but changes after World War II, both in the movement's aims and in the public's response to its appeals, brought strikingly new ideas to federal land policy.[70] The earlier turn from acquisition and disposal to reservation and conservation was largely a strategic change in thinking about the most efficient means of utilizing natural resources. In contrast, concern for the environment took aim at the concept of utility itself. Environmentalists did not charge the government with promoting resource development or with finding the right balance between various economic and recreational uses or even with promoting recreation uses above others. Instead, they asked government to recognize the integrity of nature and to regard a diffuse, encompassing, and perpetual human interest in the ecosystem as fundamental to all policies. The radical thrust of this stance as a premise for political development stems from the fact that all instrumental divisions of authority – liberal divisions between public and private spheres, bureaucratic divisions among agencies, territorial divisions among local, national, and international questions – are potential obstacles to its operation. By the same token, the developmental problem posed by environmentalism is not just that it butts up against more authorities than earlier land-use ideas but that it calls into question the instrumentalist assumptions of liberal democratic government, making it hard to determine where authority for this cause might safely reside.[71]

This quandary helps to explain why political development on behalf of environmental protection has served not just to further proliferate authorities and compound problems posed by their intercurrence, but more distinctively, to strip away the divisions among authorities and short circuit the operations of each. The political response to environmentalism has scrambled competing interests the government had previously separated, forced them to confront one another, and has cycled their different purposes through agencies that are now more thoroughly entangled in each other's affairs than ever before. Federal land policy, once the model of flexibility and instrumental efficiency, is now the paradigmatic case of institutionally encumbered governance.[72]

If this result follows in a general way from the difficulties of incorporating the idea of environmental protection into the operations of a liberal government, it stems specifically from prior political development in federal land management. In the course of events, environmentalists could not advance their cause by promoting the transfer of more authority to bureaucrats. Their own diagnosis of the situation was that the proliferation of agencies with different mandates attentive to distinct resource uses empowered single-interest clienteles at the expense of broader public interests. [73] They plotted strategy in reaction to what had come before. Their program took shape as an assault on the separate bureaucracies that had been built up between the Progressive era and the New Deal and as an effort to shift authority back to principal constitutional officers in hopes of redirecting the whole.[74]

The courts proved as responsive as ever, though this time their responsiveness thrust them into the center of land policy politics. Over the course of the 1960s, the judiciary reversed its historical indulgence of resource users and their various bureaucratic overseers by adopting new standards of "strict scrutiny" over decisions of federal agencies and by altering the rules of standing to facilitate lawsuits by "public" interest groups.[75] Congress followed along, rewriting agency mandates handed down from the Progressive era with new prescriptive detail and extensive provision for public involvement, revising the Administrative Procedures Act and passing a Federal Advisory Committee Act along similar lines, crafting new laws to force old agencies to attend to environmental concerns, and charging a new Council on Environmental Quality in the Executive Office of the President with the daunting task of formulating a unified national environmental policy. All extended judicial authority. One thing Congress did not do was scrap the old institutions and redesign land use policy from scratch.

The Forest Service, long the model of the Progressive-era discretionary bureaucracy, bore the most sustained assault from the courts and Congress, though the Park Service, the Bureau of Land Management, the Bureau of Mines, and to a lesser extent the Fish and Wildlife service have been subject to similar treatment.[76] Forest Service autonomy in allocating land use ended in 1964 when the Wilderness Act withdrew agency discretion over wilderness designations and put Congress directly in control of these set-asides. The agency was hemmed in further by the requirements of the Wild and Scenic Rivers Act (1968), the Endangered Species Acts (1966, 1968, 1973), the Federal Water Pollution Control Act, and the Federal Environmental Pesticide Control Act (1972), and, most importantly, the National Environmental Protection Act (1970), which required an environmental impact statement for any proposed change in land use. When in the early 1970s successful lawsuits against clear cutting on national forest land threatened a nationwide moratorium on timber harvests, Congress stepped in again, this time to rewrite the forest service's Organic Statute of 1897. The National Forest Management Act of 1976 demanded a comprehensive fifteen-year plan for each national forest and prescribed in detail the procedures and environmental standards by which these plans would be promulgated.

This decade-long hammering at the discretion and entrenched priorities of Progressive-era bureaucracies has changed the way the government does business and made each actor more solicitous of ecological interests. But notable as these developments have been, the actual shifts in authority bear only a tenuous relationship to policies alleged to stand behind them. The institutional foothold gained by the environmentalists against their adversaries has proven to be more precarious than was held earlier by the conservationists, because there is no domain in which their authority excludes others. Limiting agency discretion and making the relevant bureaucracies more accountable to politicians and public interest groups has done less to secure environmental aims than to set the various stakeholders at loggerheads.

At every stage of land management policy, the mandates of the law have proven less binding in practice than they appear on paper, but in this instance, the deployment of authority for new purposes has called into question the managerial capacities of liberal government itself. The self-limiting nature of these shifts is evident on several fronts. In the first place, the new planning priorities stipulated in the law, with their complex schemes for balancing contending values, insured that agency discretion in rule making, however hemmed in, would not be eliminated; in some ways, it would be enhanced. Coordination through the creation of a new overhead authority, the Environmental Protection Agency, has also proven problematic, as that agency was thrown together by an executive order that simply collected disparate authorities from different divisions under a common roof. Even more notable as a self-limiting feature of these shifts are the still weak formal linkages between the planning and priority mandates of the law and the government's annual budget and appropriations processes.[77]

All this means that although laws might force agencies to attend to new priorities in long-term planning, neither the Congress nor the president need defer to these plans in their year-to-year interventions. Congress has in fact used its new hands-on approach to agency decision making in contradictory ways. It has on occasion increased funding for the noncommodity work of the Forest Service over agency budget requests, but it also has forced commodity production on the agency at the expense of the planning priorities and mandates promulgated in the legislative directives of 1974 and 1976.[78] One notorious example involved the head forester of the northern region, who, by 1990, had become a leading symbol of a new environmental consciousness in the agency and of agency responsiveness to congressional priorities as stipulated in laws of the 1970s. He was forced out of his job in 1991 by a senator angry over his directive to district subordinates to give precedence to the environmental laws over the congressionally prescribed timber targets when the two conflicted.[79]

Finally, the assault on agency discretion has proven self-limiting in that the shift back to constitutional authorities has served to increase conflict among Congress, the presidency, and the courts over their respective prerogatives vis-a-vis the bureaucracy. An early signal of this antagonism was the passage of the Forest and Rangeland Renewable Resources Planning Act (RRP) of 1974. This measure, though it followed in a long line of environmental law writing was, in fact, prompted by intercurrent changes outside it. To explain RRP, we need to double back, to Richard Nixon's campaign to reform national budgeting and expenditure processes. Nixon had by this time turned the executive budget office into a political arm of presidential control over the bureaucracy, and he had shown his determination to impose his own priorities on the executive branch by impounding congressionally appropriated funds. RRP was a congressional response to one such effort, the impoundment of funds for new logging roads. It sought to compel agencies to detail their plans more thoroughly and to tie them to these plans by specifying how modifications were to be made, reported, and implemented. Environmental protection was a secondary concern in this controversy; the impoundment of congressionally appropriated funds for new logging roads was, if anything, a "green" intervention. Though the RRP paid homage to new environmental priorities, its real target was the Office of Management and Budget, and its first objective was to promote Congress as the final arbiter of agency priorities.[80]

Because the shifts in authority that have responded to the environmental movement have had the effect of entangling authorities rather than separating them, they have made for even more irresolvable political controversies than the conservation movement. If there is a single counterpart to the Pinchot–Ballinger controversy in the contemporary struggle to secure new authority relations, it is probably the one over the spotted owl in the forests of the Pacific Northwest that raged between 1985 and 1993. In this instance, a confrontation was driven by conservative presidents determined to derail the environmental offensive and by environmentalists determined to expose flagrant defiance of the law by the executive branch. The Reagan and Bush administrations lent their support to the timber industry in these old growth forests by delaying action by the Fish and Wildlife Service, the Bureau of Land Management, and the Forest Service to protect the spotted owl's habitat. Once the owl was listed as a threatened species, the Bush administration went further, nullifying the effect of the listing by invoking authority in the law to make exceptions to administrative rulings in extraordinary circumstances. Meanwhile, environmental groups had seized on the plight of the owl as a strategy for staving off the advance of old-growth logging in the region, and they successfully used the courts to break executive intransigence and force agency action. For its part, Congress offered compromises in 1987 and 1989 providing the agencies with judicial relief pending the formulation of plans to protect the owl, and heading off any injunction against timber sales. Nonetheless, environmentalists secured such an injunction in 1991, citing agency refusal to comply with laws protecting wildlife and directly implicating "higher authorities in the executive branch of government" in the subversion of those laws.[81]

By this time, political mobilization on both sides had exposed the severe limitations of court decrees in providing a practical solution. Environmental victories in court were matched by an industry-led public-relations campaign that aimed to submerge the issue of saving old-growth forests and to present instead a national choice between protecting owls and protecting jobs, endangered species or endangered workers. The confrontation persisted until the inauguration of Bill Clinton. The new administration negotiated an ad hoc settlement among the contending parties, though this itself contravened the spirit if not the letter of the law by dividing up the land in dispute and allowing each interest to dominate use of a part of it.[82]

Both the Pinchot–Ballinger controversy and the spotted owl controversy were politically calculated train wrecks. The difference is that this time, no authority emerged secure. The principal developmental effect of environmentalism to date has been to throw more authority into greater contention; a moving stalemate alert to momentary changes in the ideological alignment of institutions has been the rule. New schemes for shifting authority seek relief from these hyperpoliticized encounters by way of devolution, privatization, coordination, or collaboration, but the problem at bottom lies in the purposes which government is now called on to reconcile, and any rearrangement that fails to resolve these conflicting priorities is unlikely to perform much better. To the extent that the environmental threat is real and pressing, it has placed the developmental capacities of liberal democracy itself on the line.

FIVE

Political Development: The Issues

If we could first know where we are and whither we are tending,
we might better judge what to do and how to do it.

Abraham Lincoln

IF OUR DEFINITION OF POLITICAL DEVELOPMENT seems as comfortable as we hope, it will be because APD researchers discover they have been studying shifts in authority all along. Inclined as we are to quit while we are ahead, we feel an obligation to pick up again at the point where we bracketed larger issues of meaning and value in order to pursue a neutral definition of political development, one that could stand up empirically against the diverse historical materials engaged by scholarship in the field. The plan was not to leave these larger issues behind permanently; they were, and to many APD scholars still are, what makes political development worth thinking about. A clearer-cut definition anticipated a return, and now we are better equipped to look for answers. There is no expectation that profound matters of political philosophy will be settled by the idea of historical construction or our temporal matrix of intercurrent controls. But insofar as these profound matters contemplate, for instance, the prospects of different arrangements of authority being established and successfully sustained over time, we believe APD will have something of its own to contribute.

In this chapter we can provide only the briefest of previews of how the study of political development we describe might deliver on this promise, but we will try to do that much. For a first pass at meaning, we take up the matter of direction. In our perspective, direction concerns whether the constant rearrangement of authority among and within institutions shows a movement over time in favor of some forms or principles over others. Direction is of interest in itself, objectively, because it speaks to the coherence of political change and to continuities presumed by the idea of historical construction; it also provides a good test of whether shifts-in-authority can be enlisted in this inquiry. But direction is only a pass at – an overture to – meaning, because whatever movement the evidence supports must be interpreted by the observer, who may or may not have come to the material with meanings in advance. Repeated movements to legislative agencies from judicial ones is a direction; what it means remains to be said. Shifts-in-authority do not cook the books; our definition is a tool for meaningfully reading the record.

Another section of this chapter engages meaning directly. In a discussion that is again far shorter than is warranted by the subject matter, we ask what a polity conceived in terms of development suggests about the meaning of politics and of political action. Recall that these questions prompted the current wave of APD scholarship that began in the 1970s. A presentation of the polity as one that is intercurrent and constantly changing, one in which the attempt to control others is a perpetual motor, cannot help but inform the question of what to do and how to do it and just what it is people are doing when they act in political life. More to the point, such a presentation of the polity is, in itself, a study of people acting politically in diverse ways, despite our having placed them so often in institutional settings. To be sure, their actions are subject to interpretation as well, but a good deal of the meaning will be apparent in what the actors say and do. In this section, we consider how a focus on the dimension of time and temporality redirects our understanding of what it means to act politically, or, as it is more commonly referred to in political science, agency.

A third section between these two takes up the relationship of APD scholarship to social science. This subject has a critical bearing on all issues of meaning attached to political development; anything we might find or argue must rest on sound principles of research design and inference from evidence. As long as APD remains a miscellany of research efforts, its connection to nondevelopmental research on

American politics will be held in limbo. Once research is organized around shifts in authority, articulating methodological entailments becomes both possible and necessary. These do not boil down to a difference between qualitative and quantitative research: some APD researchers employ large data sets, standard indicators of economic growth, regression analysis, and the rest. What distinguishes APD was stated at the outset of our search: it is a substantive enterprise guided by a theoretical precept, namely, that politics is historically constructed. Adhering to that precept requires that frameworks, concepts, and methods be adapted to the aim of studying politics over time, wherever that leads, descriptively or analytically.

Political Development as Direction

It is fair to say that direction, insofar as it applies to the history of a polity overall, has been a taboo subject among political scientists for several decades. The reason was partly aired in our discussion in Chapter Two, on the unraveling of the concept of political development. In general, propositions about direction in politics, when they are not forthrightly deterministic, have had an uncanny way of educing evidence that leads straight to whatever end result, good or bad, is supported by the accompanying theory. They are, in a word, normative. These strictures seem not to apply to direction within shorter time spans, a topic taken up by researchers routinely: the decline and resurgence of Congress,[1] the rise of the imperial presidency,[2] the quest for judicial supremacy,[3] the emerging Republican majority.[4] But politics understood as historically constructed implicates direction over the long haul, junctures and all; if politics can change the platform of future action, if it can "develop," it should display something more than random movement. We think that our definition of political development in terms of shifts in authority will allow us to travel the distance without teleologies or metaphors from biology and without unduly imposing our own presuppositions about where things are headed.

The case for adopting a new approach to investigating direction in American politics must rest, at least in part, on what approaches are available to political science now. Most of the miles covered so far on the general question have been on the backs of the three great developmental war horses – democracy, bureaucracy, and liberalism; it makes sense, then, to look there for guidance. Reread in our terms, these studies can be seen to ask, did American politics develop in a democratic direction, in a liberal direction, in a bureaucratic direction? Considering that by this point in our discussion we have done our share of literature reviews, we hope we may be permitted to make our observations on the usefulness of this body of work brief and summary.

The first observation is how little the basic logic of these studies differs from the logic employed by Burgess and Wilson in the late nineteenth century. That is, a substantive political tendency or end-state is identified in advance, and its presence is sought in the historical record through different indicators, much as Burgess sought for the constitutional state through the indicators of national sovereignty and civil liberties. In Chapter Two, we argued that this a priori procedure left the concept of political development undefended against subsequent unraveling; framing political direction around democratization, bureaucratization, and liberalization produces a like result, with political development left hostage to a fairly restricted configuration of events. Put differently: when the vehicle for inquiring into direction anticipates movement of a certain kind, the search has nowhere to go should events not turn out as expected. This in itself might not be fatal were the vehicle provided well suited to the task. But there is also discouragement on this front, where problems of evidence, conceptualization, and interpretation may, for our purposes at least, be insurmountable.

Perhaps the most basic pitfall concerns indicators: what counts as evidence of, for instance, democratization. Democratization is frequently tracked by means of the indicator of suffrage. Eligibility to vote in the U.S. has expanded over time; this is true, notwithstanding the long hiatus in African-American voting that followed Reconstruction and the intermittent back-tracking on illiterate citizens and those categorized as vagrants and felons. This trend suggests a meaningful direction toward more democracy. But another important indicator of democratization is voting turnout, according to which the results look very different. Turnouts for national elections in recent decades have not risen far above the halfway mark; and for all the noise in the numbers showing turnout in the 1880s upwards of 80 percent, the demobilization of the electorate in later decades raises questions about the course and meaning of democratization. Or consider yet another way to chart democratization, in terms of the relative activity of different branches of government and their susceptibility to democratic control. The widening scope of the legislature's activity over time might suggest a democratic direction; but increasing judicial and bureaucratic activism would suggest the opposite. The point is not that all these things cannot be studied at once; they can. It is that disputes over priorities among different indicators, often engaging normative as well as empirical issues, are not easily settled. Meanwhile, the question of direction is held in abeyance, dependent on the outcome of the argument.

A related problem occurs with conceptualization. Consider here bureaucratization, which, among the three proposed vehicles of development, arguably shows the cleanest one-way pattern. Looked at in terms of the number of public agencies and bureaucrats employed, American political development has moved in a steadily bureaucratic direction; this would appear to be the case even allowing for measures designed to slow its course, such as contracting out, downsizing, and greater legislative oversight. But what conception of bureaucratization does this support? If bureaucratization is understood as a rationalization or depersonalization of authority, then the spoils system represented a considerable advance over earlier forms, whereas the proliferation of competing agencies over the first two-thirds of the twentieth century and the appearance in more recent years of a hyperpoliticized managerial class at the subcabinet level has arguably arrested this trend.[5] Alternatively, if bureaucracy is conceived more broadly in terms of detailed public rules that reach deep into society to regulate everyday life, common law regulation by the states before the Civil War presents us with this as well, neutralizing the implication of more comprehensive government through time that is captured by modern administrative forms alone.[6]

Finally, another hazard lies in the interpretation of results. Earlier we discussed Roger Smith's study of whether American politics showed any discernible direction toward liberalism. Smith uses the indicator of "ascriptive hierarchies," defined as externally constituted arrangements of personal subordination, to show nonliberal direction. Looking for these in historical materials of the late nineteenth century – laws, ideas, political tracts, letters – he concludes that in this period a liberalism dominant in politics at an earlier time was now in full retreat. Assuming the soundness of these results, what is one to make of them? They do not counter claims of a broad movement over time to greater liberalism, with the weakening of common-law hierarchies like master-and-servant and husband-and-wife. Nor do they give us much purchase on hierarchies based on bureaucratic designation – immigration status, welfare eligibility, educational and professional status – that have taken the place of their common-law forebears, but that are linked also to changes in a distinctly non-hierarchical or liberal direction, for instance to less restrictive immigration policies, income provision, and mass education.

No study can take up all time periods and contingencies at once, even in a single country. But our strong hunch is that amassing all of the evidence that could be collected on hierarchies over time would still leave us in the same predicament. The point here is not to depreciate studies along these a priori lines, for they have, among other things, served to bring the analytic problem of finding direction in politics more clearly into focus. The fact that arguments about direction when approached this way can so quickly bog down on the finer points of definition and evidence is, most of all, an invitation to alter the approach and look for movement over time through some other method. The instinct to place direction within some substantive historical context is correct: without it, narrowing the field of evidence would be impossible. But the context ought not be one with indicators that are chronically problematic and where the selection of one set over the other affects the normative thrust of results.

Our alternative proposal, one we believe will make the problem of determining direction (or no-direction) more tractable, builds on our definition of political development: we look for direction in durable shifts in governing authority, wherever these occur. Our definition of development is, to be sure, not free of political content, but the focus on authority within institutions is more versatile than the above, less tinged with historical substance and hampered by imagined end-states. It also changes the question for research from, for instance, What does the presence or absence of hierarchy tell us about the course of American liberalism? to one more direct: Do durable shifts in authority exhibit any direction over time and, if so, in what direction? While admittedly there are no collections of durable shifts in authority on-line waiting to be analyzed, neither is the search wide open; it is directed instead to the history of governing institutions, their relations with one another and with citizens. With such an independent indicator of political development, political direction becomes a matter of seeing shared features and patterns. This remains an interpretive exercise, in which cases must be selected and evidence weighed and any characterization held open to contrary findings; however, if we have limited the detours of alternative routes, we should be more effective in moving the discussion forward.

To demonstrate, we will look for direction in the three cases of political development sketched in the previous chapter. These were originally selected to illustrate the versatility of our definition in addressing diverse historical materials, without an eye to direction. Let us agree in advance that it is far-fetched to come to any firm conclusions about direction in history based on three cases alone. Still, we venture the following: political development in America shows a movement from prescriptive to positive lawmaking; that is, from finding the law, based on precedent, in the stylized manner of courts, to making the law, based on present circumstances, in the stylized manner of legislatures. Inspecting this pattern further, we will claim that movement in this direction, although highly contested at every turn, has not been subject to significant back-and-forth motion, and that even when shifts in this direction are not followed up immediately by surrounding authorities, neither are they reversed. In our brief rereadings, we stay within the facts provided in our previous accounts, but, as should be expected of a proposal of this sort, we know of no reason in advance why this interpretation of a direction in American political development would not stand up against the historical record generally.

Each of the three developmental episodes illustrates the movement we observe in a different way. On the face of it, the case of Reconstruction substitutes one prescriptive (constitutional) rule of American law, protecting property in slaves, with another prescriptive (constitutional) rule, declaring slavery illegal. Whereas the first rule, however, affirmed a right put into the Constitution to protect it from legislative action, one that could be implemented in many cases by courts alone, the second rule looked expressly toward legislative action to give it force, accompanied by an express provision to that effect. In fact, the post-Civil War Congress entered into the boldest and most contentious period of its history by producing a spate of legislation to expand national power at the expense of the states. Moreover, the notorious 80-year time-out that followed, during which Congress, for reasons of its own, failed to move any further on its mandate to eliminate the badges of slavery, was finally broken by positive lawmaking by the Supreme Court, in *Brown v. Board of Education* (1954). The Brown decision was not based on precedent but expressly on consequences, in this case on the psychological damage inflicted on school children by racial subordination; to the critics of the Warren Court it became a symbol of aberrant jurisprudence for that reason.

The question next arises whether the U.S. Constitution might appropriately be termed prescriptive law. The acts of national founding and of establishing a fundamental law in writing that in many respects overrode English common law in the states were themselves momentous occasions of positive lawmaking. That said, many of the Constitution's provisions, including slaveholders' rights in their property and proceedings to recapture slaves, were directly carried over, prescriptively, from common law. Speaking more generally, the Constitution stands midway between prescriptive and positive law and in that sense is a perfect example of multiple orders. The Framers clearly intended to throw over the past in important respects, but they also sought a relative permanence against the future; thus, on the one hand, the difficulty of amending the Constitution and, on the other hand, the fact that the Constitution can be amended at all. This way-station quality can be seen in many features: the institution of judicial review, for instance, and its importance in carrying on common law legalism throughout the government; and the office of the Presidency, a magistrate on the common law model, but with a starkly open-ended jurisdiction.

Second case: American relations of church and state took shape originally as an effort to stem the move toward positive lawmaking in religious affairs in England at the time of Henry VIII, when religious regulation was moved to Parliament from the ecclesiastical courts. The First Amendment blocked Congress in this regard; however, it also locked in privileges churches enjoyed under their colonial charters and at common law. It is this arrangement we see operating in the free-exercise order over the better part of two centuries: churches thrusting outward to education, philanthropy, other good works of all kinds, and public morality, while at the same time enjoying immunities against dissident members, assorted citizen detractors, tax collectors, and legislators. The shift to strict separation that came to a head in the 1960s was initiated through positive lawmaking, first by state and local legislatures and thereafter by the Supreme Court, which, as in *Brown*, relied on no legal precedents. Especially striking in this regard was the Court's entry into matters of internal church governance. The justices' set-to with Congress over the Religious Freedom Restoration Act appears in this sequence as a curious reassertion by the Court of a prescriptive right of its own: so thoroughly had it turned church-state relations into a domain of positive law that the only defense left against the legislature was its privilege under the Constitution to define the content of the First Amendment.

Because the shift in church-state relations occurred so much later than the shift in the case of Reconstruction, it happened in a polity that was farther advanced in the direction of positive lawmaking and less encumbered by traditional ways of thinking about governance. Federal land policy, however, moved farthest, fastest, and most decisively of our three cases in the direction of positive lawmaking because, unlike the others, it started on its course after the

Revolution without prescriptive barriers of consequence, constitutional or otherwise, to overcome. In this domain from the outset, state court judges acted like legislators, inventing new rules as needed to facilitate economic development; federal judges for their part fell willingly into line with changing priorities expressed in the elected branches. In later decades, this trend continued in episodic diffusions of rule-making authority to institutions outside the legislature.

As all three of these cases indicate, Congress does not necessarily govern, or govern alone, in the "fully legislative polity" of positive lawmaking; rather, this is a polity in which all institutions – Congress, courts, the president, and the bureaucracy – act simultaneously as positive lawmakers in their own right.[7] In the setting of federal land management, courts and bureaucracies act legislatively to the extent of convening social interests under their auspices – their own constituent assemblies as it were – for purposes of arriving at decisions. The continuing pretense of a separation of powers in the era of environmentalism offers few clues to actual operations. In practice all authorities are thoroughly entangled in each others affairs, and they regularly drive toward confrontations over policy; legislating by bureaucrats confounds conventional ideas of bureaucracy and perhaps of democracy and liberalism as well.

The direction identified, assuming it holds up against the wider range of evidence to which it might apply, commands attention quite apart from any explanation we might provide for it. In fact, while the idea of a direction toward positive lawmaking may not by itself be counterintuitive, it is notable that this movement should so permeate American political history as to readily show itself in three very different episodes selected for other purposes. Finding similar robustly descriptive characterizations of change over time and examining their several implications will be, in themselves, advances for APD. But a direction having been discovered, there is still the matter of explanation. Why should American politics move in this way over time? In Chapter One, we said that we were not going to provide our own theory of American political development; we have now arrived at a point where theorizing of this sort appropriately begins. The development of the legislative polity is a large subject, worthy of a full-scale study; let us simply glimpse at this promised land, without attempting to cross over.

The concept of intercurrence, of a polity constructed through multiple, asymmetric orderings of authority, provides a perch from which we get a clear view. Intercurrence puts movement and change at the center of political analysis. The intercurrent polity may be held together in a relatively quiescent state for a time by artful arrangements hammered out at rarified levels of government; prescriptive lawmaking is one of these. But its historical-institutional character sponsors incongruity as an essential feature, relegating all else to the status of hedges against the outward-reaching, mutually impinging relations all around. The intercurrent polity, then, is one in which positive lawmaking, introduced in one sphere, is likely of its own accord to expose and undermine contrary principles of governance operating elsewhere. Prescriptive lawmaking and the constant changes fomented as a matter of course in an intercurrent polity are at odds from the start.

But even if intercurrence provides the deepest source of the move toward positive lawmaking, there still needs to be an explanation of how this change occurs; this is where specific hypotheses about causes will need to be tested. Cultural considerations present themselves immediately: how people perceive and deal with the inconsistency inherent in political development. Ideas may serve variously to justify incongruities or to force their resolution in practice, so a cultural explanation must account for the privileged position of positive lawmaking as such. We argued in Chapter Two that the recent deployment of cultural analysis against developmental premises has clouded this prospect, and it is uncertain now whether a cultural explanation sensitive to multiple traditions, to the ideological limitations of the liberal tradition itself, and to the political appeal of antiliberal ideas, can accommodate direction. Here then is some outstanding business within the APD community: redeploy cultural explanations or find something else, perhaps comparative research, that does the job.

Any explanation of a direction toward positive lawmaking is also likely to draw on ideas about path dependence, especially as these help to account for particular institutional arrangements in which this direction is manifest. In the movement toward a fully legislative polity, for instance, one that readily presents itself for explanation is the formal persistence of the separation of powers. As we said above, the institution of judicial review might reasonably be seen as rooted in the Framers' endorsement of multiple orderings of authority, including prescriptive rights, both constitutional and common law. As prescriptive rights have been dislodged, the judicial function of protecting them has narrowed, leaving the Court to seek other rationales for its constitutional role. Its embrace in recent years of original intent, textualism, and such theories as "the equity of the statute" expresses the Court's contemporary institutional dilemma, as does its strident policing, on a case-by-case basis, of its self-defined constitutional jurisdiction. Together, these may or may not succeed in keeping at bay the positive-law wolf that is Congress.

These remarks should not leave the impression that a move from prescriptive to positive law is necessarily a master key to American political development or that it exhausts the inquiry into direction. Our definition allows a search for direction to proceed from any collection of shifts in authority, and any direction found in this way is likely to hold insights of its own into debates about traditional themes like democracy. But more targeted searches could be undertaken as well, without the pitfalls mentioned earlier. If, for instance, democratic direction is of interest, relevant shifts of authority could be followed in several institutional arenas directly associated with democracy: political parties, voting laws, rules of representation, and rules governing speech and association. The standard for evaluating change is now portable and consistent, less subject to the noise encountered in contradictory results arrived at through different indicators. Comparisons can be sustained within and across arenas, over long periods of time; overall interpretation can be made on the basis of conceptual and methodological agreement. Nothing in the definition of political development requires that a democratic, a liberal, or any other direction need be found, but whatever the findings, it will be clearer what is expressed.

Another, more intricate, application might be to search for direction in relationships between two targeted sets of institutions. One common pairing in the literature considers the relationship between democracy and bureaucracy: in some respects, more democracy seems to foster more bureaucracy; in other respects, they undercut one another.[8] Untangling these interactions over time would benefit enormously from greater institutional specificity on each side and from analytic consistency with reference to both. It may be that both of these relationships hold with reference to different institutional indicators; perhaps, for instance, the expansion of the suffrage consistently promotes depersonalized forms of administration, whereas the short-circuiting of political parties in favor of candidate- and public opinion-centered campaigns promotes sideways interference into administrative processes, eroding hierarchy. Again, interpretation will be required, but the evidence presented, to the extent that shifts in authority are themselves well documented, should not be a matter of debate.

Political Development as Political Science

A research program with durable shifts in authority at the center of inquiry will in many cases entail an approach to social science explanation that is different from research programs in American politics that are essentially nondevelopmental. This is because the study of shifts, by definition, resists containment within predefined institutional boundaries and because relationships among variables are altered as these boundaries change over time. Whereas other research in political science characteristically looks for a causal relationship between two kinds of variables (independent variables that affect changes in dependent variables), development as shifts-in-authority presumes configurative and cross-cutting effects, in which feedback and interdependency are omnipresent. That said, political development is a capacious subject, one that invites investigations of various kinds, many of which are not distinguishable in design or execution from empirical work found in nondevelopmental research. We will speak of investigations that are.

Of first importance in this regard are the attributes of political authority: these include institutions located on sites and having as their first order of business the attempt to control persons or other institutions outside their boundaries; also the targets of the latter, who may be expected to resist and who may have agendas of control of their own; and larger arrangements of political authority that are mutually impinging and opportunistic. These characteristics orient the study of shifts theoretically toward movement and change that expands constantly outward to the polity's edges. This bias in favor of the polity as a whole is, as we have said, a significant departure in a field where the standard curriculum is divided into operations of the parts, and even textbooks purporting to give an overview of American politics will treat the branches of government, the parties, the interest groups, the electorate, and so on separately. In this respect, APD is different also from the "new institutionalism" of rational choice, where modeling techniques likewise focus analysis on the behavior of actors in particularized settings of rules or game forms. These differences widen further in the face of the proposition of historical construction, because the whole polity must refer to the polity in the past, sometimes far into the past, and in some cases to other, impinging polities, over this same expanse.

Much of this book has sought to explain why widening temporal and spatial boundaries are vital to an understanding of political development. More needs to be said, however, about how APD research is crafted to keep the whole of the polity in view, even if only propositionally, and as much of it as is possible in active play. Obviously, scholars do not try to analyze everything at once; usually they focus on single institutions or single episodes of development. They design studies, however, that relate the impact of the part on the whole or of the whole on the part in specific ways, directly or cumulatively. This has been done, first and foremost, through substantive topics that reach over several institutions – slavery, state building, social policy, citizenship, liberalism – and in these especially, the normative instincts, the "what-kind-of-country-is-this-anyway?" beat that rumbles just below the surface of much of APD research, has kept attention keyed to whole polity. Certainly this book has sought to

foreground the whole: sites, plenary authority, outward-reaching institutions, the temporal matrix, intercurrence. All attempt to show
a connection among separate institutions and events over time and
to lend a semblance of substantive, as well as conceptual, unity to
diverse studies in the field.

This argument for the importance of the whole is all the more
distinctive for the associated claim that the whole is itself is a collection of parts – multiple orders and loose ends – riddled by tension
and conflict. What defines these as a whole is, again, the centrality of
political authority, and in particular the existence of an arrangement
by which at any point in time some institution or set of institutions
has the authority to settle these conflicts when they are presented
for decision. This, too, may be riddled with contradictions – think
of the conflicts among federal courts throughout American history –
but it signifies a polity as a whole nonetheless. Intercurrence among
parts, the constant requirements of negotiation and renegotiation, is
not only consistent with the analytic priority of the whole but would
seem to require it: separating the operations of parts from considerations of the whole is a far more tenuous proposition when the latter
is characterized in its normal state by asymmetries and incongruities
than if parts were consistent with one another and synthetic in their
operations.

Each of the individual instances that comprise the historical patterns APD scholars use to organize their subjects – for example, any
one of the party systems over time,[9] or of the different modes of
presidential leadership,[10] or of the competing policy types in progressive reform,[11] or of the succession of different welfare states[12] –
can be treated separately; in fact, many of them are treated separately in nondevelopmental analysis. What is telling, though, is that
separate treatments would cause them to lose more than half their
meaning. It is the position of each piece relative to the others in the
pattern that conveys their significance in the study of political development. One piece might suggest what could have occurred if some
other piece, with other characteristics, had been there instead at that
time, or what would have been the case if all the other pieces were
missing and this one piece had constituted a coherent party system,

institution, or policy over time. Here too, it is the interrelations of the pieces as these comprise the whole pattern that is arresting and worth study.

To indicate how this perspective changes the relationship among variables from their analysis in nondevelopmental research, let us address some issues that in the latter setting raise red flags. We begin with the issue of endogeneity. Here is a discussion of endogeneity offered up as admonitory instruction in the leading primer on the design of qualitative research, based on *The Protestant Ethic and the Spirit of Capitalism* by Max Weber:

> Weber attempted to demonstrate that a specific type of economic behavior – the capitalist spirit – was (inadvertently) induced by Protestant teachings and doctrines. But ... Weber and his followers could not answer one objection that was raised to their thesis: namely that the Europeans who already had an interest in breaking the bonds of precapitalist spirit might well have left the church precisely for that purpose. In other words, the economic interests of certain groups could be seen as inducing the development of the Protestant ethic. Without a better controlled study, Weber's line of causation could be turned the other way.[13]

What makes this passage interesting is that from the viewpoint of nondevelopmental political science, it constitutes withering criticism. By contrast in the perspective of APD, even taken strictly at face value, the passage expresses several ideas or themes that play important and entirely positive roles in research. Note first that the anchoring event in Weber's story is a political development: the Protestant revolution was a durable shift in authority if ever there was one. A second theme is that durable shifts in authority are accomplished through broad-scale breakage: in this case protocapitalist Europeans moved not only against offensive economic policies of the time but against religious institutions that supported them. A third theme is how purposes are engraved in political institutions and movements and carried forward over long periods, even if their traces may not be obvious on the surface. A fourth is how streams of economic and ideological change become separated and rejoined over time and how each has potential explanatory importance. A fifth is how establishing connections of this kind opens to a better understanding of the sources of particular changes.

These observations suggest that the language of endogeneity and exogeneity is strained to the point of irrelevance when applied to research that assumes that parts routinely collide and rearrange, that institutional purposes carry on, that authority is plenary. To the extent that the standard language connotes clean separations – between parts, between inside and outside – and places those separations at the foundations of political analysis, it cannot but confound the processes of change that a developmental research program seeks to clarify. In a nutshell: endogeneity is a feature of APD research, not a malady. This fact does not hobble analysis or reduce it to the chaotic claim that everything is connected to everything else or that exogenous events never intrude. Endogeneity is accounted for through sites, thick descriptions that delineate contingent connections and separations among parts and facilitate a clear and precise tracing of impacts and influences. In any given episode of change, these influences move backward and forward, as from the material to the ideological to the material in Weber's analysis. Developmental research of the sort we have proposed recommends itself precisely on this basis.

At this point, it is useful to recall again Theodore Lowi's article on public policy, which inverted the usual formulation, "politics causes policy." Lowi categorized public policies according to the divisibility of the resources involved, and he predicted the different political configurations that were likely to form around each. As we have seen, however, the insight that policy causes politics defies the containment characteristic of nondevelopmental research. Indeed, Lowi's analysis prompts another step back to explain divisibility itself, perhaps as a function of prior political configurations: land policy was "distributive" in early America not only because there was so much of it but also because English land law was by then far advanced toward commodification. By extension, such endogenous effects remind us that predictions generated by the mutual entailments of intercurrent parts are limited by their historical context. The implication here is not that America is more exceptional than any other country; it is that to the extent that one country's politics differs from politics observed elsewhere, it is likely because of endogenous political relationships operating over time and through mechanisms similar to what we have described as historical construction.

A different implication of the research focus on shifts in authority – on shifts in authority as, so to speak, the dependent variable – involves the question of causation. In APD, causes are multiple and sometimes remote. Shifts always have more than a single cause. Consider in this regard an analysis of the Pullman strike of 1894, arguing that the Supreme Court's holding went beyond what legal precedent required to enjoin the strikers and signaled a long-lasting shift of the Court's authority toward supporting actions of the executive branch and away from its alignment with Congress following Reconstruction. Orren has shown such a result cannot be explained by less than three causes: the Court's anger at the Congress for failing to provide it necessary resources, including salary raises for the justices; the Congress' anger at the Court for its probusiness tilt; and the administration's desire to strengthen its law enforcement arm.[14] Moreover, it is also useful to know the coalitions in Congress that turned hostile to the Court initially and the political figures and interests that made the Court's new alignment seem advantageous. Thus, for instance, the prominence of populists in Congress and their own relationship to the characters in Cleveland's second administration become causes as well. All these weighed over the longer haul of political development, just as did actions of the unions and the power of the railroads.

It is unlikely that social scientists working nondevelopmentally would ever undertake such research to begin with. Among other things, it features more causes than cases – n's – to which they apply, another red flag. There are several responses to the problem of n's in social science research, but those that speak to the APD project must, we think, be informed by the $n = 1$ premise, reflected in the "A" of its name. With analysis trained on a single historically constructed whole polity, intercurrence of parts appears in highly particularized relations: how the American presidency relates over time to the American party system, for instance, or to the American Congress, to the American system of federalism, or to American political culture. So, too, with the dynamics present at "critical" junctures or events: what happened to these relations in America's New Deal, in America's Civil War, in America's Pullman strike? The research program will, in other words, subordinate an interest in generalization as necessary to foster an understanding of shifts of substantive importance for the future operations of this polity in particular.

But only as necessary. Even at the level of the single case, where issues of $n = 1$ are posed most starkly, APD scholars have employed several analytic strategies to increase the number of observations and generate greater explanatory power while still acknowledging multicausality as an essential feature. Perhaps the first thing to say is that case studies in APD have been from their earliest undertaking theoretically informed, involving more than mere history, and at the very least, probing propositions about political development in other settings. To name just a few, recent case studies take issue with propositions about the role of farmers in state building,[15] the role of working class agitation in the reform of labor policy,[16] and the relationship between regulatory agencies and the interests they regulate.[17] The discovery of multiple causes in this research has in each instance challenged earlier strong single-cause explanations.

Also along these lines, efforts to overcome the difficulties of $n = 1$ include the use of counterfactuals to gain explanatory leverage from single cases. APD has, as we have seen, spawned several studies on alternative paths, on what-might-have-been-except-for research, in which the except-for element has a dominant role in the narrative. Strategies of this sort have proven useful in eliminating existing explanations for development shown to be overly simple, for instance, by demonstrating how those that rely on uniformity or inevitability in historical experience fail to account for stark variations in time and place. Note again, however, that arguments proposing that one or another factor made a critical difference, and not some other factor as previously thought, are not in themselves single-cause explanations. The judicial interruption of the move toward an alternative kind of labor movement, or toward a regionally based railroad network, by itself is the cause neither of the alternative preempted nor of the one that finally took hold.[18] Headway is gained here instead by subsuming multicausality for a targeted explanation of why alternative paths were brought to a critical juncture at a particular time and how that juncture was negotiated to a historical result.

A third method by which observations are increased is through the identification of historical patterns, abstracted across or within institutions. The study of American "state building," for example, draws out common patterns in different institutional developments during the same period;[19] the study of various policy developments – welfare, the environment, others – draws out patterns across different historical periods from the way a single public purpose is addressed institutionally over time.[20] Individual episodes of change have also been explained by their position within patterned sequences of events that recur over time within different institutions. Examples here would include "constitutional moments,"[21] party system realignments,[22] periods of creedal passion,[23] and recurrent structures of presidential leadership.[24] This strategy reduces the ratio of causes to cases by bundling together causes more or less present in each sequence or position, accounting for similarities found among n's without eliminating multiple causality as such. Reasoning of this sort is compatible with both generalization and prediction. Once the inherent incompatibility between the American ideals and institutional realities was identified, it became possible for Samuel Huntington to generalize about interactions that provoke outbursts of creedal passion;[25] once the dynamics of leadership associated with opposition presidents in resilient regimes were distinguished from others it became possible for Stephen Skowronek to point to a high risk that Bill Clinton would be impeached.[26]

These last remarks point to a second level of inquiry, up from explaining individual cases of political development to explaining patterns of development in the polity as a whole. Here we include elements that reappear or circumstances that are similarly configured over time to form a pattern. Weber, in *The Protestant Ethic*, was not only or even primarily interested in whether ideological motives prevailed over material interest in the particular case of the Puritans; he was attempting to refute Marxists of his time who claimed ideas were never more than a superstructure of material interest. Weber aimed to clarify the place of religion "in forming the developing web of our specifically worldly modern culture, in the complex interaction of innumerable different historical factors."[27] In the same spirit, the value added by learning, say, why it was that Bryan's currency ideas were dismissed out of hand,[28] or why the formation of political machines in the South and the West differed from those in the East,[29] or how much violence occurred among blacks and whites in the American army during WWII[30] is not just knowledge of the case in itself but a clarification of the patterns of development overall, within the same constraints of working historically that Weber mentions.

At this second level of patterns, the problem of n's is less imposing. Our discussion of direction in the previous section suggests how broader meaning can be gleaned from an accumulation of cases and what explanations might be offered for our findings. Other matters that might be pursued include, for instance, the developmental potential in "fit" versus "non-fit," testing through an accumulation of cases the intuition that robust development is more likely to ensue from "non-fit" than from filling niches in existing relations of governance. At this second level also we might more clearly delineate shifts in authority, moving from the stage of impetus to signaling to testing and negotiation, and so forth, analyzing each stage for its own features and consequences across historical examples.

There are already studies that proceed directly to this second level, mainly on political development's "input" side. Among these are those that stress the "primacy" of one interest or another as it is asserted time and again at major political turning points – the primacy of race,[31] the primacy of sectionalism,[32] the primacy of labor.[33] Primacy arguments are not so much about causes in their ordinary social science meaning as they are about persistent tensions wound tightly into authority relations at large, which sometimes erupt and shape realignments. One scholar has described these as "massive facts," inescapable features of the American landscape, likely to enter in a wide range of causal arguments about political development.[34] So far this scholarship has lacked an anchoring framework, taking for granted standard turning points in American history and only in gross terms – emancipation, the progressive era, the New Deal, the "sixties." Among the gains from a common framework for analyzing development would be the ability to align and assess these "primacies" against one another and to consider how they might be mutually illuminating.

At this second level, the outstanding question of cause becomes whether "primacy," "fit," "intercurrence," "path dependence," or a particular position in a patterned sequence can be considered causes in themselves of political development, in any acceptable definition of that word. Taking acceptable to mean a definition of cause that both draws on recognizable principles of social science reasoning and comports with the multicausal, inherently endogenous, and smallish-n features of APD research, we argue for the affirmative: an element is a cause if it is not possible to give an equally plausible account of the effect observed without its inclusion in the analysis. Put into the language of falsification: a claim that an element in an APD analysis is causal can be falsified to the extent that it can be left out without sacrificing the plausibility of the account.

We see this as a rigorous test. It has already been used to challenge the theory of critical elections, once a mainstay of APD research.[35] Note, however, that substitutes, stand-ins for known factors that have the same characteristics and play the same role in the argument by a different name, do not count as disqualifiers. The rules of the test require that the result or results of the alternative explanation be clearly specified and established as equivalent to the original account. In APD, results often refer to several different iterations of a patterned event and transitions from one time frame to another, in which case the scope of any "de-causing" must be parallel. An alternative explanation of a social movement's rise, for instance, does not disprove a cause that explained movement strategy and success as well, unless the alternative also explains all three. Conversely, if multiple causes are tolerated to explain developments over time, they must also be tolerated in disproving single-causal elements and processes. In other words, parsimony by itself does not establish cause in the face of more complex explanations.

This definition of cause, and the activity of causality testing it outlines, cuts in different directions. The concepts we have elaborated all find their rationale in the need to depict politics as constantly changing over time. Although we have not pressed the point, the picture of politics as we have conceived it raises an implicit challenge to any understanding that is static, that is indifferent to patterns over time, that does not grasp the clash of mandates and procedures that defy equilibria and push politics forward in time. In this spirit, it arguably becomes incumbent on APD scholars to demonstrate, for instance, that historical predictions based on static causes (or "universal laws") do not hold across time periods or, more importantly, do not hold their own on their chosen temporal ground. We say this without illusions that either side in such an argument will pick up their data and go home. But, generally speaking, engagement of this sort seems a better way to proceed than to embrace methodological pluralism for its own sake. To the extent that explaining politics in history is what is at issue, and not only model building or refining methodology, we think it an intellectually fruitful way of advancing common interests.

Political Development as Politics

The "biggest" issue, the nature of the "best" regime, was originally a featured part of APD research. When early practitioners turned to history, they looked first for the "ultimate type" toward which political development in the West might be moving.[36] Today, the question of the ultimate type, however much it may be informed by history, is pondered more safely within the realm of political philosophy, and the normative edge of APD research has become less pronounced. As we said in Chapter 1, historical researchers have been reluctant to cut themselves off from these issues completely; much of their work is still motivated by them, and much of its meaning is found in reference to them. Fondness for critiques of progress and for assessments of direction within periods both suggest the lingering influence of such concerns. But the difficulty of reconciling the normative and empirical aspirations of the APD project within contemporary political science produces a good deal of hedging as well. We suspect that the value commitments that are most fundamental in APD's research program are those lodged in its initial premise of a historically constructed polity, and that the enterprise we would be bolstered in all its aspirations by a more explicit elaboration of these. A premise like historical construction makes a great deal of difference, on the normative as well as the empirical plane, as it helps determine the insights a research program seeks and the kind of information it accumulates.

Even in its original and most presumptuous incarnation, APD had a decidedly practical bent, its premise of historical construction not far removed in spirit from premises routinely invoked by aspiring public officers in their public appeals. To paraphrase the most eloquent of political candidates, the idea was to articulate more clearly "where we are and whither we are tending" so as to speak more authoritatively about "what to do and how to do it." In Chapter 2, we saw how academic assessments of this kind often play on those aired by politicians in the culture at large, how assumptions invoked in popular evaluations of the current state of national affairs have served as critical points of departure in APD scholarship. Nonetheless, the question addressed by these academics is the same as that addressed instinctively by politicians: "What time is it?"

Answers to this question, the time question if you will, direct themselves to the status of the polity as a historical formation and they speak to all those within that polity who would promote or resist its alteration. For scholars no less than for politicians, the time question is inextricably tied to political action; it affirms the value and efficacy of political engagements. The normative commitments implicit in the question are, first, to political conflict as a vital human activity and then to the potential that these conflicts have for bringing about durable changes in governing.

What time it is in politics shares much with other practical questions that political scientists have posed: Who governs? Who gets what? How does the ruling class rule? Posing a different question does not mean that the others are unimportant or that a research program organized around the developmental property of politics can afford to be indifferent to them, but APD's focus sets it apart. It conveys skepticism that answers to any important question about politics will hold true apart from the considerations of the moment at hand, and it turns the historical contingency inherent in all answers into a premier feature of political analysis. Giving pride of place to situational over more generic considerations, it marks each moment with a set of alternatives and incorporates change more readily into the assessment of politics itself. Put another way, by anticipating change, the time question attributes to political activity something more than a demonstration of how a given system works or perpetuates itself; it casts politics as an activity concerned with creating something new, with reconstructing existing governing arrangements in some significant respect.

Throughout this book, we have argued that although a research program directed to issues of political development calls for extensive knowledge of the past, it does not aim at knowledge of the past. The aim is to understand the way politics moves, to highlight the tensions, ingrained and accumulated, that leave it at all moments unsettled, and to reckon with the scope and limits of its transformations. These ambitions tie APD's practical political commitments to the analytic issues that have preoccupied us and driven our search for new tools and concepts. In proposing the use of a matrix to array political elements of different origin in relation to one another, we have offered a way of telling time politically. Prior solutions to developmental challenges are of interest on such a chart not just for what they say about how such junctures have been negotiated in the past, but for what they tell us about problems left outstanding for political resolution and about the effects of prior solutions on subsequent negotiations. It will be seen that all of APD's analytic procedures – finding and sorting through patterns; specifying disjunctions and continuities; comparing divergent results; locating voters, protesters, policy makers and other actors as they connect to institutions on sites – work to the same end.

On this point, the post-Civil War scholars who founded the discipline of political science had especially keen instincts. They sensed that political developments in their own day were complicating the time question, that the political problem of figuring out "where we are and whither we are tending" was becoming more difficult and pressing as government itself became more open to change, that a science of politics could provide no more useful service than to make accounts of time in politics more precise and reliable. Woodrow Wilson's observation that "government does now whatever experience permits or times allow" spoke both to what political development had accomplished – the elimination of traditional impediments to change – and to a rising tide of political possibilities.

The crucial difference between government past and present is not, as some politicians today charge, that there is more of it now than before. It is, as Wilson understood, that government is less cleanly compartmentalized and fixed in its purposes. The resistance of the antebellum South to federal authority did not make for less government in that region than before slavery was abolished; what abolition did do, however, was vastly expand the range of governing alternatives. Wilson saw that as traditional constraints are dislodged, more of government becomes susceptible to shift as, in this example, abolition catalyzed contests to shift authority from the state to the federal level and from the courts to the Congress. When governing institutions and governmental purposes were divided more authoritatively into separate spheres, there was less need to ask where things stood or how they might be changed; knowledge of time in politics becomes more pertinent, more exigent, as governing arrangements become more malleable and contestable. In this sense, APD's interests are anything but antiquarian; telling time politically, whether at a practical or analytic level, is an eminently contemporary interest.

The hypothesis about historical direction we have proposed, in which all governing institutions increasingly operate as positive lawmaking bodies, draws on and strengthens this intuition. In addition to loosening prescriptive restraints, the proliferation of lawmaking bodies implies that government has more moving parts, each of which is, as a consequence, less secure in its authority and more vulnerable to the purposes of others. Two implications that might be drawn from this hypothesis speak to aspects of contemporary politics that otherwise appear paradoxical. One is gridlock. Extending the logic of our argument, the contemporary syndrome of gridlock in government may be tied to developments that have left fewer functions of governance anchored in separate spheres. Such an assessment, should it hold up, would reflect the fact that authorities unhinged from traditional moorings are more likely to collide and that contests among them will be less easily resolved. It would testify as well to the durability of the fully legislative polity as a political development.

Another aspect of contemporary affairs ripe for investigation by our hypothesis about direction is the apparent acceleration in the pace at which developmental issues are presented as matters for decision. By our account, there is no surprise here either: to the extent that governance is understood as just so many moveable parts, it is expected that the arrangements of authority comprising it will be called into question more routinely. Indeed, this would appear a trend without discernable end. Consider in this regard the "developed" nations of the world today and the intercurrent effects of accelerating change that envelope them. Developmental issues are well recognized and all about us: in the United States, how will a century spent developing a more extensive federal presence affect a return of authority to the separate states, how will the development of the candidate-centered campaign affect the return of strong party government, how will displacement of prescriptive by positive lawmaking affect the legitimacy of the American courts? Looking elsewhere, and very much in the news: how far will the nation states of Europe go in relinquishing their authority to a new federal union, and nations generally to world of international courts and trade authorities?

If thinking about politics developmentally is an even stronger imperative for us today than for our predecessors, the thinking itself is quite different. Wilson's generation, looked to history to determine how the developmental issues of their time "should" be resolved and how to keep American government on the "right" track;

contemporary researchers who look to the past for instruction abjure the idea of inexorable trends and elevate the importance of political action in determining the course of history. With the collapse of teleological conceptions of history, the primacy of politics is accentuated. Even setting aside inexhorability: when single underlying causes – "reason," relations of production, technological innovation, the dissemination of information – are given prominence, as they were in traditional studies of political development, human agency is correspondingly subordinated.[37] As we have described it in this book, political development also shows a relationship between historical cause and human agency. But to the extent that government operates through multiple orderings of authority and arrays contrary patterns at every juncture, political development is likely to feature many and dispersed causes. To complete the circle, it remains only to note how dispersed causes of political development draw out the role of agents in politics, reinstating a normative dimension, now in the value of human action itself and its particular role in causing politics to develop.

This connection is implicit in our description of the historical construction of politics, a process that, as we have seen, brings the present constitution of authority into view as an array of old and new elements. Institutionally situated actors, inside and outside the government, are the principal motivators of these constructions, and the historical character of the constructions themselves militates against any single principal controlling the actions of all the others. The separate origins in history of authorities that come to operate simultaneously, the incomplete displacements of authority, the layering of authorities over one another, the asymmetric organization of authority overall, the mutually impinging operation of authorities, the rarefied formulas conjured for managing the whole – all provides a distinctly full-bodied answer to the time question. At the level of agency, the polity is filled with institutions, whose officers hold historically derived mandates for action, and with persons affected by the exercise of that authority, who may occasionally call it to account. In this construction, political actors matter most as agents, not causes. Their activities do not by themselves determine the course of political development, but they reverberate with greater or lesser effect throughout the whole to make political development, durable shifts in authority, possible. So far as political development is concerned, agency is first of all a matter of breaking things apart.

The leverage gained on the question, what is politics? is, we think, considerable, not just for APD but for political science. Political actors, as a category, seek to shift authority or to resist its shift, to alter or defend some part of the current historical formation: they define themselves and others as conservative, liberal, or radical on this score and they try, with the means at their command, to realign authority to their ends. Political institutions clash on this same field; they respond with their own purposes to changes and challenges from others in their domain. Development produces new meanings and incentives that construct the politics that follow.

There should be nothing surprising in this depiction. Our point is that this is the workaday world of politics. Perhaps the strongest argument to be made on behalf of a developmental approach is that among the alternatives, it provides the most direct and complete access to this world, now seen to be animated at every point by the question of its own reconstruction. Political science is famous among disciplines for reaching outside itself to theorize about its subject matter – to psychology, sociology, economics, ecology, biology, geology. The knowledge provided by such theories will, however, always be subject to a "yes, but" response, for stepping outside the political world for basic ideas about time and place cannot but muddy the reentry. By specifying the time question in terms of existing arrangements of authority, a developmental approach exposes "politics" as it presents itself, in intricate relationships of control and resistance, perception and action, structure and possibility. The partial breakthroughs and rearrangements of the organization of authority, which can only be observed over time, are at once the wellsprings and the epitome of politics.

Arguably, the conceptual distance between the historical construction of politics, where we began this book, and action in the setting of political time is not very great. What we have offered is a research agenda, a proposal for a field, a prologue to theory building. By not straying far from our point of departure, we have been able to dwell on those aspects of our subject that we think are irreducible. Sites, authority, institutions, intercurrence, development, agency do not simply apply to politics, they are politics, and they reveal the meaning of this uniquely human activity. APD cannot do better, in our view, than to dwell on them.

Notes

One. The Historical Construction of Politics

1. See, for example, William Leuchtenberg, "The Pertinence of Political History: Reflections on the Significance of the State in America," *Journal of American History* 73(3), 1986, 585–600.
2. By canonic works that turned the study of APD in new directions, we have in mind, on liberal culture, Samuel P. Huntington, *American Politics: The Promise of Disharmony* (Cambridge, Mass.: Belknap Press, 1981), and Anne Norton, *Alternative Americas: A Reading of Antebellum Political Culture* (Chicago: University of Chicago Press, 1986); on political economy, Richard Franklin Bensel, *Sectionalism and American Political Development, 1880–1980* (Madison, Wis.: University of Wisconsin Press, 1984); on state building, Stephen Skowronek, *Building a New American State: The Expansion of National Administrative Capacities, 1877–1920* (New York: Cambridge University Press, 1982); and on welfare, Theda Skocpol, *Protecting Soldiers and Mothers: The Political Origins of Social Policy in the United States* (Cambridge, Mass.: Belknap Press, 1992). For a more general discussion see James G. March and Johan P. Olsen, *Rediscovering Institutions: The Organizational Basis of Politics* (New York: Free Press, 1989).
3. Ira Katznelson, "Structure and Configuration in Comparartive Poltics," in *Comparative Politics: Rationality, Culture, and Stuctrure*, ed. Mark Irving Lichbach and Alan Zuckerman (New York: Cambridge University Press, 1997).
4. Walter Dean Burnham, "Pattern Recognition and Doing Political History: Art, Science or Bootless Enterprise," in *The Dynamics of American Politics: Approaches and Interpretations*, ed. Lawrence Dodd and Calvin Jillson (Boulder, Colo.: Westview, 1994), 59–62.
5. In these ways, APD demarcates positions of its own with regard to issues of "historicism" and "presentism." APD may be considered a historicist project in that it understands politics as a historical construct; it seeks meaning in the way political authority in a particular place – America – was arranged in the past and in the sequence through which these

arrangements were changed over time. But APD scholars also eschew certain radical historicist positions. They do not, for instance, seek to understand politics in the past solely in terms of the way the people at the time understood it. Moreover, APD researchers, especially contemporary researchers, consider the "construction" of politics an active and positive undertaking, meaning that they are wary of the historicist tendency to elevate inexorable historical processes over human volition in the analysis of change. APD may also be considered a presentist project in that it looks to history to gain a better understanding of politics today, of where things now stand and how we came to be where we are. This presentist orientation counters historicism in that it stresses our present-day connections to politics in the past rather than the foreignness of politics in the past. At the same time, however, APD hews a historicist line against certain presentist fallacies, like the notion that people in the past shared our assumptions and our standards of action and that these can be applied indiscriminately to the politics of other eras.

6. Walter Dean Burnham, *Critical Elections and the Mainsprings of American Politics* (New York: Norton, 1970).

7. Nelson Polsby, "The Institutionalization of the House of Representatives," *American Political Science Review* 62, 1968, 144–68.

8. Louis Hartz, *The Liberal Tradition in America* (New York: Harcourt Brace, 1955); J. David Greenstone, "Political Culture and Political Development," in *Studies in American Political Development*, 1, 1986 (New Haven, Conn.: Yale University Press).

9. Skowronek, *Building A New American State.*

10. Bruce A. Ackerman, *We the People* (Cambridge, Mass.: Belknap Press, 1991).

11. Stephen Skowronek, *The Politics Presidents Make: Leadership from John Adams to Bill Clinton* (Cambridge, Mass.: The Belknap Press, 1997).

12. James A. Morone, *The Democratic Wish: Popular Participation and the Limits of American Government* (New Haven, Conn.: Yale University Press, 1998); Huntington, *American Politics: The Promise of Disharmony.*

13. Rogers M. Smith, *Civic Ideals: Conflicting Visions of Citizenship in U.S. History* (New Haven, Conn.: Yale University Press, 1997).

14. Elizabeth Sanders, "Industrial Concentration, Sectional Competition, and Antitrust Politics in America, 1880–1980," in *Studies in American Political Development* 1, 1986 (New Haven, Conn.: Yale University Press), 142–214.

15. Scott C. James, *Presidents, Parties, and the State: A Party System Perspective on Democratic Regulatory Choice, 1884–1936* (Cambridge/New York: Cambridge University Press, 2000).

16. See Norbert Elias, *Time: An Essay* (Cambridge, UK: Basil Blackwell, 1992); see p. 10 and *passim.*

17. Skowronek, *The Politics Presidents Make.*

18. Christopher McGrory Klyza, *Who Controls Public Lands?: Mining, Forestry, and Grazing Policies, 1870–1990* (Chapel Hill: University of North Carolina Press, 1996).

19. Richard Bensel, *Sectionalism and American Political Development;* Elizabeth Sanders, *Roots of Reform: Farmers, Workers, and the American State, 1877–1917* (Chicago: University of Chicago Press, 1999); Ira Katznelson, Kim Geiger, and Daniel Kryder, "Limiting Liberalism: The Southern Veto in Congress," *Political Science Quarterly* 108, 1993, 283–306.

20. Peter Trubowitz's work on sectionalism and the development of American foreign policy provides an excellent example of this sort of historical construction. See *Defending the National Interest: Conflict and Change in American Foreign Policy* (Chicago: University of Chicago Press, 1998).

21. Karen Orren and Stephen Skowronek, "Beyond the Iconography of Order: Notes for a 'New' Institutionalism," in *The Dynamics of American Politics*, ed. L. C. Dodd and C. Jillson (Boulder, Colo.: Westview, 1993), 311–32.

22. The realignment synthesis is described in Chapter Two. For a recent exchange on the value of synthesis versus disaggregation, see Richard L. McCormick, "Walter Dean Burnham and 'The System of 1896,'" *Social Science History* 10, 1986, 245–63, and Walter Dean Burnham, "Periodization Schemes and Party Systems: 'The System of 1896' as a Case in Point," *Social Science History* 10, 1986, 264–75. For a more general discussion see Karen Orren and Stephen Skowronek, "Institutions and Intercurrence: Theory Building in the Fullness of Time," in *Nomos XXXVIII* (New York: New York University Press, 1993), 87–111; David R. Mayhew, *Electoral Realignments: A Critique of an American Genre* (New Haven, Conn.: Yale University Press, 2002).

23. John Gerring, *Party Ideologies in America: 1828–1996* (New York: Cambridge University Press, 1998).

24. Eileen McDonagh, "The 'Welfare Rights State' and the 'Civil Rights State': Policy Paradox and State Building in the Progressive Era," *Studies in American Political Development* 7, 1993, 225–74.

25. Louis Hartz, *The Liberal Tradition in America*.

26. Louis Galambos, "The Emerging Organizational Synthesis in Modern American History," *Business History Review* 44, 1970, 279–90; Brian Balogh, "Reorganizing the Organizational Synthesis: Federal-Professional Relations in Modern America," *Studies in American Political Development* 5(1), 1991, 119–72.

27. Walter Dean Burnham, *Critical Elections*.

28. Morris Fiorina, *Congress, Keystone of the Washington Establishment* (New Haven, Conn.: Yale University Press, 1977).

29. Keith Whittington, *Constitutional Construction: Divided Powers and Constitutional Meaning* (Cambridge, Mass.: Havard University Press, 1999); Stephen Griffen, *American Constitutionalism: From Theory to Politics* (Princeton, N.J.: Princeton University Press, 1996); Bruce Ackerman,

We the People: Foundations (Cambridge, Mass.: Harvard University Press, 1991); Louis Fisher, *Constitutional Dialogues: Interpretation as a Political Process* (Princeton, N.J.: Princeton University Press, 1988); Kevin McMahon, *Reconsidering Roosevelt on Race: How the Presidency Paved the Road to Brown* (Chicago: University of Chicago Press, 2004).

30. Jacob Hacker, *The Divided Welfare State: The Battle over Public and Private Social Benefits in the United States* (New York: Cambridge University Press, 2002).

31. Paul Pierson, *Dismantling the Welfare State?: Reagan, Thatcher, and the Politics of Retrenchment* (Cambridge/New York: Cambridge University Press, 1994); Paul Pierson, "Increasing Returns, Path Dependence, and the Study of Politics," *American Political Science Review* 94(2), 2000, 251–67.

32. Orren and Skowronek, "Beyond the Iconography of Order"; Orren and Skowronek, "Institutions and Intercurrence." These issues are addressed in more detail in Chapter Three of this book.

33. A good example is Daniel Carpenter, *The Forging of Bureaucratic Autonomy: Reputations, Networks, and Policy Innovation in Executive Agencies, 1862–1928* (Princeton, N.J.: Princeton University Press, 2001).

34. Examples of these effects can be found in Marie Gottschalk, *The Shadow Welfare State: Labor Relations and the Politics of Health Care in the United States* (Ithaca, N.Y.: Cornell University Press, 2000); Margaret Weir, *Politics and Jobs: The Boundaries of Employment Policy in the United States* (Princeton, N.J.: Princeton University Press, 1992). For a more general discussion see Elizabeth Clemens and James Cook, "Politics and Institutionalism: Explaining Durability and Change," *Annual Review of Sociology* 25, 1999, 441–466; Sidney Tarrow, *Power in Movement* (New York: Cambridge University Press, 1994).

35. Orren and Skowronek, "Beyond the Iconography of Order."

36. A similar contrast is drawn by William Robert Clark, "Agents and Structures: Two Views of Preferences, Two Views of Institutions," *International Studies Quarterly* 42(2), 1998, 245–70.

37. Peter B. Evans, Dietrich Rueschemeyer, and Theda Skocpol, eds., *Bringing the State Back In* (New York: Cambridge University Press, 1985).

38. Martin Shefter, "Regional Receptivity to Reform in the United States," *Political Science Quarterly* 98, 1983, 459–83.

39. Elizabeth Sanders, *Roots of Reform;* David Sarasohn, *The Party of Reform: Democrats in the Progressive Era* (Jackson: University Press of Mississippi, 1989).

40. See the discussion of Paul Ricoeur in *Time and Narrative*, Volume 1 (Chicago: University of Chicago, 1984), 182–92. Ricoeur attributes to Weber the remark that historians both resemble criminologists and differ from them: "By investigating guilt they also investigate causality, although to causal imputation they add ethical imputation," p. 184.

41. Richard R. John, *Spreading the News: The American Postal System from Franklin to Morse* (Cambridge, Mass.: Harvard University Press, 1995); S. Kernell and M. P. McDonald, "Congress and America's Political Development: The Transformation of the Post Office from Patronage to Service," *American Journal of Political Science* 43 (3), 1999, 103–112; Samuel Kernell, "Rural Free Delivery as a Critical Test of Alternative Models of American Political Development," *Studies in American Political Development* 15 (1), 2001, 103–112; Richard Kielbowicz, "Government Goes into Business: Parcel Post in the Nation's Political Economy, 1880–1915," *Studies in American Political Development* 8 (1), 1994, 150–72; Jean Schroedel and Bruce Snyder, "People's Banking: The Promise Betrayed," *Studies in American Political Development* 8 (1), 1994, 173–193; Elizabeth Sanders, *Roots of Reform*; Daniel Carpenter, *The Forging of Bureaucratic Autonomy*.

42. See, for example, Jean-François Lyotard, *The Post-Modern Condition: A Report on Knowledge*, Geoff Bennington and Brian Massumi translators (Minneapolis: University of Minnesota Press, 1979); Catherine Kohler Riessman, *Narrative Analysis* (Newbury Park, Calif.: Sage, 1993).

43. Examples may be traced back to Tocqueville. Just a few of the many contemporary political theorists who continue to forge these bonds are Clyde W. Barrow, *Universities and the Capitalist State: Corporate Liberalism and the Reconstruction of American Higher Education, 1894–1928* (Madison, Wis.: University of Wisconsin Press, 1990); James W. Ceaser, *Presidential Selection* (Princeton, N.J.: Princeton University Press, 1979); Eldon J. Eisenach, *The Lost Promise of Progressivism, American Political Thought* (Lawrence, Kans.: University Press of Kansas, 1994); David F. Ericson, *The Debate over Slavery: Antislavery and Proslavery Liberalism in Antebellum America* (New York: New York University Press, 2000); Rogan Kersh, *Dreams of a More Perfect Union* (Ithaca, N.Y.: Cornell University Press, 2001). Especially influential for their efforts to bring postmodern methods and currents of interpretation into APD are Ann Norton, *Republic of Signs: Liberal Theory and American Popular Culture* (Chicago: University of Chicago Press, 1993), and Michael Rogin, *Fathers and Children: Andrew Jackson and Subjugation of the American Indian* (New York: Random House, 1975).

44. Walter Dean Burnham, "Pattern Recognition."

Two. Unraveling the Premise: The Cultural Critique

1. One of our subjects, Charles Beard, is better known as a historian, but he was educated by political scientists and maintained close ties to that discipline. He was elected president of American Political Science Association in 1926. Among the many historians who have had profound affects on American political science, and the study of American political

development in particular, Fredrick Jackson Turner, Richard Hofstadter, Eric Foner, and Gordon Wood stand out for special mention.

2. Thomas L. Haskell, *The Emergence of Professional Social Science: The American Social Science Association and the Nineteenth-Century Crisis of Authority* (Urbana: University of Illinois Press, 1977); Dorothy Ross, "Historical Consciousness in Nineteenth Century America," *The American Historical Review* 80(4), 1984, 909–28.

3. *Ibid.* Also, Dorothy Ross, *The Origins of American Social Science, Ideas in Context* (Cambridge/New York: Cambridge University Press, 1991), 64–77. Wilfred, M. McClay, "John W. Burgess and the Search for Cohesion in American Political Thought," *Polity* 26(1), 1993, 51–73.

4. John Burgess, *Political Science and Comparative Constitutional Law* (Boston, Mass.: Ginn, 1902), 38–9.

5. John Burgess, "Political Science and History," *The American Historical Review* 2(3), 1987, 401–8.

6. John Burgess, *Political Science and Comparative Constitutional Law*, Vol. 1, 264, Vol. 2, 13 and 39.

7. John Burgess, *Political Science and Comparative Constitutional Law*, Vol. 1, 100–8.

8. John Burgess, *The Civil War and the Constitution, 1859–1865* (New York: C. Scribner's Sons, 1901), 135.

9. John Burgess, "The Ideal of the American Commonwealth," *Political Science Quarterly*, 10(3), 1895, 404–25.

10. John Burgess, *Political Science and Comparative Constitutional Law*, Vol. 1, 3–4, 44–5, 1504. Also Burgess, "The Ideal of the American Commonwealth."

11. Woodrow Wilson, *Congressional Government: A Study in American Politics* (Boston, Mass.: Houghton Mifflin Co., 1885).

12. Woodrow Wilson, *Congressional Government*, 30.

13. Terri Bimes and Stephen Skowronek, "Woodrow Wilson's Critique of Popular Leadership: Reassessing the Modern-Traditional Divide in Presidential History," *Polity* 29(1), 1996, 27–63.

14. Most notable among Wilson's other reflections is Woodrow Wilson, *The State: Elements of Historical and Practical Politics* (Boston, Mass.: D. C. Heath & Co., 1889). In its historical sweep, its Eurocentric (Teutonic) biases, and its reference to development as a natural, conservative, and evolutionary process, the book is more perfectly a parallel to Burgess's *Political Science*. But on the crucial points – its critique of the Constitution, its critique of contemporary American politics, its appeal to "the facts," its realism, and its more aggressive stance toward reform – it pulls forward the distinctive features that gave the *Congressional Government* its greater appeal and staying power.

15. Woodrow Wilson, *Congressional Government: A Study in American Politics*, p. 187.

16. This argument has been reworked several times. For a more recent version see Samuel P. Huntington, *Political Order in Changing Societies* (New Haven Conn.: Yale University Press, 1968), Chapter 2: Political Modernization: America vs. Europe.

17. Wilson, *Congressional Government: A Study in American Politics.*

18. Wilson, *The State: Elements of Historical and Practical Politics* p. 651, italics in the original.

19. A recent critique along these lines, which explicitly appeals to Wilson's insights, is Daniel Lazare, *The Frozen Republic: How the Constitution is Paralyzing Democracy* (New York: Harcourt Brace, 1996).

20. Woodrow Wilson, "A System of Political Science and Constitutional Law," *Atlantic Monthly* 67, 1891, 694–9.

21. Morton Gabriel White, *Social Thought in America, the Revolt against Formalism* (New York: Viking Press, 1949).

22. Woodrow Wilson, "Mr. Goldwin Smith's 'Views of our Political History',", *Forum* 16, 1893, 489–99; Woodrow Wilson, "The Proper Perspective of American History," *Forum* 19,1895; 544–559; Woodrow Wilson, *Division and Reunion, 1829–1889* (New York/London: Longmans Green and Co., 1894); Woodrow Wilson, *A History of the American People* (New York/London: Harper & Brothers, 1902). In examining the issues that had brought on the Civil War, for example, Wilson found two credible readings of the Constitution. The one in the South had been largely unaffected by developments that had transformed thinking in the North: "Neither change of thought nor change of political conditions in the nation at large had altered the thought of the South with regard to the character of the government; for she herself had not changed and her own thought had kept steadfastly to the first conception of the Union." Wilson, *A History of the American People*, Vol. 4, 201.

23. Henry Jones Ford, *The Rise and Growth of American Politics: A Sketch of Constitutional Development* (New York: Da Capo Press, 1967), 38–71.

24. *Ibid.*, 56, 279, 293.

25. *Ibid.*, 370.

26. The "ultimate type" is Ford's phrase, and the title of his final chapter in Ford, *The Rise and Growth of American Politics: A Sketch of Constitutional Development*

27. Woodrow Wilson, *Constitutional Government in the United States* (New York: Columbia University Press, 1908). Ford's influence on Wilson's last academic statement on the Constitution has been underscored most recently by Daniel D. Stid, *The President as Statesman: Woodrow Wilson and the Constitution, American Political Thought* (Lawrence: University Press of Kansas, 1998).

28. Charles Austin Beard, *Politics: A Lecture Delivered at Columbia University in the Series on Science, Philosophy and Art, February 12, 1908* (New York: The Columbia University Press, 1908).

29. Another of Beard's teachers at Columbia codified the selective borrowing from Marx by Progressive-era social scientists in America. See Edwin R. A. Seligman, *The Economic Interpretation of History* (London: Macmillan and company, 1902). On Seligman's influence on Beard and progressive history more generally see Richard Hofstadter, *The Progressive Historians: Turner, Beard, Parrington* (New York: Knopf, 1968), 196–200.

30. See, for example, the close of Charles Austin Beard and Mary Ritter Beard, *The Rise of American Civilization*, one-volume edition (New York: Macmillan, 1930), 800.

31. Clyde W. Barrow, "Beyond Progressivism: Charles Beard's Social Democratic Theory of American Political Development," *Studies in American Political Development* 8(2), 1994, 255. More generally, see Clyde W. Barrow and Charles Austin Beard, *More Than a Historian: The Political and Economic Thought of Charles A. Beard* (New Brunswick, N.J.: Transaction, 2000). The analysis that follows draws heavily on Barrow's work.

32. Charles Austin Beard, *The Supreme Court and the Constitution* (New York: The Macmillan Company, 1912), 94.

33. Beard, *The Supreme Court and the Constitution*, 76.

34. Beard, *An Economic Interpretation*, 151.

35. Charles Austin Beard, *Contemporary American History, 1877–1913* (New York: The MacMillan Company, 1914), 252; Beard, "Politics," 27–8; Barrow, *op cit.*

36. On Beard's concept of a "lag" in "political development" see Ernst Breisach, *American Progressive History: An Experiment in Modernization* (Chicago: University of Chicago Press, 1993), 93.

37. Charles Austin Beard, *The American Party Battle* (New York: The Macmillan Company, 1928).

38. Charles Beard, "The Historical Approach to the New Deal," *The American Political Science Review* 28, 1934, 11–15. Also see Lloyd R. Sorenson, "Charles A. Beard and German Historiographic Thought," *Mississippi Valley Historical Review* 42, June 1955–March 1956, 274–85.

39. In one particularly strident tract aimed at warding off American involvement in a new world war, Beard went so far as to reject appeals to facts or trends as these are used by elites to justify in public opinion a particular course of action. He urged instead a sharper and more candid political debate over desirable ends. "There is nothing in any known set of facts that dictates policy ... every large public policy is *an interpretation of history –* past, in the making, and to be made. A policy is a value asserted, not a proposition that can be demonstrated in itself." Charles Beard, *The Devil Theory of War: An Inquiry into the Nature of History and the Possibility of Keeping Out of War* (New York: Vanguard Press, 1936), 109–11. This critique anticipates the position examined later in this chapter of contemporary scholars examining America's lost alternatives.

40. Though we are primarily interested in the work of Louis Hartz in this section, Richard Hofstadter made equally important contributions on these

themes. See *Anti-Intellectualism in American Life* (New York: Knopf, 1963) and *The Paranoid Style of American Politics and Other Essays* (New York: Knopf, 1965). It should be noted that APD work along these lines ran parallel to the vogue of modernization theory in the study of comparative politics in which the United States often figured at least implicitly as a model of development. The cultural critique in APD scholarship at this time might be read as an important demur from the work of the modernization school. See Gabriel Almond and Sidney Verba, *The Civic Culture: Political Attitudes and Democracy in Five Nations* (Princeton, N.J: Princeton University Press, 1963), and W. W. Rostow, *The Stages of Economic Growth: An Non Communist Manifesto* (New York: Cambridge University Press, 1960).

41. Louis Hartz, *The Liberal Tradition in America* (New York: Harcourt Brace, 1955), 14.

42. *Ibid.*

43. Walter Dean Burnham, *Critical Elections and the Mainsprings of American Politics* (New York: Norton, 1970), 181.

44. *Ibid.*, 4.

45. A sampling of the influence of Burnham's scheme might include: Allen Bogue, "The New Political History in the 1970s," in *The Past Before Us: Contemporary Historical Writing in the United States*, ed. Michael Kammen (Ithaca, N.Y.: Cornell University Press, 1980). On parties, John Aldrich, *"Why Parties? The Origin and Trasnformation of Political Parties in America* (Chicago: University of Chicago Press, 1995); on the Constitution, Bruce A. Ackerman, *We the People* (Cambridge, Mass.: Belknap Press of Harvard University Press, 1991); on the presidency, Stephen Skowronek, *The Politics Presidents Make: Leadership from John Adams to Bill Clinton* (Cambridge, Mass.: The Belknap Press of Harvard University Press, 1997); on Congress, David Brady, *Critical Elections and Congressional Policy Making* (Stanford, Calif.: Stanford University Press, 1988); on cultural conflict, Samuel P. Huntington, *American Politics: The Promise of Disharmony* (Cambridge, Mass.: Belknap Press, 1981); on American political thought, Eldon Eisenach "Reconstituting American Political Thought from a Regime Change Perspective," *Studies in American Political Development* 4, 1990, 169–228; on bureaucracy, James A. Morone, *The Democratic Wish: Popular Participation and the Limits of American Government* (New Haven, Conn.: Yale University Press, 1998) and Martin Shefter, "Party, Bureaucracy, and Political Change in the United States," in *Political Parties: Development and Decay*, ed. Joseph Cooper (Beverly Hills, Calif.: Sage Publications, 1978); on public policy, Benjamin Ginsberg, "Elections and Public Policy," *American Political Science Review* 70, 1976, 41–50. On political regimes, Andrew Polsky "Why Regimes? Ideas, Incentives and Politics in American Politics Orders," *Policy*, 29(2), 1997, 625–40, and David Plotke, *Building A Democratic Political Order: Reshaping American Liberalsim in the 1930s and 1940s* (New

York: Cambridge University Press, 1996); on labor, Gwendolyn Mink, *Old Labor and New Immigrants in American Poltical Development: Union, Party and the State, 1875–1920* (Ithaca, N.Y.: Cornell University Press, 1986).

46. For a review see Richard L. McCormick, "The Realignment Synthesis in American History," *The Journal of Interdisciplinary History* 13, 1982, 85–105. See also John Gerring, *Party Ideologies in America, 1828–1996* (Cambridge/New York: Cambridge University Press, 1998); David R. Mayhew, *Electoral Realignments: A Critique of an American Genre* (New Haven, Conn.: Yale University Press, 2002); Richard L. McCormick, *The Party Period and Public Policy: American Politics from the Age of Jackson to the Progressive Era* (New York: Oxford University Press, 1986).

47. Burnham, *Critical Elections and the Mainsprings of American Politics*, 187.

48. R. M. Smith, "Beyond Tocqueville, Myrdal, and Hartz – the Multiple Traditions in America," *American Political Science Review* 87(3), 1993; E. Foner, "Why Is There No Socialism in the United-States," *History Workshop Journal* 17, 1984, 57–80.

49. Gerring, *Party Ideologies in America*.

50. It is notable that this literature has focused on the struggles to redirect the course of American politics leftward and that equal attention has not been given to right-wing alternatives. We suspect that the same sort of analysis might be applied to either.

51. Alan Brinkley, *The End of Reform: New Deal Liberalism in Recession and War* (New York: Alfred A. Knopf, 1995).

52. Eldon J. Eisenach, *The Lost Promise of Progressivism, American Political Thought* (Lawrence: University Press of Kansas, 1994).

53. Gretchen Ritter, *Goldbugs and Greenbacks: The Antimonopoly Tradition and the Politics of Finance in America* (Cambridge/New York: Cambridge University Press, 1997); Lawrence Goodwyn, *The Populist Moment: A Short History of the Agrarian Revolt in America* (New York: Oxford University Press, 1978).

54. Victoria Charlotte Hattam, *Labor Visions and State Power: The Origins of Business Unionism in the United States* (Princeton, N.J.: Princeton University Press, 1993).

55. Eric Foner, *Reconstruction: America's Unfinished Revolution, 1863–1877* (New York: Harper & Row, 1988).

56. Amy Bridges, *A City in the Republic, Ante Bellum Politics and the Origins of Machine Politics* (New York: Cambridge University Press, 1984).

57. Gordon S. Wood, *The Creation of the American Republic, 1776–1787* (New York: Norton, 1972).

58. Gerald Berk, *Alternative Tracks: The Constitution of American Industrial Order, 1865–1917* (Baltimore; Md.: Johns Hopkins University Press, 1994); also Hattam, *Labor Visions and State Power*; Ritter, *Goldbugs and Greenbacks*; and Goodwyn, *The Populist Moment*.

59. Consider in this regard the denouement of revolutionary republicanism in Gordon Wood's, *The Creation of the American Republic, 1776–1787*, 562: "In effect, [the Federalists] appropriated and exploited the language that more rightfully belonged to their opponents. The result was the beginning of a hiatus in American politics between ideology and motives that was never again closed. By using the most popular and democratic rhetoric available to explain and justify their aristocratic system, the Federalists helped to foreclose the development of an American intellectual tradition in which differing ideas of politics would be intimately and genuinely related to differing social interests." For a critique of Wood on this point see Ackerman, *We the People*, 212–21.

60. Victoria Hattam, "Economic Visions and Political Strategies: American Labor and the State 1865–1896," *Studies in American Political Development* 4, 1990, 82–129. A modified version of the argument appears in *Labor Visions and State Power: The Origins of Business Unionism in the United States*.

61. J. David Greenstone, *The Lincoln Persuasion: Remaking American Liberalism* (Princeton, N.J.: Princeton University Press, 1993); J. David Greenstone, "Political Culture and Political Development," *Studies in American Political Development* 1, 1986 (New Haven, Conn.: Yale University Press); Daniel T. Rodgers, *Contested Truths: Keywords in American Politics Since Independence* (New York: Basic Books, 1987).

62. Rogers M. Smith, *Civic Ideals: Conflicting Visions of Citizenship in U.S. History* (New Haven, Conn.: Yale University Press, 1997); see also Smith, "Beyond Tocqueville, Myrdal, and Hartz – the Multiple Traditions in America," For an interesting position between these views see Catherine A. Holland, *The Body Politic: Foundings, Citizenship, and Difference in the American Political Imagination* (New York: Routledge, 2001).

63. Though Burgess attempts trace the evolution of the liberal state, Smith is quite right to point out that he does not defend the liberal tradition as Hartz understands it.

64. J. David Greenstone, "Political Culture and Political Development," 1.

Three. The Institutional Turn: Rethinking Order and Change over Time

1. James G. March and Johan P. Olsen, *Rediscovering Institutions: The Organizational Basis of Politics* (New York: Free Press, 1989); Jack Knight, *Institutions and Social Conflict* (Cambridge/New York: Cambridge University Press, 1992); James March and Johan Olsen, "The New Institutionalism: Organizational Factors in Political Life," *American Political Science Review* 78(3), 1984, 734–49.

2. We use this term to refer to the entire group. Historical-institutionalism is but one current of the "new institutionalism," and it has applications well beyond APD. See Paul Pierson and Theda Skocpol, "Historical Institutionalism in Contemporary Political Science" in *Political Science: State*

of the Discipline, eds. Ira Katznelson and Helen V. Milner (New York: W. W. Norton & Company, 2002); also Peter A. Hall and R. C. R. Taylor, "Political Science and the Three New Institutionalisms," *Political Studies* 44 (5), 1996; also Sven Steinmo, Kathleen Ann Thelen, and Frank Longstreth, *Structuring Politics: Historical Institutionalism in Comparative Analysis* (New York: Cambridge University Press, 1992).

3. For example, Thomas Jefferson to Samuel Kercheval, July 1816, in Paul Leicester Ford, ed., *The Writings of Thomas Jefferson* (New York/London: G. P. Putnam's sons, 1892), Vol. 10, 37–45. A similar concern for how institutions may come to be perceived as part of a natural order of things may be found in Woodrow Wilson's critique of the Constitution and in Charles Beard's concern with archaic institutional forms that insinuate themselves into the life of the polity and distort the natural processes of development. For a treatment of this issue in the work of other liberal political philosophers, see Stephen Holmes, *Benjamin Constant and the Making of Modern Liberalism* (New Haven, Conn.: Yale University Press, 1984).

4. Theda Skocpol, *Protecting Soldiers and Mothers: The Political Origins of Social Policy in the United States* (Cambridge, Mass.: Belknap Press, 1992), 41–62.

5. In this we depart from those who take a more expansive view of institutions that blurs the distinction between them and stable sets of ideas or traditions. See Peter Hall and Rosemary C. R. Taylor, "Political Science and the Three New Institutionalisms."

6. For the distinction just mentioned, the institutional attribute that is most problematic among those mentioned is boundaries. The family is an institution in our meaning; however, it does not include the idiosyncrasies of individual families but only those aspects that concern families as a whole; should women, for instance, form a national wives' organization, this would fall outside the institution's boundaries.

7. Robert Higgs, *Crisis and Leviathan: Critical Episodes in the Growth of American Government* (New York: Oxford University Press, 1987), 6.

8. James Madison, "Federalist No. 10" in Hamilton, Madison, and Jay, *The Federalist with Letters of "Brutus,"* Terence Ball, ed. (New York: Cambridge University Press, 2003), 40–6.

9. Martin Van Buren, *Inquiry into the Origin and Course of Political Parties in the United States* (New York: A. M. Kelley, 1967).

10. Barry R. Weingast, "Political Stability and Civil War: Institutions, Commitment, and American Democracy," *Analytic Narratives*, ed. Robert Bates et al. (Princeton, N.J.: Princeton University Press, 1998).

11. Richard Franklin Bensel, *The Political Economy of American Industrialization, 1877–1900* (New York: Cambridge University Press, 2000).

12. Terry Moe, "Interests, Institutions, and Positive Theory: The Politics of the NLRB," in *Studies in American Political Development* 2, 1987 (New Haven, Conn:. Yale University Press), 236–302; Terry Moe, "Control and

Feedback in Economic Regulation – the Case of the NLRB," *American Political Science Review* 79(4), 1985, 1094–1116.

13. Daniel P. Carpenter, *The Forging of Bureaucratic Autonomy: Reputations, Networks, and Policy Innovation in Executive Agencies, 1862–1928* (Princeton, N.J.: Princeton University Press, 2001).

14. Weingast, "Political Stability and Civil War: Institutions, Commitment, and American Democracy," 149.

15. Bensel, *The Political Economy of American Industrialization, 1877–1900*, 16.

16. Gregory Wawro, "Minority Rights in the Senate and Property Rights in Slaves: Sectional Balance, Dilatory Tactics, and Political Stability in the Antebellum Era" (Working Paper, 2003).

17. Other studies focusing on prime movers include Morris P. Fiorina, *Congress, Keystone of the Washington Establishment* (New Haven; Conn.: Yale University Press, 1977); and Gary W. Cox and Mathew D. McCubbins, *Legislative Leviathan: Party Government in the House* (Berkeley: University of California Press, 1993).

18. On Carpenter's critique of Congress as prime mover, see Daniel P. Carpenter, "The Political Foundations of Bureaucratic Autonomy: A Response to Kernell," *Studies in American Political Development* 15(1), 2001, 113–122; Samuel Kernell, "Rural Free Delivery as a Critical Test of Alternative Models of American Political Development," *Studies in American Political Development* 15(1), 2001, 103–112.

19. Carpenter, *The Forging of Bureaucratic Autonomy: Reputations, Networks, and Policy Innovation in Executive Agencies, 1862–1928*, 19.

20. Terry Moe, "Interests, Institutions, and Positive Theory: The Politics of the NLRB," 298.

21. Stephen Skowronek, *Building a New American State: The Expansion of National Administrative Capacities, 1877–1920* (New York: Cambridge University Press, 1982).

22. On the political significance of early American bureaucracy see Richard R. John, *Spreading the News: The American Postal System from Franklin to Morse* (Cambridge, Mass.: Harvard University Press, 1995); also Matthew A. Crenson, *The Federal Machine: Beginnings of Bureaucracy in Jacksonian America* (Baltimore, Md.: Johns Hopkins University Press, 1975) and William Edward Nelson, *The Roots of American Bureaucracy, 1830–1900* (Cambridge, Mass.: Harvard University Press, 1982).

23. Theda Skocpol, *Protecting Soldiers and Mothers: The Political Origins of Social Policy in the United States.*

24. Theda Skopcol, "Against Evolution: Social Policies and American Political Development," *Studies in American Political Development* 8(2), 1994, 140–9.

25. The subordination of women in later New Deal welfare provision is elaborated by Suzanne Mettler, *Dividing Citizens: Gender and Federalism in New Deal Public Policy* (Ithaca, N.Y.: Cornell University Press, 1998).

26. Robert Lieberman, *Shifting the Color Line: Race and the American Welfare State* (Cambridge, Mass.: Harvard University Press, 1998).

27. As Lieberman puts it, "Institutionally national policies were possible only when they could be restricted to a narrowly designed target population that was predominately white. More inclusive programs with the potential to bridge the racial divide were possible only when they could be made less national." *Shifting*, 38.

28. Jacob Hacker, "The Historical Logic of National Health Insurance: Structure and Sequence in the Development of British, Canadian, and U.S. Medical Policy," *Studies in American Political Development* 12 (1), 1998, 57–130.

29. On this point see also Marie Gottschalk, *The Shadow Welfare State: Labor, Business, and the Politics of Health Care in the United States* (Ithaca, N.Y.: ILR Press, 2000).

30. On this point see also Jacob Hacker, *The Road to Nowhere: The Genesis of President Clinton's Plan for Health Security* (Princeton, N.J.: Princeton University Press, 1997); Theda Skocpol, *Boomerang: Health Care Reform and the Turn against Government* (New York: W. W. Norton & Co., 1997).

31. Ira Katznelson, "Structure and Configuration in Comparative Politics," in *Comparative Politics: Rationality, Culture, and Structure*, ed. Mark Irving Lichbach and Alan Zuckerman (New York: Cambridge University Press, 1997); Paul Pierson and Theda Skocpol, "Historical Institutionalism in Contemporary Political Science"; Paul Pierson, "Increasing Returns, Path Dependence, and the Study of Politics," *American Political Science Review* 94(2), 2000, 251–267. Paul Pierson, "Not Just What, but When: Timing and Sequence in Political Processes," *Studies in American Political Development* 14(1), 2000, 72–92.

32. E. E. Schattschneider, *Politics, Pressures and the Tariff* (New York: Prentice Hall, 1935), p. 288; Theodore Lowi, "American Business, Public Policy, Case Studies and Political Theory," *World Politics* 16(4), 1964, 677–715.

33. Paul Pierson, "Not Just What but When: Timing and Sequence in Political Processes," *Studies in American Political Development* 14(1), 2000, 72.

34. This point is made by Elisabeth Stephanie Clemens in *The People's Lobby: Organizational Innovation and the Rise of Interest Group Politics in the United States, 1890–1925* (Chicago: University of Chicago Press, 1997).

35. John Mark Hansen, *Gaining Access: Congress and the Farm Lobby, 1919–1981* (Chicago: University of Chicago Press, 1991); Clemens, *The People's Lobby: Organizational Innovation and the Rise of Interest Group Politics in the United States, 1890–1925*; Ruth Ann O'Brien, *Workers' Paradox: The Republican Origins of New Deal Labor Policy, 1886–1935* (Chapel Hill, N.C.: The University of North Carolina Press, 1998); Anna L. Harvey, *Votes without Leverage: Women in American Electoral Politics, 1920–1970* (New York: Cambridge University Press, 1998).

36. Howard, *The Hidden Welfare State: Tax Expenditures and Social Policy in the United States* (Princeton: Princeton University Press, 1997); Howard, "Protean Lure for the Working Poor: Party Competition and the Earned Income Tax Credit" *Studies in American Development*, 9 (2) Fall 1995, 404–436; Pierson, "When Effect Becomes Cause: Policy Feedback and Political Change."

37. Jeffrey Tulis, *The Rhetorical Presidency* (Princeton, N.J.: Princeton University Press, 1987).

38. Louis Fisher, *Presidential War Power* (Lawrence: University Press of Kansas, 1995); Theodore Lowi, *The Personal President* (Ithaca, N.Y.: Cornell University Press, 1985); Tulis, *The Rhetorical Presidency*.

39. Andrew Polsky, "The Odyssey of the Juvenile Court: Policy Failure and Institutional Persistence in the Therapeutic State," *Studies in American Political Development* 3, 1989, 157–198; Andrew Polsky, *The Rise of the Therapeutic State* (Princeton, N.J.: Princeton University Press, 1991).

40. Kenneth Finegold and Theda Skocpol, *State and Party in America's New Deal* (Madison: University of Wisconsin Press, 1995).

41. Karen Orren, *Belated Feudalism: Labor, the Law, and Liberal Development in the United States* (New York: Cambridge University Press, 1991).

42. Eric Schickler, *Disjointed Pluralism: Institutional Innovation and the Development of the U.S. Congress* (Princeton: Princeton University Press, 2001), 267; see also William Riker, "The Experience of Creating Constitutions: The Framing of the United States Constitution," in *Explaining Social Institutions*, ed. Jack Knight and Itai Sened (Ann Arbor: University of Michigan Press, 1995), 121; Robert Lieberman appropriates the notion in studying the relationship between ideas and institutions in "Ideas, Institutions and Political Order: Explaining Political Change," *American Political Science Review* 96(4), 2002, 697–712.

43. Karen Orren and Stephen Skowronek, "Beyond the Iconography of Order: Notes for a 'New' Institutionalism," in *The Dynamics of American Politics*, ed. L. C. Dodd and C. Jillson (Boulder, Colo.: Westview, 1994); Karen Orren and Stephen Skowronek, "Institutions and Intercurrence: Theory Building in the Fullness of Time," *Nomos* 38, 1996; Karen Orren and Stephen Skowronek, "In Search of Political Development," in *The Liberal Tradition in America: Reassessing the Legacy of American Liberalism*, eds., David Ericson and Lousia Bertch Green (New York: Routledge, 1999); Karen Orren and Stephen Skowronek, "Regimes and Regime Building in American Government: A Review of Literature on the 1940s," *Political Science Quarterly* 113(4), 1998, 689–702.

44. In addition to *Belated Feudalism* reviewed above, this issue is addressed in a comparison of different countries over several centuries in Karen Orren, "Constitutional Development in the United States and Argentina," in *Multiple Modernities: Comparative Perspectives on the Americas*, eds. Luis Roniger and Carlos Waisman (Brighton: Sussex Academic Press, 2002).

45. Of course, disruptions more totalitarian in their sweep than the American Revolution have occurred in world history, but even in the more extreme cases, Nazi Germany for instance, there is research to support our strong historical intuition that some governing arrangements carry over and that politics remains, to that extent, intercurrent. For one treatment closely aligned with the idea of intercurrence, see Kathy Thelen, "Institutions and Social Change: The Evolution of Vocational Training in Germany," forthcoming, in Stephen Skowronek, Ian Shapiro, and Daniel Galvin, eds., *Crafting and Operating Institutions* (Cambridge University Press, forthcoming).

46. See Adam Sheingate, "Political Entrepreneurs, Institutional Change and American Political Development," *Studies in American Political Development* 17(2), 2003.

47. Orren and Skowronek, "Institutions and Intercurrence: Theory Building in the Fullness of Time."

48. Douglass North, *Institutions, Institutional Change, and Economic Performance* (Cambridge/New York: Cambridge University Press, 1990), 95.

49. Orren and Skowronek, "Regimes and Regime Building in American Government: A Review of Literature on the 1940s."

Four. Political Development: The Definition

1. Martin J. Sklar, *The Corporate Reconstruction of American Capitalism, 1890–1916: The Market, the Law, and Politics* (New York: Cambridge University Press, 1987); Scott C. James, *Presidents, Parties, and the State: A Party System Perspective on Democratic Regulatory Choice, 1884–1936* (New York: Cambridge University Press, 2000); Elizabeth Sanders, *Roots of Reform: Farmers, Workers, and the American State, 1877–1917, American Politics and Political Economy* (Chicago: University of Chicago Press, 1999).

2. Robert C. Lieberman, *Shifting the Color Line: Race and the American Welfare State* (Cambridge, Mass.: Harvard University Press, 1998).

3. Christopher Howard, *The Hidden Welfare State: Tax Expenditure and Social Policy in the United States* (Princeton, N.J.: Princeton University Press, 1997).

4. Louis Fisher, *Presidential War Power* (Lawrence: University Press of Kansas, 1995).

5. On the conflicts among government authorities that surrounded virtually every step taken by James I and Charles I, not only at the point of Parliament's rebellion against Charles, but more widely and before, and in contrast in this regard with previous reigns, see F. W. Maitland, *The Constitutional History of England* (Cambridge: The University Press, 1950). See, for instance, 258–71 and 307–9 on the laying of imposts and on finance; 268–71, on the administration of criminal law; and 278–80, on disposal of the army.

6. Alexis de Tocqueville, *Democracy in America, Vol. 1* (New York: Vintage, 1945), 258.
7. For instance, here are the first sentences of three successive paragraphs from a chapter entitled "The Reconstruction of the North" in Eric Foner, *Reconstruction 1864–1877: America's Unfinished Revolution*, 471–2. (1) "Partly because of Congressional measures that applied throughout the country, and partly due to actions at the state and local level, the decade following the Civil War witnessed astonishing advances in the political, civil, and social rights of Northern blacks." (2) "Despite the rapid toppling of traditional racial barriers, the North's racial Reconstruction proved in many respects less far-reaching than the South's." (3) "Nonetheless, blacks now found the North's public life open to them in ways inconceivable before the war." Also see the controversy surrounding the 1876 presidential elections.
8. William M. Wiecek, *The Sources of Antislavery Constitutionalism in America, 1760–1848* (Ithaca, N.Y.: Cornell University Press, 1977).
9. John C. Calhoun, *A Disquisition on Government: and Selections from the Discourse*, ed. C. Gordon Post (New York: Liberal Arts Press, 1953).
10. James Kent, *Commentaries on American Law* II (New York: W. Kent, 1844), 5th ed., no. 2, 258.
11. Ex Parte Milligan, 4 Wall. 2 (1866).
12. Test Oath Cases, 4 Wall. 277, 4 Wall 333 (1867).
13. Ex Parte McCardle, 6 Wall. 318 (1868); 7 Wall. 506 (1869). McCardle was a Georgia publisher, convicted in military court for statements harmful to the present occupation. He appealed over the ruling of the District Court under provisions provided under the Reconstruction Act of 1867.
14. The best general account remains Stanley Kutler, *Judicial Power and Reconstruction Politics* (Chicago: University of Chicago Press, 1968).
15. Foner, for instance, makes no mention of *McCardle*.
16. 7 Wall 506, at 515–16. The fullest discussion of the controversy is Charles Fairman, *The Oliver Wendell Holmes Devise History of the Supreme Court, Vol. VI, Part One: Reconstruction and Reunion, 1864–88* (New York: Macmillan, 1971), Chapter X, 433–514.
17. 16 Wall. 36 (1873).
18. Morgan J. Kousser, *The Shaping of Southern Politics: Suffrage Restriction and the Establishment of the One-party South, 1880–1910* (New Haven, Conn.: Yale University Press, 1974), 28.
19. Rogers M. Smith, "Beyond Tocqueville, Myrdal, and Hartz: The Multiple Traditions in America," *American Political Science Review* 87 (3), 549–66, especially 559 ff.
20. Smith's argument is one that seems to rest the case for development simply on the passage of time. The argument is that because black suffrage lasted a certain number of years, it constituted political development. In our

view it makes better sense both analytically and on the historical record to distinguish between political developments and changes that last a number of years. Development is a distinctive problem because it requires a durable rearrangement of authority on the site of change.

21. Alexander Keyssar, *The Right to Vote: The Contested History of Democracy in the United States* (New York: Basic Books, 2000), p. 89. See generally on the 13th Amendment's passage.

22. But see Eldon J. Eisenach, *The Next Religious Establishment: National Identity and Political Theology in Post-Protestant America* (Lanham: Rowman & Littlefield Publishers, 2000), and James Morone, *Hellfire Nation: The Politics of Sin in American History* (New Haven, Yale Conn.: University Press, 2003).

23. For concise treatments of religion in the American colonies, voluntarism, and American religion generally see Sidney E. Mead, *The Lively Experiment: The Shaping of Christianity in America* (New York: Harper & Row, 1976).

24. On revivals and social reform see William G. McLoughlin, *Revivals, Awakenings, and Reform* (Chicago: University of Chicago Press, 1978.)

25. Donald M. Scott, *From Office to Profession* (Philadelphia: University of Pennsylvania Press, 1978), Chapter 2, 18–35.

26. James W. Ceaser, *Presidential Selection, Theory and Development* (Princeton, N.J.: Princeton University Press, 1979).

27. An indispensable study of the lesser known elements of this potpourri is Allen Bloom, *The American Religion: The Emergence of the Post-Christian nation* (New York: Simon & Schuster, 1992).

28. On civil service exemptions, see Richard F. Hamm, *Shaping the 18th Amendment: Temperance Reform, Legal Culture, and the Polity, 1880–1920* (Chapel Hill: University of North Carolina Press, 1995), 254.

29. See John Witte Jr., *Religion and the American Constitutional Experiment, Essential Rights and Liberties* (Boulder, Colo.: Westview, 2000), Appendix 3.

30. *Cantwell v. Connecticut*, 310 U.S. 396.

31. *Terrett v. Taylor*, 13 U.S. 43; *Goesele v. Bimeler*, 55 U.S. 589 and *Baker v. Nachtrieb*, 60 U.S. 126; *Bouldin v. Alexander*, 82 U.S. 131.

32. *Cummings v. Missouri*, 71 U.S. 277; *Bradford v. Roberts*, 175 U.S. 291; *Quick Bear v Leupp*, 210 U.S. 50; *Pierce v. Society of Sisters*, 268 U.S. 510.

33. *Jones v. Opelika*, 319 U.S. 103; *West Virginia State Board of Education v. Barnette*, 319 U.S. 624; *Prince v. Massachusetts*, 321 U.S. 158.

34. Selective Draft Law Cases, 245 U.S. 366.

35. *Reynolds v. United States*, 98 U.S. 145 (1879); *Murphy v. Ramsey*, 114 U.S (1885). 15; *Davis v. Beason*, 133 U.S. 337 (1890); Church of Jesus Christ of Latter Day Saints v. U.S., 136 U.S. 1 (1890).

36. The quote is from Church of the Holy Trinity v. United States, 143 U.S. 457 (1892), at 470–1.
37. *Engle v. Vitale*, 370 U.S. 421 (school prayer); and Abington School *District v. Schempp*, 374 U.S. 203 (1963) (Bible reading.).
38. See John C. Jeffries, Jr. and James E. Ryan, "A Political History of the Establishment Clause," *Michigan Law Review* 100, 279–369 (2001), p. 305, note 129, and 306.
39. Lucas A. Powe, *The Warren Court and American Politics* (Cambridge Mass.: Belknap Press, 2000), p. 187. The suggestion was by Democratic Senator Sam Ervin of South Carolina. See Robert Alley, *School Prayer: The Court, the Congress, and the First Amendment* (Buffalo, N.T.: Prometheus Books, 1994), p. 110.
40. *Griswold v. Connecticut*, 381 U.S. 479; *Friedman v. Maryland*, 380 U.S. 51; *Epperson v. Arkansas*, 393 U.S. 97; *Roe v. Wade*, 410 U.S. 113; *Jones v. Wolf*, 443 U.S. 595; *Wallace v. Jaffree*, 472 U.S. 38; *Lee v. Weissman*, 505 U.S. 577.
41. *U.S. v. Carolene Products*, 304 U.S. 144 (1938), note 4. See discussion in Powe, *The Warren Court and American Politics*, 487.
42. *Everson v. Board of Education*, 330 U.S. 855 (1947). As late as 1961, the court had upheld Sunday closing laws (*McGowan v. Maryland*, 366 U.S. 420 and attached cases.) During the same session it unanimously struck down a 185-year-old Maryland law requiring all public officers to affirm a belief in God (*Torcaso v. Watkins*, 367 U.S. 488); this decision apparently surprised no one.
43. The racial underpinnings of support for Goldwater in 1964 is the thesis of Edward G. Carmines and James A. Stimson, *Issue Evolution: Race and the Transformation of American Politics* (Princeton, N.J.: Princeton University Press, 1989).
44. See James L. Guth, "Southern Baptist Clergy: Vanguard of the Christian Right?," in Robert C. Liebman and Robert Wuthnow, *The New Christian Right* (Hawthorn, N.Y.: Aldine, 1983), 121.
45. U. S. Congress, *Investigation on illegal or improper activities in connection with the 1996 federal election campaign: Hearings before the Committee on Governmental Affairs*, United States Senate, 105th Congress, 1st Session, 1998, Chapter 10, 11. This figure is over three times the total contributions to all tax exempt organizations reported for the 1996 election cycle by the Democratic National Committee. *Ibid.* On party change, see John H. Aldrich, *Why Parties? The Origin and Transformation of Party Politics in America* (Chicago: University of Chicago Press, 1995), 254 ff.
46. *Chicago Sun-Times*, November 29, 2002.
47. This realignment is the subject of Geoffrey Layman, *The Great Divide: Religion and Cultural Conflict in American Party Politics* (New York: Columbia University Press, 2001).
48. In 1998 the vote to recommit was 201–23 Republicans against; 22–170 Democrats in favor. On the amendment itself: 197–28 Republicans in

favor; 27–174 Democrats against. In 1971, by contrast, on the vote to discharge the school prayer amendment from the judiciary committee, House Republicans voted 129–33 (yeas to nays) and Democrats 113–123 (of which northern Democrats were 58–101 and southern Democrats were 55–22). The vote on the amendment itself was Republicans 138–26, Democrats 102–137 (northern Democrats 48–114, southern Democrats 54–23). The measure failed for lack of the necessary two-thirds majority. On the increasing prominence of Republicans in support after 1962 generally see John A Murley, "School Prayer" in Raymond Tatalvoch and Byron W. Daynes, *Social Regulatory Policy: Moral Controversies in American Politics* (Boulder: Colo.: Westview, 1988), 26.

49. *City of Boerne v. Flores*, 521 U.S. 507.

50. James Willard Hurst, *Law and the Conditions of Freedom in the Nineteenth Century United States* (Madison: University of Wisconsin Press, 1956), 12.

51. On the long lingering controversy in New York see Charles McCurdy, *The Anti-Rent Era in New York Law and Politics, 1839–1865* (Chapel Hill: University of North Carolina, 2001).

52. The Northwest Ordinance were passed in 1785 and 1787; Marion Clawson, *The Land System of the United States* (Lincoln: University of Nebraska:, 1968), 25–26; Leonard White, *The Federalists: A Study in Administrative History* (Westport, Conn.: Greenwood, 1948), 382.

53. As is well known uncertainties of a quite fundamental sort drove the postindependence call for constitutional revision as the newfound authority of state legislatures, and the even more radical authority claimed by the people "out of doors," raised concerns about governmental protections for property rights.

54. Everett Dick, *The Lure of the Land: A Social History of the Public Lands from the Articles of Confederation to the New Deal* (Lincoln: Univeristy of Nebraska Press, 1970), 1–69.

55. Clawson, 27–59; White, *The Federalists*, 384; Leonard White, *The Jeffersonians: A Study in Administrative History, 1801–1829* (New York: Free Press, 1951), 474–95, 513–27.

56. Morton Horwitz, *The Transformation of American Law, 1780–1860* (Cambridge, Mass.: Harvard University Press, 1977), 31–62.

57. This correspondence is integral to the work of Samuel P. Hayes. See *Conservation and the Gospel of Efficiency: The Progressive Conservation Movement, 1890–1920* (New York: Athenium, 1974) and *Beauty Health and Permanence, Environmental Politics in the United States 1955–1985* (New York: Cambridge). This is not to say that industrialization caused the conservation crusade or that the consumer economy caused the environmental movement. Consumers pollute and conservationists derided industrial irresponsibility. The point is that the changes brought about by

these economic developments gave rise to new interests and movements concerned with the land.

58. Dick, 70–84.
59. Clawson, *The Land System*, 65–6.
60. On land grants to soldiers see Laura Jensen, *Patriots, Settlers, and the Origins of American Social Policy* (New York: Cambridge University Press, 2003).
61. Clawson, *The Land System*, 56–71; Marion Clawson, *The Bureau of Land Management* (New York; Praeger, 1971), 26–42; White, *The Jeffersonians*, 519–21; Elmo Richardson, *BLM's Billion Dollar Checkerboard: Managing the O&C Lands* (Santa Cruz, Calif.: Forest Hill Society, 1980).
62. Dick *The Lure of the Land;* Clawson, *The Bureau of Land Management*, 28–34.
63. On variation see Christopher McGrory Klyza, *Who Controls Bush Lands: Mining Forestry and Grazing Policies, 1870–1990* (Chapel Hill: University of North Carolina Press, 1996). Also Daniel Carpenter's excellent study *The Forging of Bureaucratic Autonomy: Reputations, Networks, and Policy Innovation in Executive Agencies, 1862–1928* (Princeton, N.J.: Princeton University Press, 2001).
64. On forestry and courts see Charles Wilkinson and H. Michael Anderson, *Land and Resource Planning in the National Forests*, 46–60; On legal problems in reclamation see Hayes, *Conservation*, 15–17.
65. Carpenter, 283; Theodore Roosevelt, *An Autobiography* (New York: DeCapo, 1985), 414–420; Edmund Morris, *Theodore Rex* (New York: Random House, 2001), 486–7.
66. Hayes, *Conservation*, 199–218;
67. Carpenter, 285–86; Alpheas Thomas Mason, *Bureaucracy Convicts Itself: The Pinchot Ballinger Controversy of 1910* (New York: Viking, 1941); Martin Fausold, *Gifford Pinchot: Bull Moose Progressive* (Syracuse: Syracuse University Press, 1961).
68. An excellent discussion of cooperation may be found in Harold Steen, *The U.S. Forest Service: A History* (Seattle: University of Washington, 1976), 47–144.
69. Steen, 118–122; Ben Twight, *Oganizational Values and Political Power, The Forest Service versus the Olympic National Park* (University Park: Penn State University Press, 1982); Frank Gregg, "Public Land Policy: Controversial Beginnings for the Third Century" in *Government and Environmental Politics; Essays on Historical Developments Since World War II,* ed. Micheal Lacey, (Washington, D.C.: The Woodrow Wilson Center Press, 1991), 143–46.
70. On "the movement" see Hayes, *Beauty;* Robert Cameron Mitchell, "From Conservation to Environmental Movement: The Development of the Modern Environmental Lobbies" in Lacy, 81–113; more recent

developments are captured by Christopher Bosso, "Environmental Groups and the New Political Landscape" in *Environmental Policy: New Directions for the Twentieth Century*, eds. Norman, Vig and Michael Kraft (Washington, D.C.: Congressional Quarterly, 2000), 55–76.

71. Matthew Alan Cahn, *Environmental Deceptions: The Tension Between Liberalism and Environmental Policymaking in the United States* (Albany: State University of New York Press, 1995).

72. See for example "The Process Predicament: How Statutory, Regulatory and Administrative Factors Affect National Forest Management," *Report of the USDA Forest Service*, June 2002.

73. Theodore J. Lowi, *The End of Liberalism: The Second Republic of the United States*, (New York: Norton, 1979), 2d ed.

74. Samuel P. Hayes, "Three Decades of Environmental Politics: the Historical Context," in *Government and Environmental Politics*, ed. Michael Lacy (Washington, D.C.: Woodrow Wilson Center Press, 1991), 19–79.

75. See Karen Orren, "Standing to Sue: Interest Group Conflict in the Federal Courts," *American Political Science Review* 70 (3), 1976, 723–741; Richard Stewart, "The Reformation of American Administrative Law," *Harvard Law Review* 88, 1975, 1669–813; Lettie M. Wenner, *The Environmental Decade in Court* (Bloomington: Indiana University Press, 1982); for more recent developments see Lettie McSpadden, "Environmental Policy in the Courts" in *Environmental policy: New Directions for the Twenty First Century*, eds. Normal Vig and Michael Kraft (Washington, D.C.: Congressional Quarterly, 2000), 145–64.

76. Joseph Sax, "Parks, Wilderness and Recreation" in Lacy, 131.

77. Paul Hirt, *A Conspiracy of Optimism: Management of the National Forests Since World War II* (Lincoln: University of Nebraska Press, 1994); V. Alaric Sample, *The Impact of the Federal Budget Process on National Forest Planning* (New York, Greenwood, 1990).

78. See Timothy Farnahm, "Forest Service Budge Requests and Appropriations: What do Analyses of Trends Reveal?" *Policy Studies Journal* 23(2), 1995, 253–67; and Ellis S. Jones and Will Callaway, "Neutral Bystander, Intrusive Micromanager, or Useful Catalyst?: The Role of Congress in Effecting Change Within the Forest Service," *Policy Studies Journal* 23(4), 1995, 337–350.

79. See Jones and Callaway, 342–44; Wirt, 285–95.

80. Wirt, 244–5; Gregg, 167; Wilkinson and Anderson, 37–40. OMB urged Nixon to veto the measure, but the bill was forced on Gerald Ford after Nixon's resignation.

81. Cassandra Moseley, "New Ideas, Old Institutions: Environment, Community and State in the Pacific Northwest," doctoral dissertation Yale University, 1999, 118–46.

82. Moseley, "New Ideas, Old Institutions"; Steven Lewis Yaffee, *The Wisdom of the Spotted Owl: Policy Lessons for a New Century* (Covelo, Calif.: Island Press, 1994).

Five. Political Development: The Issues

1. James Sundquist, *The Decline and Resurgence of Congress* (Washington, D.C.: Brookings Institution, 1981).

2. Arthur M. Schlesinger, Jr., *The Imperial Presidency* (Boston, Mass.: Houghton Mifflin Company, 1973).

3. Robert Houghwout Jackson, *The Struggle for Judicial Supremacy: A Study of a Crisis in American Power Politics* (New York: Vintage Books, 1941).

4. Kevin P. Phillips, *The Emerging Republican Majority* (New Rochelle, N.Y.: Arlington House, 1969).

5. On rationalization, see Matthew A. Crenson, *The Federal Machine: Beginnings of Bureaucracy in Jacksonian America* (Baltimore, Johns Hopkins University Press, 1975); William Edward Nelson, *The Roots of American Bureaucracy, 1830–1900* (Cambridge, Mass.: Harvard University Press, 1982); Richard R. John, *Spreading the News: The American Postal System from Franklin to Morse* (Cambridge, Mass.: Harvard University Press, 1995); on hyperpoliticization, see Paul Light, *Thickening Government: Federal Hierarchy and the Diffusion of Accountability* (Washington, D.C.: The Brookings Institution, 1995); Terry Moe, "The Politics of Bureaucratic Structure," in *Can the Government Govern?*, eds. John E. Chubb and Paul E. Peterson (Washington, D.C.: The Brookings Institution, 1989), 267–329.

6. William J. Novak, *The People's Welfare Law and Regulation in Nineteenth-Century America* (Chapel Hill: University of North Carolina Press, 1996).

7. The "fully legislative polity" is discussed in Orren, *Belated Feudalism*.

8. For instance, bureaucracy and democracy seem to foster one another in policy studies of welfare state, where a conception of social democracy is implicit. For the contrary view, see Theodore Lowi, *The End of Liberalism: Ideology, Policy and the Crisis of Public Authority* (New York: Norton, 1969) and Robert H. Wiebe, *Self-Rule: A Cultural History of American Democracy* (Chicago: University of Chicago Press, 1995).

9. Walter Dean Burnham, *Critical Elections and the Mainsprings of American Politics* (New York: Norton, 1970).

10. Stephen Skowronek, *The Politics Presidents Make: Leadership from John Adams to Bill Clinton* (Cambridge, Mass.: The Belknap Press, 1997).

11. Eileen McDonagh, "The 'Welfare Rights State' and the 'Civil Rights State': Policy Paradox and State Building in the Progressive Era," *Studies in American Political Development* 7, 1993, 225–74.

12. Theda Skocpol, *Protecting Soldiers and Mothers: The Political Origins of Social Policy in the United States* (Cambridge, Mass.: Belknap Press of Harvard University Press, 1992).

13. Gary King, Robert O. Keohane, and Sidney Verba, *Designing Social Inquiry: Scientific Inference in Qualitative Research* (Princeton, N.J.: Princeton University Press, 1994), 186–7. King et al. are quoting David Laitin.

14. Karen Orren, "The Belly and the Members: A Historical-Institutionalist Perspective on the Pullman Strike," *Studies in Law, Society, and Politics,* 15, 1995, 9–28.
15. Elizabeth Sanders, *Roots of Reform: Farmers, Workers, and the American State 1877–1917* (Chicago: University of Chicago Press, 1999).
16. Theda Skocpol, Kenneth Finegold, and Michael Goldfield, "Explaining New-Deal Labor Policy," *American Political Science Review* 84(4), 1990, 1297–1315.
17. Terry Moe, "Interests, Institutions, and Positive Theory: The Politics of the NLRB," *Studies in American Political Development* (2), 1987, 236–299.
18. Victoria Charlotte Hattam, *Labor Visions and State Power: The Origins of Business Unionism in the United States* (Princeton, N.J.: Princeton University Press, 1993); Gerald Berk, *Alternative Tracks: The Constitution of American Industrial Order, 1865–1917* (Baltimore, Md.: Johns Hopkins University Press, 1994).
19. Stephen Skowronek, *Building A New American State: The Expansion of National Administrative Capacities, 1877–1920* (Cambridge, UK: Cambridge University Press, 1982).
20. In addition to the examples of Skocpol, Lieberman, and Hacker reviewed in Chapter Three, see Adam Sheingate, *The Rise of the Agricultural Welfare State: Institutions and Interest Group Power in the United States, France, and Japan* (Princeton, N.J.: Princeton University Press, 2001).
21. Bruce A. Ackerman, *We the People* (Cambridge, Mass.: Belknap Press, 1991).
22. Walter Dean Burnham, *Critical Elections and the Mainsprings of American Politics.*
23. Samuel P. Huntington, *American Politics: The Promise of Disharmony* (Cambridge, Mass.: Belknap Press, 1981).
24. Stephen Skowronek, *The Politics Presidents Make: Leadership from John Adams to Bill Clinton.*
25. Huntington, *American Politics: The Promise of Disharmony.*
26. Skowronek, *The Politics Presidents Make: Leadership from John Adams to Bill Clinton,* 464.
27. Max Weber, *The Protestant Ethic and the Spirit of Capitalism,* trans. Talcott Parsons (New York: Charles Scribner's Sons, 1958), 90.
28. Gretchen Ritter, *Goldbugs and Greenbacks: The Antimonopoly Tradition and the Politics of Finance in America* (New York: Cambridge University Press, 1997).
29. Martin Shefter, "Regional Receptivity to Reform – the Legacy of the Progressive- Era," *Political Science Quarterly* 98(3), 1983, 459–483.
30. Daniel Kryder, *Divided Arsenal: Race and the American State During World War II* (New York: Cambridge University Press, 2000).
31. Michael Goldfield, *The Color of Politics: Race and the Mainsprings of American Politics* (New York: W. W. Norton & Co., 1997).

32. Richard Franklin Bensel, *Sectionalism and American Political Development, 1880–1980* (Madison, Wis.: University of Wisconsin Press, 1984).
33. Karen Orren, "The Primacy of Labor in American Constitutional Development," *American Political Science Review* 89(2), 1995, 377–388.
34. Richard Franklin Bensel, *Sectionalism and American Political Development*, 5–6.
35. David R. Mayhew, *Electoral Realignments: A Critique of an American Genre* (New Haven, Conn.: Yale University Press, 2002).
36. *The ultimate type* is Henry Jones Ford's term and the title of the last chapter of *The Rise and Growth of American Politics*.
37. See, for example, Isaiah Berlin, "Historical Inevitability," in *Four Essays on Liberty* (London: Oxford University Press, 1969), 41–118.

Index

agency, 21, 30, 35, 36, 47, 74, 80, 173,
  199–201
alternatives
  absence of, 58
  conceptualization of, 35, 78
  empowered, 68–71
  historical contingency of, 54, 65
  lost, 66–68
American Constitution, 2, 9, 35, 47, 156
  and separation of powers, 38, 43, 44,
    123, 181, 183
  and slavery, 135–136, 137–138, 156
  as constraint on development, 131
  as institutional "system," 86–87
  as prescriptive law, 179–180
  Beard's critique of, 52
  Burgess's conception of, 38–39
  Burnham's conception of, 61
  compared to parliamentary system, 46,
    49–50
  Ford's conception of, 48–50, 52
  Framers of, 33–39, 42, 43, 48, 58, 63,
    115, 145
  Hartz's conception of, 58
  in realignment theory, 62
  intercurrent relations in, 115
  separation of church and state in, 145,
    146, 151
  Wilson's conception of, 42–44, 45,
    208, 214
American exceptionalism, 7, 33, 56, 57,
  62, 63
"American Idea," 64
American political culture (see also
  boundaries, boundary conditions,
  and ideas)
  and political development, 3, 76, 182

as "toolbox," 69, 75
as source of ideas, 35, 47, 54–55, 65,
  68, 69–71
assumptions of, 33–34, 51
multiple traditions in, 65, 71–73,
  114–118, 182
American Political Development (APD)
  subfield (see also political
  development)
  as descriptive enterprise, 21, 123, 181,
    188
  as interpretive or normative enterprise,
    26–31, 122, 132, 172–173, 178,
    185, 194–196
  comparative analysis in, 6–7, 8, 9, 13,
    101, 120, 182, 196, 217
  critical stance of, 2–3, 33–34, 35, 120,
    121
  institutional turn in, 77, 78–119, 120
  interdisciplinary nature of, 5
  methodological entailments of, 8–9,
    11, 14–15, 19–26, 173–174,
    184–194
  origins of, 1, 29, 33, 35, 36
  problems faced by, 3–5, 27, 29–31, 74
  recent resurgence of interest in, 1–3,
    35, 75
  redirection of, 74–77
  theory-building in, 1, 6, 27–32, 123

Bagehot, Walter, 43
Beard, Charles, 51–55, 56, 58, 59, 64,
  75, 207, 210, 214
Bensel, Richard, 88–89, 92, 93, 94, 95
boundaries
  as institutional attribute, 82, 83, 184,
    185